International Conventions Affecting Children

International Conventions Affecting Children

by

Jeremy Rosenblatt

KLUWER LAW INTERNATIONAL
THE HAGUE – LONDON – BOSTON

Published by:
Kluwer Law International
P.O. Box 85889, 2508 CN The Hague, The Netherlands
sales@kli.wkap.nl
http://www.kluwerlaw.com

Sold and Distributed in North, Central and South America by:
Kluwer Law International
675 Massachusetts Avenue, Cambridge, MA 02139, USA

Sold and Distributed in all other countries by:
Kluwer Law International
Distribution Centre, P.O. Box 322, 3300 AH Dordrecht, The Netherlands

Library of Congress Cataloging-in-Publication Data is available.

Printed on acid-free paper.

ISBN 90-411-1386-X

Kluwer Law International incorporates the publishing programmes
of Graham & Trotman Ltd, Kluwer Law and Taxation Publishers
and Martinus Nijhoff Publishers

Printed and bound in Great Britain by Antony Rowe Limited.

for Stella Sweetman

CONTENTS

INTRODUCTION

The purpose of this book is to set out International Conventions Affecting Children that can be relied upon by the child practitioner in legal submissions before respective courts. It is hoped this book will be used in any State whose jurisprudence recognises the importance of such international Conventions in their own decision-making process, whether such States have incorporated such Conventions or are as yet just signatories of them.

I also acknowledge the excellence of the volume edited by Geraldine Van Bueren, *International Documents on Children,* though distinguish it and *International Conventions Affecting Children* in that I have tried to amass solely those Conventions that have direct bearing in legal practice.

It would fortunately appear that more Conventions are coming into being in order to reinforce a legal standard affecting children and to attempt to ensure uniformity between States and legal systems, which is of equal importance. Particularly in European Countries the comity and competence of similar legal jursidictions has allowed a variety of such Conventions to actually work in practice rather than simply be left as a threshold requirement regarding standards of behaviour towards children that is seldom applied. The same can begin to be said globally.

The Hague Convention on Intercountry Adoption 1993 ensures that a child placed for adoption by applicants in another State will not have to endure a duplicate adoption process in their home and receiving country, with the additional safeguard that the applicants will have been deemed appropriate as prospective parents in their home country prior to the process getting underway, ensuring that the immigration authorities will also consider immigration status, all within the single umbrella of one such international Convention. Similarly, The Hague Convention on the Civil Aspects of International Child Abduction now has some fifty-eight signatory countries with the expectation of proper enforcement of the return of abducted children to their place of habitual residence unless stringent Defences are proven to prevent an expedited return.

The Brussels and Lugano Conventions assist in the arena of maintenance with mutual enforcement considerations and processes, with the Dublin Convention attempting at least to ensure consistency in respect of asylum seekers within the European Union. The Worst Forms of Child Labour Convention 1999 and the Geneva Convention Relative to the Protection of Civilian Persons in Time of War 1949 might not be as esoteric as some might assume, as they have direct bearing in countries which lack the regulation of systems and norms of behaviour, even within a legal process, that other practitioners take for granted: persistent Conventions that are assumed with care, remind the practitioner of the requirement of standards and safeguards at all times, especially when even most Western States find themselves in breach of the expected standard within the UN Convention on the Rights of the Child 1993, let alone other less-sophisticated States.

As such then, this book seeks to set out such necessary Conventions and to actually remind practitioners to be confident in using them in their respective domestic courts. Change can come about if more reluctant Judges are forced to consider submissions regarding Conventions, if only to remind themselves of the wider influence they might have, even within their domestic systems.

Jeremy Rosenblatt
Barrister
Chambers of Lionel Swift QC
41 Paper Building
Temple
London EC4Y 7EX
clerks@4pb.com

Children and Social Security

CHILDREN AND SOCIAL SECURITY

Citizens and family dependants of EU States enjoy social security rights within the European Community, rights which are also conferred on nationals of the European Free Trade Association and their dependants through the European Economic Area Agreement. For the purpose of ensuring the free movement of persons within the EU, States must ensure such movement takes place without any loss of State benefits. EU employees and their dependants can therefore seek such benefits under social security schemes of other States and have passages of time spent in one State as opposed to another aggregated, to ensure the assessment of the applicant's eligibility. EU law coordinates rather than harmonises different national social security systems, with one State being prevented from subjecting applicants from an EU State where they are not ordinarily domiciled to discrimination for applying for benefits by reason of such a status.

The main EU provision on social security is found within Regulation 1408/71 as amended and updated, which details applications by the employed and self-employed and their dependants. Benefits are also to be sought under Article 7(2) of Regulation 1612/68 which ensures that EU workers and their dependants should enjoy the same social advantages as national workers of the host State concerned. Under this principle, payments can be made to large families, handicapped persons, old persons and widows and widowers. This Regulation applies to all general social security schemes whether contributory or non-contributory, as well as to applications regarding sickness, maternity benefits, invalidity benefits, old-age benefits, survivors' benefits, death grants, benefits regarding accidents at work and occupational diseases, unemployment and family benefits in addition.

Besides EU nationals and their dependants being covered by this Regulation, family members or surviving family members of EU nationals, or habitually resident refugees in a State concerned are also covered, whether or not EU nationals.

A family member is a member of the claimant's household by the law of the State where the benefit is payable. Family members who have survived a deceased worker have EU social security rights. A child would be deemed a family member and dependant. Regulation 1408/71 distinguishes between family benefits and family allowances. Family benefits relate to benefits in cash or kind under domestic legislation, with the latter being cash benefits allowed by reference to the number and age of the family dependants concerned. Family benefits and family allowances may be aggregated by a State where its legislation grants entitlement through periods of insurance or employment. An employed person can seek family benefits in a State even if their family dependants reside in another State. This same rule applies to unemployed persons with family benefit entitlement under Article 74 of Regulation 1408/71 as amended. A dependent child under the age of 21 may be required to be available for employment in the State where they reside.

Children and Legal Aid

THE EUROPEAN AGREEMENT ON THE TRANSMISSION OF LEGAL AID APPLICATIONS 1977

The European Agreement on the Transmission of Legal Aid Applications 1977, also known as the Strasbourg Agreement, sets out the States participating in the transmission of civil legal aid applications between signatory States, with each State having a designated sending and receiving department. In each State the applicant should submit the domestic legal aid form with questions of means answered in the language required, being that of the sending jurisdiction, with the exception of France and Austria who require translations in their own respective languages.

The receiving State will make its assessment of legal aid entitlement on provision and criteria, within its own jurisdictional department, with the receiving department advising the sending department of the outcome.

The following countries are signatories of the Treaty:

Austria
Belgium
Denmark
France
Greece
Italy
Luxembourg
Norway
Portugal
Republic of Ireland
Sweden
Turkey
United Kingdom.

Children and Legal Protection

THE HAGUE CONVENTION ON THE PROTECTION OF CHILDREN:

The Convention on Jurisdiction, Applicable Law, Recognition, Enforcement and Cooperation in Respect of Parental Responsibility and Measures for the Protection of Children

The Hague Convention on the Protection of Children seeks to offer a framework for contracting States to determine which State has jurisdiction when an application is made to a State court. The court will require to consider the appropriate forum, which law is applicable and ensure that there is cooperation between the Central Authorities of contracting States for the purpose of the Convention to be properly implemented. The Convention relates to both private and public law issues. Historically this new 1996 Convention is a revision of the 1961 Convention on the Protection of Minors with only eleven countries then ratifying it.

The 1996 Convention lacks substantive law regarding child protection or parental responsibility matters. Its purpose is to regulate the basis upon which a contracting State can assume jurisdiction regarding child protection measures. All States would be bound as to which State assumes jurisdiction to deal with child protection measures, also recognising and enforcing the child protection measures of one contracting State in another contracting State, with the Convention being applicable to children habitually resident in a contracting State from birth to the age of eighteen.

The main contents of the Convention are: the Scope of the Convention; Jurisdiction; Applicable Law; Recognition and Enforcement; Cooperation; General Provisions and Final Clauses.

Article I contains the objects of the Convention with jurisdiction being, under Article 5, with the State where the child is habitually resident. The State of habitual residence has the power to make decisions regarding matters of parental responsibility, for the protection of the child or its property. The court entitled to jurisdiction can consider applications regarding attribution, exercise, termination, restriction and delegation of parental responsibility, as well as rights of custody.

Matters of contact, residence, removal from the jurisdiction, placement with foster parents and within the public care system, guardianship and issues surrounding administration, conservation and disposal of a child's property are all covered.

Article 6(1) grants jurisdiction regarding refugee children who, 'due to disturbances occurring in their country, are internationally displaced'. A local authority could therefore protect such children, including those arriving in one State unaccompanied or temporarily deprived of their parents. Nor could a parent avoid a court's deliberation by moving a child to another country.

The Contracting State in which the child is habitually resident may request another State to assume jurisdiction to take protective measures if it is thought the other State would be in a better position to assess the child's welfare and best interests. Therefore, the 'other State' could be the State where the child is a national, where its property exists, where the parents' divorce and ancillary applications are taking place, or where there is some proper connection. Similarly a Contracting State where a child is present but not habitually resident may wish to exercise its jurisdiction for child protection purposes.

Whilst under Article 23, the measures taken by the authorities, 'shall be recognised by operation of law in all other Contracting States', exceptions exist, including where the State has acted in contravention of the jurisdictional rules of the Convention and where measures have been taken without input from the child or hearing a person with parental responsibility. The requested State cannot review the merits of the decision of the first State and cannot reopen the case.

As with other Hague Conventions, a Central Authority required to be established and such authority will take measures to 'provide on the request of a competent authority of another Contracting State, assistance in discovering the whereabouts of a child, where it appears that the child may be present and in need of protection within the territory of the requested State'.

The Convention will come into force upon ratification by three States, which only Monaco has so far done.

Convention on Jurisdiction, Applicable Law, Recognition, Enforcement and Co-operation in Respect of Parental Responsibility and Measures for the Protection of Children

The States signatory to the present Convention, Considering the need to improve the protection of children in international situations,

Wishing to avoid conflicts between their legal systems in respect of jurisdiction, applicable law, recognition and enforcement of measures for the protection of children,

Recalling the importance of international co-operation for the protection of children,

Confirming that the best interests of the child are to be a primary consideration, Noting that the Convention of 5 October 1961 concerning the powers of authorities and the law applicable in respect of the protection of minors is in need of revision,

Desiring to establish common provisions to this effect, taking into account the *United Nations Convention on the Rights of the Child* of 20 November 1989,

Have agreed on the following provisions:

CHAPTER I
SCOPE OF THE CONVENTION

Article 1

1. The objects of the present Convention are -
   (a) to determine the State whose authorities have jurisdiction to take measures directed to the protection of the person or property of the child;
   (b) to determine which law is to be applied by such authorities in exercising their jurisdiction;
   (c) to determine the law applicable to parental responsibility;
   (d) to provide for the recognition and enforcement of such measures of protection in all Contracting States;
   (e) to establish such co-operation between the authorities of the Contracting States as may be necessary in order to achieve the purposes of this Convention.
2. For the purposes of this Convention, the term 'parental responsibility' includes parental authority, or any analogous relationship of authority determining the rights, powers and responsibilities of parents, guardians or other legal representatives in relation to the person or the property of the child.

Article 2

The Convention applies to children from the moment of their birth until they reach the age of 18 years.

Article 3

The measures referred to in Article 1 may deal in particular with -

(a) the attribution, exercise, termination or restriction of parental responsibility, as well as its delegation;
(b) rights of custody, including rights relating to the care of the person of the child and, in particular, the right to determine the child's place of residence, as well as rights of access including the right to take a child for a limited period of time to a place other than the child's habitual residence;
(c) guardianship, curatorship and analogous institutions;
(d) the designation and functions of any person or body having charge of the child's person or property, representing or assisting the child;
(e) the placement of the child in a foster family or in institutional care, or the provision of care by kafala or an analogous institution;
(f) the supervision by a public authority of the care of a child by any person having charge of the child;
(g) the administration, conservation or disposal of the child's property.

Article 4

The Convention does not apply to -
(a) the establishment or contesting of a parent–child relationship;
(b) decisions on adoption, measures preparatory to adoption, or the annulment or revocation of adoption;
(c) the name and forenames of the child;
(d) emancipation;
(e) maintenance obligations;
(f) trusts or succession;
(g) social security;
(h) public measures of a general nature in matters of education or health;
(i) measures taken as a result of penal offences committed by children;
(j) decisions on the right of asylum and on immigration.

CHAPTER II
JURISDICTION

Article 5

1. The judicial or administrative authorities of the Contracting State of the habitual residence of the child have jurisdiction to take measures directed to the protection of the child's person or property.
2. Subject to Article 7, in case of a change of the child's habitual residence to another Contracting State, the authorities of the State of the new habitual residence have jurisdiction.

Article 6

1. For refugee children and children who, due to disturbances occurring in their country, are internationally displaced, the authorities of the Contracting State on the territory of which these children are present as a

result of their displacement have the jurisdiction provided for in paragraph 1 of Article 5.

2. The provisions of the preceding paragraph also apply to children whose habitual residence cannot be established.

Article 7

1. In case of wrongful removal or retention of the child, the authorities of the Contracting State in which the child was habitually resident immediately before the removal or retention keep their jurisdiction until the child has acquired a habitual residence in another State, and
   (a) each person, institution or other body having rights of custody has acquiesced in the removal or retention; or
   (b) the child has resided in that other State for a period of at least one year after the person, institution or other body having rights of custody has or should have had knowledge of the whereabouts of the child, no request for return lodged within that period is still pending, and the child is settled in his or her new environment.
2. The removal or the retention of a child is to be considered wrongful where
   (a) it is in breach of rights of custody attributed to a person, an institution or any other body, either jointly or alone, under the law of the State in which the child was habitually resident immediately before the removal or retention; and
   (b) at the time of removal or retention those rights were actually exercised, either jointly or alone, or would have been so exercised but for the removal or retention.

   The rights of custody mentioned in subparagraph (a) above, may arise in particular by operation of law or by reason of a judicial or administrative decision, or by reason of an agreement having legal effect under the law of that State.
3. So long as the authorities first mentioned in paragraph 1 keep their jurisdiction, the authorities of the Contracting State to which the child has been removed or in which he or she has been retained can take only such urgent measures under Article 11 as are necessary for the protection of the person or property of the child.

Article 8

1. By way of exception, the authority of a Contracting State having jurisdiction under Article 5 or 6, if it considers that the authority of another Contracting State would be better placed in the particular case to assess the best interests of the child, may either
   - request that other authority, directly or with the assistance of the Central Authority of its State, to assume jurisdiction to take such measures of protection as it considers to be necessary, or
   - suspend consideration of the case and invite the parties to introduce such a request before the authority of that other State.
2. The Contracting States whose authorities may be addressed as provided in the preceding paragraph are
   (a) a State of which the child is a national,

(b) a State in which property of the child is located,
(c) a State whose authorities are seised of an application for divorce or legal separation of the child's parents, or for annulment of their marriage,
(d) a State with which the child has a substantial connection.

3. The authorities concerned may proceed to an exchange of views.
4. The authority addressed as provided in paragraph 1 may assume jurisdiction, in place of the authority having jurisdiction under Article 5 or 6, if it considers that this is in the child's best interests.

Article 9

1. If the authorities of a Contracting State referred to in Article 8, paragraph 2 consider that they are better placed in the particular case to assess the child's best interests, they may either
   - request the competent authority of the Contracting State of the habitual residence of the child, directly or with the assistance of the Central Authority of that State, that they be authorised to exercise jurisdiction to take the measures of protection which they consider to be necessary, or
   - invite the parties to introduce such a request before the authority of the Contracting State of the habitual residence of the child.
2. The authorities concerned may proceed to an exchange of views.
3. The authority initiating the request may exercise jurisdiction in place of the authority of the Contracting State of the habitual residence of the child only if the latter authority has accepted the request.

Article 10

1. Without prejudice to Articles 5 to 9, the authorities of a Contracting State exercising jurisdiction to decide upon an application for divorce or legal separation of the parents of a child habitually resident in another Contracting State, or for annulment of their marriage, may, if the law of their State so provides, take measures directed to the protection of the person or property of such child if
   (a) at the time of commencement of the proceedings, one of his or her parents habitually resides in that State and one of them has parental responsibility in relation to the child, and
   (b) the jurisdiction of these authorities to take such measures has been accepted by the parents, as well as by any other person who has parental responsibility in relation to the child, and is in the best interests of the child.
2. The jurisdiction provided for by paragraph 1 to take measures for the protection of the child ceases as soon as the decision allowing or refusing the application for divorce, legal separation or annulment of the marriage has become final, or the proceedings have come to an end for another reason.

Article 11

1. In all cases of urgency, the authorities of any Contracting State in whose territory the child or property belonging to the child is present have jurisdiction to take any necessary measures of protection.

2. The measures taken under the preceding paragraph with regard to a child habitually resident in a Contracting State shall lapse as soon as the authorities which have jurisdiction under Articles 5 to 10 have taken the measures required by the situation.
3. The measures taken under paragraph 1 with regard to a child who is habitually resident in a non-Contracting State shall lapse in each Contracting State as soon as measures required by the situation and taken by the authorities of another State are recognised in the Contracting State in question.

Article 12

1. Subject to Article 7, the authorities of a Contracting State in whose territory the child or property belonging to the child is present have jurisdiction to take measures of a provisional character for the protection of the person or property of the child which have a territorial effect limited to the State in question, in so far as such measures are not incompatible with measures already taken by authorities which have jurisdiction under Articles 5 to 10.
2. The measures taken under the preceding paragraph with regard to a child habitually resident in a Contracting State shall lapse as soon as the authorities which have jurisdiction under Articles 5 to 10 have taken a decision in respect of the measures of protection which may be required by the situation.
3. The measures taken under paragraph 1 with regard to a child who is habitually resident in a non-Contracting State shall lapse in the Contracting State where the measures were taken as soon as measures required by the situation and taken by the authorities of another State are recognised in the Contracting State in question.

Article 13

1. The authorities of a Contracting State which have jurisdiction under Articles 5 to 10 to take measures for the protection of the person or property of the child must abstain from exercising this jurisdiction if, at the time of the commencement of the proceedings, corresponding measures have been requested from the authorities of another Contracting State having jurisdiction under Articles 5 to 10 at the time of the request and are still under consideration.
2. The provisions of the preceding paragraph shall not apply if the authorities before whom the request for measures was initially introduced have declined jurisdiction.

Article 14

The measures taken in application of Articles 5 to 10 remain in force according to their terms, even if a change of circumstances has eliminated the basis upon which jurisdiction was founded, so long as the authorities which have jurisdiction under the Convention have not modified, replaced or terminated such measures.

Article 15

1. In exercising their jurisdiction under the provisions of Chapter II, the authorities of the Contracting States shall apply their own law.
2. However, in so far as the protection of the person or the property of the child requires, they may exceptionally apply or take into consideration the law of another State with which the situation has a substantial connection.
3. If the child's habitual residence changes to another Contracting State, the law of that other State governs, from the time of the change, the conditions of application of the measures taken in the State of the former habitual residence.

Article 16

1. The attribution or extinction of parental responsibility by operation of law, without the intervention of a judicial or administrative authority, is governed by the law of the State of the habitual residence of the child.
2. The attribution or extinction of parental responsibility by an agreement or a unilateral act, without intervention of a judicial or administrative authority, is governed by the law of the State of the child's habitual residence at the time when the agreement or unilateral act takes effect.
3. Parental responsibility which exists under the law of the State of the child's habitual residence subsists after a change of that habitual residence to another State.
4. If the child's habitual residence changes, the attribution of parental responsibility by operation of law to a person who does not already have such responsibility is governed by the law of the State of the new habitual residence.

Article 17

The exercise of parental responsibility is governed by the law of the State of the child's habitual residence. If the child's habitual residence changes, it is governed by the law of the State of the new habitual residence.

Article 18

The parental responsibility referred to in Article 16 may be terminated, or the conditions of its exercise modified, by measures taken under this Convention.

Article 19

1. The validity of a transaction entered into between a third party and another person who would be entitled to act as the child's legal representative under the law of the State where the transaction was concluded cannot be contested, and the third party cannot be held liable, on the sole ground that the other person was not entitled to act as the child's legal representative under the law designated by the provisions of this Chapter, unless the third party knew or should have known that the parental responsibility was governed by the latter law.
2. The preceding paragraph applies only if the transaction was entered into between persons present on the territory of the same State.

Article 20

The provisions of this Chapter apply even if the law designated by them is the law of a non-Contracting State.

Article 21

1. In this Chapter the term 'law' means the law in force in a State other than its choice of law rules.
2. However, if the law applicable according to Article 16 is that of a non-Contracting State and if the choice of law rules of that State designate the law of another non-Contracting State which would apply its own law, the law of the latter State applies. If that other non-Contracting State would not apply its own law, the applicable law is that designated by Article 16.

Article 22

The application of the law designated by the provisions of this Chapter can be refused only if this application would be manifestly contrary to public policy, taking into account the best interests of the child.

CHAPTER IV
RECOGNITION AND ENFORCEMENT

Article 23

1. The measures taken by the authorities of a Contracting State shall be recognised by operation of law in all other Contracting States.
2. Recognition may however be refused
   (a) if the measure was taken by an authority whose jurisdiction was not based on one of the grounds provided for in Chapter II;
   (b) if the measure was taken, except in a case of urgency, in the context of a judicial or administrative proceeding, without the child having been provided the opportunity to be heard, in violation of fundamental principles of procedure of the requested State;
   (c) on the request of any person claiming that the measure infringes his or her parental responsibility, if such measure was taken, except in a case of urgency, without such person having been given an opportunity to be heard;
   (d) if such recognition is manifestly contrary to public policy of the requested State, taking into account the best interests of the child;
   (e) if the measure is incompatible with a later measure taken in the non-Contracting State of the habitual residence of the child, where this later measure fulfils the requirements for recognition in the requested State;
   (f) if the procedure provided in Article 33 has not been complied with.

Article 24

Without prejudice to Article 23, paragraph 1, any interested person may request from the competent authorities of a Contracting State that they decide on the recognition or non-recognition of a measure taken in another Contracting State. The procedure is governed by the law of the requested State.

Article 25

The authority of the requested State is bound by the findings of fact on which the authority of the State where the measure was taken based its jurisdiction.

Article 26

1. If measures taken in one Contracting State and enforceable there require enforcement in another Contracting State, it shall, upon request by an interested party, be declared enforceable or registered for the purpose of enforcement in that other State according to the procedure provided in the law of the latter State.
2. Each Contracting State shall apply to the declaration of enforceability or registration a simple and rapid procedure.
3. The declaration of enforceability or registration may be refused only for one of the reasons set out in Article 23, paragraph 2.

Article 27

Without prejudice to such review as is necessary in the application of the preceding Articles, there shall be no review of the merits of the measure taken.

Article 28

Measures taken in one Contracting State and declared enforceable, or registered for the purpose of enforcement, in another Contracting State shall be enforced in the latter State as if they had been taken by the authorities of that State. Enforcement takes place in accordance with the law of the requested State to the extent provided by such law, taking into consideration the best interests of the child.

CHAPTER V
CO-OPERATION

Article 29

1. A Contracting State shall designate a Central Authority to discharge the duties which are imposed by the Convention on such authorities.
2. Federal States, States with more than one system of law or States having autonomous territorial units shall be free to appoint more than one Central Authority and to specify the territorial or personal extent of their functions. Where a State has appointed more than one Central Authority, it shall designate the Central Authority to which any communication may be addressed for transmission to the appropriate Central Authority within that State.

Article 30

1. Central Authorities shall co-operate with each other and promote co-operation amongst the competent authorities in their States to achieve the purposes of the Convention.

2. They shall, in connection with the application of the Convention, take appropriate steps to provide information as to the laws of, and services available in, their States relating to the protection of children.

Article 31

The Central Authority of a Contracting State, either directly or through public authorities or other bodies, shall take all appropriate steps to -

a) facilitate the communications and offer the assistance provided for in Articles 8 and 9 and in this Chapter;
b) facilitate, by mediation, conciliation or similar means, agreed solutions for the protection of the person or property of the child in situations to which the Convention applies;
c) provide, on the request of a competent authority of another Contracting State, assistance in discovering the whereabouts of a child where it appears that the child may be present and in need of protection within the territory of the requested State.

Article 32

On a request made with supporting reasons by the Central Authority or other competent authority of any Contracting State with which the child has a substantial connection, the Central Authority of the Contracting State in which the child is habitually resident and present may, directly or through public authorities or other bodies,

a) provide a report on the situation of the child,
b) request the competent authority of its State to consider the need to take measures for the protection of the person or property of the child.

Article 33

1. If an authority having jurisdiction under Articles 5 to 10 contemplates the placement of the child in a foster family or institutional care, or the provision of care by kafala or an analogous institution, and if such placement or such provision of care is to take place in another Contracting State, it shall first consult with the Central Authority or other competent authority of the latter State. To that effect it shall transmit a report on the child together with the reasons for the proposed placement or provision of care.
2. The decision on the placement or provision of care may be made in the requesting State only if the Central Authority or other competent authority of the requested State has consented to the placement or provision of care, taking into account the child's best interests.

Article 34

1. Where a measure of protection is contemplated, the competent authorities under the Convention, if the situation of the child so requires, may request any authority of another Contracting State which has information relevant to the protection of the child to Communicate such information.
2. A Contracting State may declare that requests under paragraph 1 shall be communicated to its authorities only through its Central Authority.

Article 35

1. The competent authorities of a Contracting State may request the authorities of another Contracting State to assist in the implementation of measures of protection taken under this Convention, especially in securing the effective exercise of rights of access as well as of the right to maintain direct contacts on a regular basis.
2. The authorities of a Contracting State in which the child does not habitually reside may, on the request of a parent residing in that State who is seeking to obtain or to maintain access to the child, gather information or evidence and may make a finding on the suitability of that parent to exercise access and on the conditions under which access is to be exercised. An authority exercising jurisdiction under Articles 5 to 10 to determine an application concerning access to the child, shall admit and consider such information, evidence and finding before reaching its decision.
3. An authority having jurisdiction under Articles 5 to 10 to decide on access may adjourn a proceeding pending the outcome of a request made under paragraph 2, in particular, when it is considering an application to restrict or terminate access rights granted in the State of the child's former habitual residence.
4. Nothing in this Article shall prevent an authority having jurisdiction under Articles 5 to 10 from taking provisional measures pending the outcome of the request made under paragraph 2.

Article 36

In any case where the child is exposed to a serious danger, the competent authorities of the Contracting State where measures for the protection of the child have been taken or are under consideration, if they are informed that the child's residence has changed to, or that the child is present in another State, shall inform the authorities of that other State about the danger involved and the measures taken or under consideration.

Article 43

All documents forwarded or delivered under this Convention shall be exempt from legalisation or any analogous formality.

Article 44

Each Contracting State may designate the authorities to which requests under Articles 8, 9 and 33 are to be addressed.

Article 45

1. The designations referred to in Articles 29 and 44 shall be communicated to the Permanent Bureau of the Hague Conference on Private International Law.
2. The declaration referred to in Article 34, paragraph 2, shall be made to the depositary of the Convention.

Article 46

A Contracting State in which different systems of law or sets of rules of law apply to the protection of the child and his or her property shall not be bound to apply the rules of the Convention to conflicts solely between such different systems or sets of rules of law.

Article 47

In relation to a State in which two or more systems of law or sets of rules of law with regard to any matter dealt with in this Convention apply in different territorial units –

1. Any reference to habitual residence in that State shall be construed as referring to habitual residence in a territorial unit;
2. Any reference to the presence of the child in that State shall be construed as referring to presence in a territorial unit;
3. Any reference to the location of property of the child in that State shall be construed as referring to location of property of the child in a territorial unit;
4. Any reference to the State of which the child is a national shall be construed as referring to the territorial unit designated by the law of that State or, in the absence of relevant rules, to the territorial unit with which the child has the closest connection;
5. Any reference to the State whose authorities are seised of an application for divorce or legal separation of the child's parents, or for annulment of their marriage, shall be construed as referring to the territorial unit whose authorities are seised of such application;
6. Any reference to the State with which the child has a substantial connection shall be construed as referring to the territorial unit with which the child has such connection;
7. Any reference to the State to which the child has been removed or in which he or she has been retained shall be construed as referring to the relevant territorial unit to which the child has been removed or in which he or she has been retained;
8. Any reference to bodies or authorities of that State, other than Central Authorities, shall be construed as referring to those authorised to act in the relevant territorial unit;
9. Any reference to the law or procedure or authority of the State in which a measure has been taken shall be construed as referring to the law or procedure or authority of the territorial unit in which such measure was taken;
10. Any reference to the law or procedure or authority of the requested State shall be construed as referring to the law or procedure or authority of the territorial unit in which recognition or enforcement is sought.

Article 48

For the purpose of identifying the applicable law under Chapter III, in relation to a State which comprises two or more territorial units each of which has its own system of law or set of rules of law in respect of matters covered by this Convention, the following rules apply

(a) if there are rules in force in such a State identifying which territorial unit's law is applicable, the law of that unit applies;
(b) in the absence of such rules, the law of the relevant territorial unit as defined in Article 47 applies.

Article 49

For the purpose of identifying the applicable law under Chapter III, in relation to a State which has two or more systems of law or sets of rules of law applicable to different categories of persons in respect of matters covered by this Convention, the following rules apply -

(a) if there are rules in force in such a State identifying which among such laws applies, that law applies;
(b) in the absence of such rules, the law of the system or the set of rules of law with which the child has the closest connection applies.

Article 50

This Convention shall not affect the application of the *Convention of 25 October 1980 on the Civil Aspects of International Child Abduction*, as between Parties to both Conventions. Nothing, however, precludes provisions of this Convention from being invoked for the purposes of obtaining the return of a child who has been wrongfully removed or retained or of organising access rights.

Article 51

In relations between the Contracting States this Convention replaces the *Convention of 5 October 1961 concerning the powers of authorities and the law applicable in respect of the protection of minors*, and the *Convention governing the guardianship of minors*, signed at The Hague 12 June 1902, without prejudice to the recognition of measures taken under the Convention of 5 October 1961 mentioned above.

Article 52

1. This Convention does not affect any international instrument to which Contracting States are Parties and which Contains provisions on matters governed by the Convention, unless a contrary declaration is made by the States Parties to such instrument.
2. This Convention does not affect the possibility for one or more Contracting States to conclude agreements which contain, in respect of children habitually resident in any of the States Parties to such agreements, provisions on matters governed by this Convention.
3. Agreements to be concluded by one or more Contracting States on matters within the scope of this Convention do not affect, in the relationship of such States with other Contracting States, the application of the provisions of this Convention.
4. The preceding paragraphs also apply to uniform laws based on special ties of a regional or other nature between the States concerned.

Article 53

1. The Convention shall apply to measures only if they are taken in a State after the Convention has entered into force for that State.
2. The Convention shall apply to the recognition and enforcement of measures taken after its entry into force as between the State where the measures have been taken and the requested State.

Article 54

1. Any communication sent to the Central Authority or to another authority of a Contracting State shall be in the original language, and shall be accompanied by a translation into the official language or one of the official languages of the other State or, where that is not feasible, a translation into French or English.
2. However, a Contracting State may, by making a reservation in accordance with Article 60, object to the use of either French or English, but not both.

Article 55

1. A Contracting State may, in accordance with Article 60,
   (a) reserve the jurisdiction of its authorities to take measures directed to the protection of property of a child situated on its territory;
   (b) reserve the right not to recognize any parental responsibility or measure in so far as it is incompatible.

Article 60

1. Any State may, not later than the time of ratification, acceptance, approval or accession, or at the time of making a declaration in terms of Article 59, make one or both of the reservations provided for in Articles 54, paragraph 2, and 55. No other reservation shall be permitted.
2. Any State may at any time withdraw a reservation it has made. The withdrawal shall be notified to the depositary.
3. The reservation shall cease to have effect on the first day of the third calendar month after the notification referred to in the preceding paragraph.

Article 61

1. The Convention shall enter into force on the first day of the month following the expiration of three months after the deposit of the third instrument of ratification, acceptance or approval referred to in Article 57.
2. Thereafter the Convention shall enter into force -
   (a) for each State ratifying, accepting or approving it subsequently, on the first day of the month following the expiration of three months after the deposit of its instrument of ratification, acceptance, approval or accession;
   (b) for each State acceding, on the first day of the month following the expiration of three months after the expiration of the period of six months provided in Article 58, paragraph 3;
   (c) for a territorial unit to which the Convention has been extended in conformity with Article 59, on the first day of the month following the expiration of three months after the notification referred to in that Article.

Article 62

1. A State Party to the Convention may denounce it by a notification in writing addressed to the depositary. The denunciation may be limited to certain territorial units to which the Convention applies.

2. The denunciation takes effect on the first day of the month following the expiration of twelve months after the notification is received by the depositary. Where a longer period for the denunciation to take effect is specified in the notification, the denunciation takes effect upon the expiration of such longer period.

Article 63

The depositary shall notify the States Members of the Hague Conference on Private International Law and the States which have acceded in accordance with Article 58 of the following -

(a) the signatures, ratifications, acceptances and approvals referred to in Article 57;
(b) the accessions and objections raised to accessions referred to in Article 58;
(c) the date on which the Convention enters into force in accordance with Article 61;
(d) the declarations referred to in Articles 34, paragraph 2, and 59;
(e) the agreements referred to in Article 39;
(f) the reservations referred to in Articles 54, paragraph 2, and 55 and the withdrawals referred to in Article 60, paragraph 2;
(g) the denunciations referred to in Article 62.

Children and Labour

CHILDREN AND LABOUR

Article 32 of the UN Convention on the Rights of the Child makes it clear that children should not work where they may be physically or mentally harmed. Unfortunately, few countries have ratified the International Labour Convention Number 138, though most countries are signatories of the UN Convention on the Rights of the Child.

The Convention on the Worst Forms of Child Labour came into being in 1999 seeking cooperation and assistance, complementing the Convention and the Recommendation concerning Minimum Age for Admission to Employment 1973. Each member State should take effective measures pursuant to Article 1 to secure the prohibition and elimination of the worst forms of child labour as a matter of urgency, with actual programmes being implemented pursuant to Article 6 to eliminate as a priority the worst forms of child labour. Under Article 10 the Convention will bind members of the International Labour Organisation whose ratification has been registered with the Director-General.

Worst Forms of Child Labour Convention, 1999

The General Conference of the International Labour Organization,

Having been convened at Geneva by the Governing Body of the International Labour Office, and having met in its 87th Session on 1 June 1999, and

Considering the need to adopt new instruments for the prohibition and elimination of the worst forms of child labour, as the main priority for national and international action, including international cooperation and assistance, to complement the Convention and the Recommendation concerning Minimum Age for Admission to Employment, 1973, which remain fundamental instruments on child labour, and

Considering that the effective elimination of the worst forms of child labour requires immediate and comprehensive action, taking into account the importance of free basic education and the need to remove the children concerned from all such work and to provide for their rehabilitation and social integration while addressing the needs of their families, and

Recalling the resolution concerning the elimination of child labour adopted by the International Labour Conference at its 83rd Session in 1996, and

Recognizing that child labour is to a great extent caused by poverty and that the long-term solution lies in sustained economic growth leading to social progress, in particular poverty alleviation and universal education, and

Recalling the Convention on the Rights of the Child adopted by the United Nations General Assembly on 20 November 1989, and

Recalling the ILO Declaration on Fundamental Principles and Rights at Work and its Follow-up, adopted by the International Labour Conference at its 86th Session in 1998, and

Recalling that some of the worst forms of child labour are covered by other international instruments, in particular the Forced Labour Convention, 1930, and the United Nations Supplementary Convention on the Abolition of Slavery, the Slave Trade, and Institutions and Practices Similar to Slavery, 1956, and

Having decided upon the adoption of certain proposals with regard to child labour, which is the fourth item on the agenda of the session, and

Having determined that these proposals shall take the form of an international Convention;

adopts this seventeenth day of June of the year one thousand nine hundred and ninety-nine the following Convention, which may be cited as the Worst Forms of Child Labour Convention, 1999.

Article 1

Each Member which ratifies this Convention shall take immediate and effective measures to secure the prohibition and elimination of the worst forms of child labour as a matter of urgency.

Article 2

For the purposes of this Convention, the term *child* shall apply to all persons under the age of 18.

Article 3

For the purposes of this Convention, the term *the worst forms of child labour* comprises:

(a) all forms of slavery or practices similar to slavery, such as the sale and trafficking of children, debt bondage and serfdom and forced or compulsory labour, including forced or compulsory recruitment of children for use in armed conflict;
(b) the use, procuring or offering of a child for prostitution, for the production of pornography or for pornographic performances;
(c) the use, procuring or offering of a child for illicit activities, in particular for the production and trafficking of drugs as defined in the relevant international treaties;
(d) work which, by its nature or the circumstances in which it is carried out, is likely to harm the health, safety or morals of children.

Article 4

1. The types of work referred to under Article 3(d) shall be determined by national laws or regulations or by the competent authority, after consultation with the organizations of employers and workers concerned, taking into consideration relevant international standards, in particular Paragraphs 3 and 4 of the Worst Forms of Child Labour Recommendation, 1999.
2. The competent authority, after consultation with the organizations of employers and workers concerned, shall identify where the types of work so determined exist.
3. The list of the types of work determined under paragraph 1 of this Article shall be periodically examined and revised as necessary, in consultation with the organizations of employers and workers concerned.

Article 5

Each Member shall, after consultation with employers' and workers' organizations, establish or designate appropriate mechanisms to monitor the implementation of the provisions giving effect to this Convention.

Article 6

1. Each Member shall design and implement programmes of action to eliminate as a priority the worst forms of child labour.
2. Such programmes of action shall be designed and implemented in consultation with relevant government institutions and employers' and workers' organizations, taking into consideration the views of other concerned groups as appropriate.

Article 7

1. Each Member shall take all necessary measures to ensure the effective implementation and enforcement of the provisions giving effect to this Convention including the provision and application of penal sanctions or, as appropriate, other sanctions.

2. Each Member shall, taking into account the importance of education in eliminating child labour, take effective and time-bound measures to:
   (a) prevent the engagement of children in the worst forms of child labour;
   (b) provide the necessary and appropriate direct assistance for the removal of children from the worst forms of child labour and for their rehabilitation and social integration;
   (c) ensure access to free basic education, and, wherever possible and appropriate, vocational training, for all children removed from the worst forms of child labour;
   (d) identify and reach out to children at special risk; and
   (e) take account of the special situation of girls.
3. Each Member shall designate the competent authority responsible for the implementation of the provisions giving effect to this Convention.

Article 8

Members shall take appropriate steps to assist one another in giving effect to the provisions of this Convention through enhanced international cooperation and/or assistance including support for social and economic development, poverty eradication programmes and universal education.

Article 9

The formal ratifications of this Convention shall be communicated to the Director-General of the International Labour Office for registration.

Article 10

1. This Convention shall be binding only upon those Members of the International Labour Organization whose ratifications have been registered with the Director-General of the International Labour Office.
2. It shall come into force 12 months after the date on which the ratifications of two Members have been registered with the Director-General.
3. Thereafter, this Convention shall come into force for any Member 12 months after the date on which its ratification has been registered.

Article 11

1. A Member which has ratified this Convention may denounce it after the expiration of ten years from the date on which the Convention first comes into force, by an act communicated to the Director-General of the International Labour Office for registration. Such denunciation shall not take effect until one year after the date on which it is registered.
2. Each Member which has ratified this Convention and which does not, within the year following the expiration of the period of ten years mentioned in the preceding paragraph, exercise the right of denunciation provided for in this Article, will be bound for another period of ten years and, thereafter, may denounce this Convention at the expiration of each period of ten years under the terms provided for in this Article.

Article 12

1. The Director-General of the International Labour Office shall notify all Members of the International Labour Organization of the registration of all ratifications and acts of denunciation communicated by the Members of the Organization.
2. When notifying the Members of the Organization of the registration of the second ratification, the Director-General shall draw the attention of the Members of the Organization to the date upon which the Convention shall come into force.

Article 13

The Director-General of the International Labour Office shall communicate to the Secretary-General of the United Nations, for registration in accordance with article 102 of the Charter of the United Nations, full particulars of all ratifications and acts of denunciation registered by the Director-General in accordance with the provisions of the preceding Articles.

Article 14

At such times as it may consider necessary, the Governing Body of the International Labour Office shall present to the General Conference a report on the working of this Convention and shall examine the desirability of placing on the agenda of the Conference the question of its revision in whole or in part.

Article 15

1. Should the Conference adopt a new Convention revising this Convention in whole or in part, then, unless the new Convention otherwise provides –
   (a) the ratification by a Member of the new revising Convention shall ipso jure involve the immediate denunciation of this Convention, notwithstanding the provisions of Article 11 above, if and when the new revising Convention shall have come into force;
   (b) as from the date when the new revising Convention comes into force, this Convention shall cease to be open to ratification by the Members.
2. This Convention shall in any case remain in force in its actual form and content for those Members which have ratified it but have not ratified the revising Convention.

Article 16

The English and French versions of the text of this Convention are equally authoritative.

Cross references

Conventions: (C29)Forced Labour convention, 1930
Conventions: (C138)Minimum Age Convention, 1973

Recommendations:(R35)Forced Labour (Indirect Compulsion) Recommendation, 1930
Recommendations:(R36)Forced Labour (Regulation) Recommendation, 1930
Recommendations:(R146)Minimum Age Recommendation, 1973
SUPPLEMENTED: (R190)Complemented by the Worst Forms of Child Labour Recommendation, 1999
Constitution: 22:article 22 of the Constitution of the International Labour Organisation

Children and International Abduction

THE HAGUE CONVENTION ON THE CIVIL ASPECTS OF INTERNATIONAL CHILD ABDUCTION 1980

The purpose of The Hague Convention on the Civil Aspects of International Child Abduction is to ensure a reciprocal arrangement between signatory States for the expeditious return of children who have been abducted or retained in one State that is not their State of habitual residence. Article 11(2) of the Convention on the Rights of the Child requests States to accede to existing agreements on child abduction, with Article 11(1) imposing an obligation on States to take measures to 'combat the illicit transfer and non-return of children abroad'.

Each State has a Central Authority and that home Central Authority will contact the foreign state Central Authority to commence proceedings in the foreign court if a child has been abducted or retained in that foreign state. For an application to be commenced the applicant must pursuant to Article 3, have a 'right of custody' regarding the child subject of proceedings. Different states have different considerations of the applicant father, the mother automatically having such a right of custody, the married father also having such a right, but not so the unmarried father. Certain states under domestic statute permit the father to receive an order granting him the same rights to a child as if he were married to the mother of the child. Such a father would come within Article 3 and be able to trigger the Convention and make the application; other States might find that a father in the throes of seeking such a domestic order will still fall within the provisions of a Hague Convention application for return.

The jurisprudential complexities do not come upon applications as often as they come upon Defences. A parent who has abducted or retained a child can seek to persuade the foreign court not to return the child to the home state, namely, the State of the child's habitual residence, pursuant to Article 8. Article 13 (a) and (b) sets out the Defences that can be raised. One consideration already mentioned is the applicant lacking a right of custody, but the more common Defence is that a return would place the child in a situation of 'psychological harm' or place the child in an 'intolerable' situation.

Extraordinary Defences have sought to be raised over the years to come within such criteria by parents who simply do not want to return to unhappy relationships or to countries that they have sadly never come to terms with. These Conventions came into being after all, reflecting the global nature of relationships and more importantly, the consequences upon children when some breakdown and abduction or retention arises. Different countries have different reputations for the effective implementation of the Hague Convention. England, for example, now has a reputation for putting the Convention properly into practice and rejecting most Defences raised under Article 13(b). Other countries have a softer reputation that encourages complaints of disparity regarding the Convention practice amongst the fifty-eight signatory countries.

Intercountry Adoption – Hague Convention Countries

The following lists show the position as regards the Hague Convention on the Protection of Children and Co-operation in Respect of Intercountry Adoption (The Hague, 29 May 1993):

The following States have signed the Convention:

Contracting State	*Date of signing*
Australia	25 August 1998
Austria	18 December 1998
Belarus	10 December 1997
Belgium	27 January 1999
Brazil	29 May 1993
Burkina Faso	19 April 1994
Canada	12 April 1994
Colombia	1 September 1993
Costa Rica	29 May 1993
Cyprus	17 November 1994
Denmark	2 July 1997
Ecuador	3 May 1994
El Salvador	21 November 1996
Finland	19 April 1994
France	5 April 1995
Germany	7 November 1997
Ireland	19 June 1996
Israel	2 November 1993
Italy	11 December 1995
Luxembourg	6 June 1995
Mexico	29 May 1993
Netherlands	5 December 1993
Norway	20 May 1996
Panama	15 June 1999
Peru	16 November 1994
Philippines	17 July 1995
Poland	12 June 1995
Romania	29 May 1993
Slovakia	1 June 1999
Spain	27 March 1995
Sri Lanka	24 May 1994
Sweden	10 October 1996
Switzerland	16 January 1995
United Kingdom	12 January 1994
United States	31 March 1994

(Continued)

Contracting State	*Date of signing*
Uruguay	1 September 1993
Venezuela	10 January 1997

Total number of signatories – 37

The following States have ratified the Convention:

Contracting State	*Date of ratification*	*Entry into force*
Australia	25 August 1998	1 December 1998
Austria	19 May 1999	1 September 1999
Brazil	10 March 1999	1 July 1999
Burkina Faso	11 January 1996	1 May 1996
Canada	19 December 1996	1 April 1997
Colombia	13 July 1998	1 November1998
Costa Rica	30 October 1995	1 February 1996
Cyprus	20 February 1995	1 June 1995
Denmark	2 July 1997	1 November 1997
Ecuador	7 September 1995	1 January 1996
El Salvador	17 November 1998	1 March 1999
Finland	27 March 1997	1 July 1997
France	30 June 1998	1 October 1998
Israel	3 February 1999	1 June 1999
Mexico	14 September 1994	1 May 1995
Netherlands	26 June 1998	1 October 1998
Norway	25 September 1997	1 January 1998
Peru	14 September 1995	1 January 1996
Philippines	2 July 1996	1 November 1996
Poland	12 June 1995	1 October 1995
Romania	28 December 1994	1 May 1995
Spain	11 July 1995	1 November 1995
Sri Lanka	23 January 1995	1 May 1995
Sweden	28 May 1997	1 September 1997
Venezuela	10 January 1997	1 May 1997

Total number of ratifications – 25

The following States have acceded to the Convention:

Contracting State	*Date of accession*	*Entry into force*	*Expiry date under Art 44(3)*[1]
Andorra	3 January 1997	1 May 1997	August 1997
Burundi	15 October 1998	1 February 1999	15 May 1999
Georgia	9 April 1999	1 August 1999	1 November 1999

(Continued)

Contracting State	*Date of accession*	*Entry into force*	*Expiry date under Art 44(3)*[1]
Lithuania	29 April 1998	1 August 1998	1 December 1998
Mauritius	28 September 1998	1 January 1999	15 May 1999
Moldova	10 April 1998	1 August 1998	1 November 1998
Monaco	29 June 1999	1 October 1999	15 January 2000
New Zealand	18 September 1998	1 January 1999	15 April 1999
Paraguay	13 May 1998	1 September 1998	1 December 1998

Total number of accessions – 9
The Convention entered into force on 1 May 1995
Source – Permanent Bureau listing as at 5 July 1999.

Abduction – Hague Convention Countries

The following list shows the contracting States to the Hague Convention on the Civil Aspects of International Child Abduction (The Hague, 25 October 1980):

Contracting State	*Specified territories*	*Date in force between the UK and the State or Territory*
Argentina	–	1 June 1991
Australia	Australian States and mainland Territories	1 January 1987
Austria	–	1 October 1988
The Bahamas	–	1 January 1994
Belize	–	1 October 1989
Bosnia and Herzegovina	–	7 April 1992
Burkina	–	1 August 1992
Canada	Ontario	1 August 1986
	New Brunswick	1 August 1986
	British Columbia	1 August 1986
	Manitoba	1 August 1986
	Nova Scotia	1 August 1986
	Newfoundland	1 August 1986
	Prince Edward Island	1 August 1986
	Quebec	1 August 1986
	Yukon Territory	1 August 1986
	Saskatchewan	1 November 1986

Continued

[1]In accordance with Art 44(3) of the Convention, the accession has effect only as regards the relations between the acceding State and those contracting States which have not raised an objection to its accession in the 6 months following the date on which the depositary gave notice of the accession. The date specified here is the expiry of that 6-month period.

Contracting State	*Specified territories*	*Date in force between the UK and the State or Territory*
	Alberta	1 February 1987
	Northwest Territories	1 April 1988
Chile	–	1 May 1994
Columbia	–	1 March 1996
Croatia	–	1 December 1991
Cyprus	–	1 February 1995
Czech Republic	–	1 March 1998
Denmark	–	1 July 1991
Ecuador	–	1 April 1992
Finland	–	1 August 1994
France	–	1 August 1986
Georgia	–	1 October 1997
Germany	–	1 December 1990
Greece	–	1 June 1993
Honduras	–	1 March 1994
Hungary	–	1 September 1986
Iceland	–	1 November 1996
Republic of Ireland	–	1 October 1991
Israel	–	1 December 1991
Italy	–	1 May 1995
Luxembourg	–	1 January 1987
Macedonia	–	1 December 1991
Mauritius	–	1 June 1993
Mexico	–	1 September 1991
Monaco	–	1 February 1993
Netherlands	–	1 September 1990
New Zealand	–	1 August 1991
Norway	–	1 April 1989
Panama	–	1 December 1991
Poland	–	1 November 1992
Portugal	–	1 August 1986
Romania	–	1 February 1993
Slovenia	–	1 June 1994
South Africa	–	1 October 1997
Spain	–	1 September 1987
St Kitts and Nevis	–	1 August 1994
Sweden	–	1 June 1989
Switzerland	–	1 August 1986
Turkmenistan	–	1 March 1998
The Federal Republic of Yugoslavia	–	27 April 1992
United States	–	1 July 1988
Venezuela	–	1 January 1997
Zimbabwe	–	1 July 1995

Source - Child Abduction and Custody (Parties to Conventions) Order 1986 (SI 1986/1159) (as last amended by SI 1998/256).

Custody – European Convention Countries

The following list shows the contracting States to the European Convention on Recognition and Enforcement of Decisions concerning Custody of Children and on the Restoration of Custody of Children (Luxembourg, 20 May 1980):

Contracting State	*Specified territories*	*Date in force between the UK and the State or Territory*
Austria	–	1 August 1986
Belgium	–	1 August 1986
Cyprus	–	1 October 1986
Denmark	–	1 August 1991
Finland	–	1 August 1994
France	–	1 August 1986
Germany	–	1 February 1991
Greece	–	1 July 1993
The Republic of Ireland	–	1 October 1991
Iceland	–	1 November 1996
Italy	–	1 June 1995
Liechtenstein	–	1 August 1997
Luxembourg	–	1 August 1986
Netherlands	–	1 September 1990
Norway	–	1 May 1989
Poland	–	1 March 1996
Portugal	–	1 August 1986
Spain	–	1 August 1986
Sweden	–	1 July 1989
Switzerland	–	1 August 1986

Source – Child Abduction and Custody (Parties to Conventions) Order 1986 (SI 1986/1159) (as last amended by SI 1998/256).

Convention on the Civil Aspects of International Child Abduction

The States signatory to the present Convention.

Firmly convinced that the interests of children are of paramount importance in matters relating to their custody.

Desiring to protect children internationally from the harmful effects of their wrongful removal or retention and to establish procedures to ensure their prompt return to the State of their habitual residence, as well as to secure protection for rights of access.

Have resolved to conclude a Convention to this effect, and have agreed upon the following provisions –

CHAPTER 1
SCOPE OF THE CONVENTION

Article 1

The objects of the present Convention are –

(a) to secure the prompt return of children wrongfully removed to or retained in any Contracting State: and

(b) to ensure that rights of custody and of access under the law of one Contracting State are effectively respected in the other Contracting States.

Article 2

Contracting States shall take all appropriate measures to secure within their territories the implementation of the objects of the Convention. For this purpose they shall use the most expeditious procedures available.

Article 3

The removal or the retention of a child is to be considered wrongful where –

(a) it is in breach of rights of custody attributed to a person, an institution or any other body, either jointly or alone, under the law of the State in which the child was habitually resident immediately before the removal or retention; and

(b) at the time of removal or retention those rights were actually exercised, either jointly or alone, or would have been so exercised but for the removal or retention.

The rights of custody mentioned in subparagraph (a) above may arise in particular by operation of law or by reason of a judicial or administrative decision, or by reason of an agreement having legal effect under the law of that State.

Article 4

The Convention shall apply to any child who was habitually resident in a Contracting State immediately before any breach of custody or access rights. The Convention shall cease to apply when the child attains the age of sixteen years.

Article 5

For the purposes of this Convention –

(a) 'rights of custody' shall include rights relating to the care of the person of the child and, in particular, the right to determine the child's place of residence;

(b) 'rights of access' shall include the right to take a child for a limited period of time to a place other than the child's habitual residence.

CHAPTER II
CENTRAL AUTHORITIES

Article 6

A Contracting State shall designate a Central Authority to discharge the duties which are imposed by the Convention upon such authorities.

Federal States, States with more than one system of law or States having autonomous territorial organizations shall be free to appoint more than one Central Authority and to specify the territorial extent of their powers. Where a State has appointed more than one Central Authority, it shall designate the Central Authority to which applications may be addressed for transmission to the appropriate Central Authority within that State.

Article 7

Central Authorities shall co-operate with each other and promote cooperation amongst the competent authorities in their respective States to secure the prompt return of children and to achieve the other objects of this Convention.

In particular, either directly or through any intermediary, they shall take all appropriate measures –

(a) to discover the whereabouts of a child who has been wrongfully removed or retained;
(b) to prevent further harm to the child or prejudice to interested parties by taking or causing to be taken provisional measures;
(c) to secure the voluntary return of the child or to bring about an amicable resolution of the issues;
(d) to exchange, where desirable, information relating to the social background of the child;
(e) to provide information of a general character as to the law of their State in connection with the application of the Convention;
(f) to initiate or facilitate the institution of judicial or administrative proceedings with a view to obtaining the return of the child and, in a proper case, to make arrangements for organizing or securing the effective exercise of rights of access;
(g) where the circumstances so require, to provide or facilitate the provision of legal aid and advice, including the participation of legal counsel and advisers;
(h) to provide such administrative arrangements as may be necessary and appropriate to secure the safe return of the child;
(i) to keep each other informed with respect to the operation of this Convention and, as far as possible, to eliminate any obstacles to its application.

CHAPTER III
RETURN OF CHILDREN

Article 8

Any person, institution or other body claiming that a child has been removed or retained in breach of custody rights may apply either to the Central Authority

of the child's habitual residence or to the Central Authority of any other Contracting State for assistance in securing the return of the child.
The application shall contain –
(a) information concerning the identity of the applicant, of the child and of the person alleged to have removed or retained the child;
(b) where available, the date of birth of the child;
(c) the grounds on which the applicant's claim for return of the child is based;
(d) all available information relating to the whereabouts of the child and the identity of the person with whom the child is presumed to be.
The application may be accompanied or supplemented by –
(e) an authenticated copy of any relevant decision or agreement;
(f) a certificate or an affidavit emanating from a Central Authority, or other competent authority of the State of the child's habitual residence, or from a qualified person, concerning the relevant law of that State;
(g) any other relevant document.

Article 9

If the Central Authority which receives an application referred to in Article 8 has reason to believe that the child is in another Contracting State, it shall directly and without delay transmit the application to the Central Authority of that Contracting State and inform the requesting Central Authority, or the applicant, as the case may be.

Article 10

The Central Authority of the State where the child is shall take or cause to be taken all appropriate measures in order to obtain the voluntary return of the child.

Article 11

The judicial or administrative authorities of Contracting States shall act expeditiously in proceedings for the return of children.

If the judicial or administrative authority concerned has not reached a decision within six weeks from the date of commencement of the proceedings, the applicant or the Central Authority of the requested State, on its own initiative or if asked by the Central Authority of the requesting State, shall have the right to request a statement of the reasons for the delay. If a reply is received by the Central Authority of the requested State, that Authority shall transmit the reply to the Central Authority of the requesting State, or to the applicant, as the case may be.

Article 12

Where a child has been wrongfully removed or retained in terms of Article 3 and, at the date of the commencement of the proceedings before the judicial or administrative authority of the Contracting State where the child is, a period of less than one year has elapsed from the date of the wrongful removal or retention, the authority concerned shall order the return of the child forthwith.

The judicial or administrative authority, even where the proceedings have been commenced after the expiration of the period of one year referred to in the preceding paragraph, shall also order the return of the child, unless it is demonstrated that the child is now settled in its new environment.

Where the judicial or administrative authority in the requested State has reason to believe that the child has been taken to another State, it may stay the proceedings or dismiss the application for the return of the child.

Article 13

Notwithstanding the provisions of the preceding Article, the judicial or administrative authority of the requested State is not bound to order the return of the child if the person, institution or other body which opposes its return establishes that –

(a) the person, institution or other body having the care of the person of the child was not actually exercising the custody rights at the time of removal or retention, or had consented to or subsequently acquiesced in the removal or retention; or

(b) there is a grave risk that his or her return would expose the child to physical or psychological harm or otherwise place the child in an intolerable situation.

The judicial or administrative authority may also refuse to order the return of the child if it finds that the child objects to being returned and has attained an age and degree of maturity at which it is appropriate to take account of its views.

In considering the circumstances referred to in this Article, the judicial and administrative authorities shall take into account the information relating to the social background of the child provided by the Central Authority or other competent authority of the child's habitual residence.

Article 14

In ascertaining whether there has been a wrongful removal or retention within the meaning of Article 3, the judicial or administrative authorities of the requested State may take notice directly of the law of, and of judicial or administrative decisions, formally recognized or not in the State of the habitual residence of the child, without recourse to the specific procedures for the proof of that law or for the recognition of foreign decisions which would otherwise be applicable.

Article 15

The judicial or administrative authorities of a Contracting State may, prior to the making of an order for the return of the child, request that the applicant obtain from the authorities of the State of the habitual residence of the child a decision or other determination that the removal or retention was wrongful within the meaning of Article 3 of the Convention, where such a decision or determination may be obtained in that State. The Central Authorities of the Contracting States shall so far as practicable assist applicants to obtain such a decision or determination.

Article 16

After receiving notice of a wrongful removal or retention of a child in the sense of Article 3, the judicial or administrative authorities of the Contracting State to which the child has been removed or in which it has been retained shall not decide on the merits of rights of custody until it has been determined that the child is not to be returned under this Convention or unless an application under this Convention is not lodged within a reasonable time following receipt of the notice.

Article 17

The sole fact that a decision relating to custody has been given in or is entitled to recognition in the requested State shall not be a ground for refusing to return a child under this Convention, but the judicial or administrative authorities of the requested State may take account of the reasons for that decision in applying this Convention.

Article 18

The provisions of this Chapter do not limit the power of a judicial or administrative authority to order the return of the child at any time.

Article 19

A decision under this Convention concerning the return of the child shall not be taken to be a determination on the merits of any custody issue.

Article 20

The return of the child under the provisions of Article 12 may be refused if this would not be permitted by the fundamental principles of the requested State relating to the protection of human rights and fundamental freedoms.

CHAPTER IV
RIGHTS OF ACCESS

Article 21

An application to make arrangements for organizing or securing the effective exercise of rights of access may be presented to the Central Authorities of the Contracting States in the same way as an application for the return of a child.

The Central Authorities are bound by the obligations of co-operation which are set forth in Article 7 to promote the peaceful enjoyment of access rights and the fulfilment of any conditions to which the exercise of those rights may be subject. The Central Authorities shall take steps to remove, as far as possible, all obstacles to the exercise of such rights. The Central Authorities, either directly or through intermediaries, may initiate or assist in the institution of proceedings with a view to organizing or protecting these rights and securing respect for the conditions to which the exercise of these rights may be subject.

CHAPTER V
GENERAL PROVISIONS

Article 22

No security, bond or deposit, however described, shall be required to guarantee the payment of costs and expenses in the judicial or administrative proceedings falling within the scope of this Convention.

Article 23

No legalization or similar formality may be required in the context of this Convention.

Article 24

Any application, communication or other document sent to the Central Authority of the requested State shall be in the original language, and shall be accompanied by a translation into the official language or one of the official languages of the requested State or, where that is not feasible, a translation into French or English. However, a Contracting State may, by making a reservation in accordance with Article 42, object to the use of either French or English, but not both, in any application, communication or other document sent to its Central Authority.

Article 25

Nationals of the Contracting States and persons who are habitually resident within those States shall be entitled in matters concerned with the application of this Convention to legal aid and advice in any other Contracting State on the same conditions as if they themselves were nationals of and habitually resident in that State.

Article 26

Each Central Authority shall bear its own costs in applying this Convention.

Central Authorities and other public services of Contracting States shall not impose any charges in relation to applications submitted under this Convention. In particular, they may not require any payment from the applicant towards the costs and expenses of the proceedings or, where applicable, those arising from the participation of legal counsel or advisers. However, they may require the payment of the expenses incurred or to be incurred in implementing the return of the child.

However, a Contracting State may, by making a reservation in accordance with Article 42, declare that it shall not be bound to assume any costs referred to in the preceding paragraph resulting from the participation of legal counsel or advisers or from court proceedings, except insofar as those costs may be covered by its system of legal aid and advice.

Upon ordering the return of a child or issuing an order concerning rights of access under this Convention, the judicial or administrative authorities may, where appropriate, direct the person who removed or retained the child, or who prevented the exercise of rights of access, to pay necessary expenses incurred by or on behalf of the applicant, including travel expenses, any costs incurred or payments made for locating the child, the costs of legal representation of the applicant, and those of returning the child.

Article 27

When it is manifest that the requirements of this Convention are not fulfilled or that the application is otherwise not well founded, a Central Authority is not bound to accept the application. In that case, the Central Authority shall forthwith inform the applicant or the Central Authority through which the application was submitted, as the case may be, of its reasons.

Article 28

A Central Authority may require that the application be accompanied by a written authorization empowering it to act on behalf of the applicant, or to designate a representative so to act.

Article 29

This Convention shall not preclude any person, institution or body who claims that there has been a breach of custody or access rights within the meaning of Article 3 or 21 from applying directly to the judicial or administrative authorities of a Contracting State, whether or not under the provisions of this Convention.

Article 30

Any application submitted to the Central Authorities or directly to the judicial or administrative authorities of a Contracting State in accordance with the terms of this Convention, together with documents and any other information appended thereto or provided by a Central Authority, shall be admissible in the courts or administrative authorities of the Contracting States.

Article 31

In relation to a State which in matters of custody of children has two or more systems of law applicable in different territorial units –

(a) any reference to habitual residence in that State shall be construed as referring to habitual residence in a territorial unit of that State;
(b) any reference to the law of the State of habitual residence shall be construed as referring to the law of the territorial unit in that State where the child habitually resides.

Article 32

In relation to a State which in matters of custody of children has two or more systems of law applicable to different categories of persons, any reference to the law of that State shall be construed as referring to the legal system specified by the law of that State.

Article 33

A State within which different territorial units have their own rules of law in respect of custody of children shall not be bound to apply this Convention where a State with a unified system of law would not be bound to do so.

Article 34

This Convention shall take priority in matters within its scope over the *Convention of 5 October 1961 concerning the powers of authorities and the law applicable in respect of the protection of minors*, as between Parties to both Conventions. Otherwise the present Convention shall not restrict the application of an international instrument in force between the State of origin and the State addressed or other law of the State addressed for the purposes of obtaining the return of a child who has been wrongfully removed or retained or of organizing access rights.

Article 35

This Convention shall apply as between Contracting States only to wrongful removals or retentions occurring after its entry into force in those States.

Where a declaration has been made under Article 39 or 40, the reference in the preceding paragraph to a Contracting State shall be taken to refer to the territorial unit or units in relation to which this Convention applies.

Article 36

Nothing in this Convention shall prevent two or more Contracting States, in order to limit the restrictions to which the return of the child may be subject, from agreeing among themselves to derogate from any provisions of this Convention which may imply such a restriction.

CHAPTER VI
FINAL CLAUSES

Article 37

The Convention shall be open for signature by the States which were Members of the Hague Conference on Private International Law at the time of its Fourteenth Session.

It shall be ratified, accepted or approved and the instruments of ratification, acceptance or approval shall be deposited with the Ministry of Foreign Affairs of the Kingdom of the Netherlands.

Article 38

Any other State may accede to the Convention.

The instrument of accession shall be deposited with the Ministry of Foreign Affairs of the Kingdom of the Netherlands.

The Convention shall enter into force for a State acceding to it on the first day of the third calendar month after the deposit of its instrument of accession.

The accession will have effect only as regards the relations between the acceding State and such Contracting States as will have declared their acceptance of the accession. Such a declaration will also have to be made by any Member State ratifying, accepting or approving the Convention after an accession. Such declaration shall be deposited at the Ministry of Foreign Affairs of the Kingdom of the Netherlands; this Ministry shall forward, through diplomatic channels, a certified copy to each of the Contracting States.

The Convention will enter into force as between the acceding State and the State that has declared its acceptance of the accession on the first day of the third calendar month after the deposit of the declaration of acceptance.

Article 39

Any State may, at the time of signature, ratification, acceptance, approval or accession, declare that the Convention shall extend to all the territories for the international relations of which it is responsible, or to one or more of them. Such a declaration shall take effect at the time the Convention enters into force for that State.

Such declaration, as well as any subsequent extension, shall be notified to the Ministry of Foreign Affairs of the Kingdom of the Netherlands.

Article 40

If a Contracting State has two or more territorial units in which different systems of law are applicable in relation to matters dealt with in this Convention, it may at the time of signature, ratification, acceptance, approval or accession declare that this Convention shall extend to all its territorial units or only to one or more of them and may modify this declaration by submitting another declaration at any time.

Any such declaration shall be notified to the Ministry of Foreign Affairs of the Kingdom of the Netherlands and shall state expressly the territorial units to which the Convention applies.

Article 41

Where a Contracting State has a system of government under which executive, judicial and legislative powers are distributed between central and other authorities within that State, its signature or ratification, acceptance or approval of, or accession to this Convention, or its making of any declaration in terms of Article 40 shall carry no implication as to the internal distribution of powers within that State.

Article 42

Any State may, not later than the time of ratification, acceptance, approval or accession, or at the time of making a declaration in terms of Article 39 or 40, make one or both of the reservations provided for in Article 24 and Article 26, third paragraph. No other reservation shall be permitted.

Any State may at any time withdraw a reservation it has made. The withdrawal shall be notified to the Ministry of Foreign Affairs of the Kingdom of the Netherlands.

The reservation shall cease to have effect on the first day of the third calendar month after the notification referred to in the preceding paragraph.

Article 43

The Convention shall enter into force on the first day of the third calendar month after the deposit of the third instrument of ratification, acceptance, approval or accession referred to in Articles 37 and 38.

Thereafter the Convention shall enter into force –

(1) for each State ratifying, accepting, approving or acceding to it subsequently, on the first day of the third calendar month after the deposit of its instrument of ratification, acceptance, approval or accession;
(2) for any territory or territorial unit to which the Convention has been extended in conformity with Article 39 or 40, on the first day of the third calendar month after the notification referred to in that Article.

Article 44

The Convention shall remain in force for five years from the date of its entry into force in accordance with the first paragraph of Article 43 even for States which subsequently have ratified, accepted, approved it or acceded to it.

If there has been no denunciation, it shall be renewed tacitly every five years.

Any denunciation shall be notified to the Ministry of Foreign Affairs of the Kingdom of the Netherlands at least six months before the expiry of the five year period. It may be limited to certain of the territories or territorial units to which the Convention applies.

The denunciation shall have effect only as regards the State which has notified it. The Convention shall remain in force for the other Contracting States.

Article 45

The Ministry of Foreign Affairs of the Kingdom of the Netherlands shall notify the States Members of the Conference, and the States which have acceded in accordance with Article 38, of the following –

(1) the signatures and ratifications, acceptances and approvals referred to in Article 37;
(2) the accessions referred to in Article 38;
(3) the date on which the Convention enters into force in accordance with Article 43;
(4) the extensions referred to in Article 39;
(5) the declarations referred to in Articles 38 and 40;
(6) the reservations referred to in Article 24 and Article 26, third paragraph, and the withdrawals referred to in Article 42;
(7) the denunciations referred to in Article 44.

In witness whereof the undersigned, being duly authorized thereto, have signed this Convention.

Done at The Hague, on the 25th day of October, 1980, in the English and French languages, both texts being equally authentic, in a single copy which shall be deposited in the archives of the Government of the Kingdom of the Netherlands, and of which a certified copy shall be sent, through diplomatic channels, to each of the States Members of the Hague Conference on Private International Law at the date of its Fourteenth Session.

THE EUROPEAN CONVENTION ON THE RECOGNITION AND ENFORCEMENT OF DECISIONS CONCERNING CUSTODY OF CHILDREN 1980

The European Convention on the Recognition and Enforcement of Decisions Concerning Custody of Children 1980 deals primarily with the reciprocal enforcement of custody and access orders between contracting states. Every custody decision shall, subject to exceptions, be recognised and, where enforceable in the state of origin, be made enforceable in every other contracting state.

The whole purpose of the Convention was to tighten the effect of court orders regarding children of parents from different countries or living in different countries after separation. A French father might permit the permanent removal of his child to the Netherlands with a Dutch mother if a French Court order that granted him contact with his child were to be registered in the Netherlands, as it would give him the security he evidently requires, namely the knowledge that despite removal from one state to another, his contact regime is to be legally acknowledged by the foreign state of the Netherlands and he will actually be sure to get to see his child.

A party of a state wishing to have a decision from the original home state registered and enforced in another contracting state should contact the foreign state where they wish to have the order registered through the central authority of the home state. A central authority is a government body in each contracting state that simply organises the receipt of applications to register from the home state, then sends them through to the central authority of the foreign state for it to carry out the administation through its legal system of the registration of the home state's order.

Under Article 13 a copy of the original court judgment can be sought by the foreign court and in addition, the foreign court can request a report of the home state's Department of Health, Local Authority or Probation Service regarding any matter concerning the child. Article 5 imposes certain requirements upon the foreign court when receiving an application from the home requesting state.

Defences exist to the making of an order in the foreign requested state, namely:

1. that the original home order should not have been made by reason of the child not being habitually resident there at the time the application and/or the decision was taken;

2. the original home order is irreconcilable with the order of the foreign requested state or any order of any other state, should such order exist;
3. the effects of the original home order are irreconcilable with the the law of the foreign requested state;
4. the effects of the original home order no longer accord with the welfare of the child; and
5. where an original home decision was made in the absence of a Defendant who was not served with the original application, unless the Defendant at the time of the original application was found to have concealed his whereabouts, the original home order should not be made.

Under Article 15(1) it is mandatory to ascertain the views of the child before reaching a decision unless it is impracticable to do so having regard to the child's age and understanding.

European Convention on Recognition and Enforcement of Decisions Concerning Custody of Children

The Member States of the Council of Europe, signatory hereto,

Recognising that in the Member States of the Council of Europe the welfare of the child is of overriding importance in reaching decisions concerning his custody;

Considering that the making of arrangements to ensure that decisions concerning the custody of a child can be more widely recognised and enforced will provide greater protection of the welfare of children;

Considering it desirable, with this end in view, to emphasise that the right of access of parents is a normal corollary to the right of custody;

Noting the increasing number of cases where children have been improperly removed across an international frontier and the difficulties of securing adequate solutions to the problems caused by such cases;

Desirous of making suitable provision to enable the custody of children which has been arbitrarily interrupted to be restored;

Convinced of the desirability of making arrangements for this purpose answering to different needs and different circumstances;

Desiring to establish legal co-operation between their authorities,

Have agreed as follows:

Article 1

For the purposes of this Convention:

(a) 'child' means a person of any nationality, so long as he is under sixteen years of age and has not the right to decide on his own place of residence under the law of his habitual residence, the law of his nationality or the internal law of the State addressed;

(b) 'authority' means a judicial or administrative authority;

(c) 'decision relating to custody' means a decision of an authority in so far as it relates to the care of the person of the child, including the right to decide on the place of his residence, or to the right of access to him;

(d) 'improper removal' means the removal of a child across an international frontier in breach of a decision relating to his custody which has been given in a Contracting State and which is enforceable in such a State; 'improper removal' also includes:

  (i) the failure to return a child across an international frontier at the end of a period of the exercise of the right of access to this child or at the end of any other temporary stay in a territory other than that where the custody is exercised;

  (ii) a removal which is subsequently declared unlawful within the meaning of Article 12.

PART 1
CENTRAL AUTHORITIES

Article 2

1. Each Contracting State shall appoint a central authority to carry out the functions provided for by this Convention.

1. Federal States and States with more than one legal system shall be free to appoint more than one central authority and shall determine the extent of their competence.
2. The Secretary General of the Council of Europe shall be notified of any appointment under this Article.

Article 3

1. The central authorities of the Contracting States shall co-operate with each other and promote co-operation between the competent authorities in their respective countries. They shall act with all necessary despatch.
2. With a view to facilitating the operation of this Convention, the central authorities of the Contracting States:
   (a) shall secure the transmission of requests for information coming from competent authorities and relating to legal or factual matters concerning pending proceedings;
   (b) shall provide each other on request with information about their law relating to the custody of children and any changes in that law;
   (c) shall keep each other informed of any difficulties likely to arise in applying the Convention and, as far as possible, eliminate obstacles to its application.

Article 4

1. Any person who has obtained in a Contracting State a decision relating to the custody of a child and who wishes to have that decision recognized or enforced in another Contracting State may submit an application for this purpose to the central authority in any Contracting State.
2. The application shall be accompanied by the documents mentioned in Article 13.
3. The central authority receiving the application, if it is not the central authority in the State addressed, shall send the documents directly and without delay to that central authority.
4. The central authority receiving the application may refuse to intervene where it is manifestly clear that the conditions laid down by this Convention are not satisfied.
5. The central authority receiving the application shall keep the applicant informed without delay of the progress of his application.

Article 5

1. The central authority in the State addressed shall take or cause to be taken without delay all steps which it considers to be appropriate, if necessary by instituting proceedings before its competent authorities, in order:
   (a) to discover the whereabouts of the child;
   (b) to avoid, in particular by any necessary provisional measures, prejudice to the interests of the child or of the applicant;
   (c) to secure the recognition or enforcement of the decision;
   (d) to secure the delivery of the child to the applicant where enforcement is granted;
   (e) to inform the requesting authority of the measures taken and their results.

2. Where the central authority in the State addressed has reason to believe that the child is in the territory of another Contracting State it shall send the documents directly and without delay to the central authority of that State.
3. With the exception of the cost of repatriation, each Contracting State undertakes not to claim any payment from an applicant in respect of any measures taken under paragraph 1 of this Article by the central authority of that State on the applicant's behalf, including the costs of proceedings and, where applicable, the costs incurred by the assistance of a lawyer.
4. If recognition or enforcement is refused, and if the central authority of the State addressed considers that it should comply with a request by the applicant to bring in that State proceedings concerning the substance of the case, that authority shall use its best endeavours to secure the representation of the applicant in the proceedings under conditions no less favourable than those available to a person who is resident in and a national of that State and for this purpose it may, in particular, institute proceedings before its competent authorities.

Article 6

(1) Subject to any special agreements made between the central authorities concerned and to the provisions of paragraph 3 of this Article:
   (a) communications to the central authority of the State addressed shall be made in the official language or in one of the official languages of that State or be accompanied by a translation into that language;
   (b) the central authority of the State addressed shall nevertheless accept communications made in English or in French or accompanied by a translation into one of these languages.

(2) Communications coming from the central authority of the State addressed, including the results of enquiries carried out, may be made in the official language or one of the official languages of that State or in English or French.

(3) A Contracting State may exclude wholly or partly the provision of paragraph 1(b) of this Article. When a Contracting State has made this reservation any other Contracting State may also apply the reservation in respect of that State.

PART II
RECOGNITION AND ENFORCEMENT OF DECISIONS AND RESTORATION OF CUSTODY OF CHILDREN

Article 7

A decision relating to custody given in a Contracting State shall be recognized and, where it is enforceable in the State of origin, made enforceable in every other Contracting State.

Article 8

1. In the case of an improper removal, the central authority of the State addressed shall cause steps to be taken forthwith to restore the custody of the child where:-

(a) at the time of the institution of the proceedings in the State where the decision was given or at the time of the improper removal, if earlier, the child and his parents had as their sole nationality the nationality of that State and the child had his habitual residence in the territory of that State, and

(b) a request for the restoration was made to a central authority within a period of six months from the date of the improper removal.

2. If, in accordance with the law of the State addressed, the requirements of paragraph 1 of this Article cannot be complied with without recourse to a judicial authority, none of the grounds of refusal specified in this Convention shall apply to the judicial proceedings.

3. Where there is an agreement officially confirmed by a competent authority between the person having the custody of the child and another person to allow the other person a right of access, and the child, having been taken abroad, has not been restored at the end of the agreed period to the person having the custody, custody of the child shall be restored in accordance with paragraphs 1(b) and 2 of this Article. The same shall apply in the case of a decision of the competent authority granting such a right to a person who has not the custody of the child.

Article 9

1. In cases of improver removal, other than those dealt with in Article 8, in which an application has been made to a central authority within a period of six months from the date of the removal, recognition and enforcement may be refused only if:-

(a) in the case of a decision given in the absence of the defendant or his legal representative, the defendant was not duly served with the document which instituted the proceedings or an equivalent document in sufficient time to enable him to arrange his defence; but such a failure to effect service cannot constitute a ground for refusing recognition or enforcement where service was not effected because the defendant had concealed his whereabouts from the person who instituted the proceedings in the State of origin;

(b) in the case of a decision given in the absence of the defendant or his legal representative, the competence of the authority giving the decision was not founded:

(i) on the habitual residence of the defendant; or

(ii) on the last common habitual residence of the child's parents, at least one parent being still habitually resident there, or

(iii) on the habitual residence of the child;

(c) the decision is incompatible with a decision relating to custody which became enforceable in the State addressed before the removal of the child, unless the child has had his habitual residence in the territory of the requesting State for one year before his removal.

2. Where no application has been made to a central authority, the provisions of paragraph 1 of this Article shall apply equally, if recognition and enforcement are requested within six months from the date of the improper removal.

3. In no circumstances may the foreign decision be reviewed as to its substance.

Article 10

1. In cases other than those covered by Articles 8 and 9, recognition and enforcement may be refused not only on the grounds provided for in Article 9 but also on any of the following grounds:
   (a) if it is found that the effects of the decision are manifestly incompatible with the fundamental principles of the law relating to the family and children in the State addressed;
   (b) if it is found that by reason of a change in the circumstances including the passage of time but not including a mere change in the residence of the child after an improper removal, the effects of the original decision are manifestly no longer in accordance with the welfare of the child;
   (c) if at the time when the proceedings were instituted in the State of origin:
      (i) the child was a national of the State addressed or was habitually resident there and no such connection existed with the State of origin;
      (ii) the child was a national both of the State of origin and of the State addressed and was habitually resident in the State addressed;
   (d) if the decision is incompatible with a decision given in the State addressed or enforceable in that State after being given in a third State, pursuant to proceedings begun before the submission of the request for recognition or enforcement, and if the refusal is in accordance with the welfare of the child.
2. Proceedings for recognition or enforcement may be adjourned on any of the following grounds:
   (a) if an ordinary form of review of the original decision has been commenced;
   (b) if proceedings relating to the custody of the child, commenced before the proceedings in the State of origin were instituted, are pending in the State addressed;
   (c) if another decision concerning the custody of the child is the subject of proceedings for enforcement or of any other proceedings concerning the recognition of the decision.

Article 11

1. Decisions on rights of access and provisions of decisions relating to custody which deal with the right of access shall be recognized and enforced subject to the same conditions as other decisions relating to custody.
2. However, the competent authority of the State addressed may fix the conditions for the implementation and exercise of the right of access taking into account, in particular, undertakings given by the parties on this matter.
3. Where no decision on the right of access has been taken or where recognition or enforcement of the decision relating to custody is refused, the central authority of the State addressed may apply to its competent

authorities for a decision on the right of access if the person claiming a right of access so requests.

Article 12

Where, at the time of the removal of a child across an international frontier, there is no enforceable decision given in a Contracting State relating to his custody, the provisions of this Convention shall apply to any subsequent decision, relating to the custody of that child and declaring the removal to be unlawful, given in a Contracting State at the request of any interested person.

PART III
PROCEDURE

Article 13

1. A request for recognition or enforcement in another Contracting State of a decision relating to custody shall be accompanied by:
   (a) a document authorizing the central authority of the State addressed to act on behalf of the applicant or to designate another representative for that purpose;
   (b) a copy of the decision which satisfies the necessary conditions of authenticity;
   (c) in the case of a decision given in the absence of the defendant or his legal representative, a document which establishes that the defendant was duly served with the document which instituted the proceedings or an equivalent document;
   (d) if applicable, any document which establishes that, in accordance with the law of the State of origin, the decision is enforceable;
   (e) if possible, a statement indicating the whereabouts or likely whereabouts of the child in the State addressed;
   (f) proposals as to how the custody of the child should be restored.
2. The documents mentioned above shall, where necessary, be accompanied by a translation according to the provisions laid down in Article 6.

Article 14

Each Contracting State shall apply a simple and expeditious procedure for recognition and enforcement of decisions relating to the custody of a child. To that end it shall ensure that a request for enforcement may be lodged by simple application.

Article 15

1. Before reaching a decision under paragraph (1)(b) of Article 10, the authority concerned in the State addressed:
   (a) shall ascertain the child's views unless this is impracticable having regard in particular to his age and understanding; and
   (b) may request that any appropriate inquiries be carried out.
2. The cost of inquiries in any Contracting State shall be met by the authorities of the State where they are carried out.

Requests for inquiries and the results of inquiries may be sent to the authority concerned through the central authorities.

Article 16

For the purposes of this Convention, no legalisation or any like formality may be required.

PART IV
RESERVATIONS

Article 17

1. A Contracting State may make a reservation that, in cases covered by Articles 8 and 9 or either of these Articles, recognition and enforcement of decisions relating to custody may be refused on such of the grounds provided under Article 10 as may be specified in the reservation.
2. Recognition and enforcement of decisions given in a Contracting State which has made the reservation provided for in paragraph 1 of this Article may be refused in any other Contracting State on any of the additional grounds referred to in that reservation.

Article 18

A Contracting State may make a reservation that it shall not be bound by the provisions of Article 12. The provisions of this Convention shall not apply to decisions referred to in Article 12 which have been given in a Contracting State which has made such a reservation.

PART V
OTHER INSTRUMENTS

Article 19

This Convention shall not exclude the possibility of relying on any other international instrument in force between the State of origin and the State addressed or on any other law of the State addressed not derived from an international agreement for the purpose of obtaining recognition or enforcement of a decision.

Article 20

1. This Convention shall not affect any obligations which a Contracting State may have towards a non-contracting State under an international instrument dealing with matters governed by this Convention.
2. When two or more Contracting States have enacted uniform laws in relation to custody of children or created a special system of recognition or enforcement of decisions in this field, or if they should do so in the future, they shall be free to apply, between themselves, those laws or that system in place of this Convention or any part of it. In order to avail themselves of this provision the States shall notify their decision to the Secretary General of the Council of Europe. Any alteration or revocation of this decision must also be notified.

PART VI
FINAL CLAUSES

Article 21

This Convention shall be open for signature by the Member States of the Council of Europe. It is subject to ratification, acceptance or approval. Instruments of ratification, acceptance or approval shall be deposited with the Secretary General of the Council of Europe.

Article 22

1. This Convention shall enter into force on the first day of the month following the expiration of a period of three months after the date on which three Member States of the Council of Europe have expressed their consent to be bound by the Convention in accordance with the provisions of Article 21.
2. In respect of any Member State which subsequently expresses its consent to be bound by it, the Convention shall enter into force on the first day of the month following the expiration of a period of three months after the date of the deposit of the instrument of ratification, acceptance or approval.

Article 23

1. After the entry into force of this Convention, the Committee of Ministers of the Council of Europe may invite any State not a member of the Council to accede to this Convention, by a decision taken by the majority provided for by Article 20(d) of the Statute and by the unanimous vote of the representatives of the Contracting States entitled to sit on the Committee.
2. In respect of any acceding State, the Convention shall enter into force on the first day of the month following the expiration of a period of three months after the date of deposit of the instrument of accession with the Secretary General of the Council of Europe.

Article 24

1. Any State may at the time of signature or when depositing its instrument of ratification, acceptance, approval or accession, specify the territory or territories to which this Convention shall apply.
2. Any State may at any later date, by a declaration addressed to the Secretary General of the Council of Europe, extend the application of this Convention to any other territory specified in the declaration. In respect of such territory, the Convention shall enter into force on the first day of the month following the expiration of a period of three months after the date of receipt by the Secretary General of such declaration.
3. Any declaration made under the two preceding paragraphs may, in respect of any territory specified in such declaration, be withdrawn by a notification addressed to the Secretary General. The withdrawal shall become effective on the first day of the month following the expiration of a period of six months after the date of receipt of such notification by the Secretary General.

Article 25

1. A State which has two or more territorial units in which different systems of law apply in matters of custody of children and of recognition and enforcement of decisions relating to custody may, at the time of signature or when depositing its instrument of ratification, acceptance, approval or accession, declare that this Convention shall apply to all its territorial units or to one or more of them.
2. Such a State may at any later date, by a declaration addressed to the Secretary General of the Council of Europe, extend the application of this Convention to any other territorial unit specified in the declaration. In respect of such territorial unit the Convention shall enter into force on the first day of the month following the expiration of a period of three months after the date of receipt by the Secretary General of such declaration.
3. Any declaration made under the two preceding paragraphs may, in respect of any territorial unit specified in such declaration, be withdrawn by notification addressed to the Secretary General. The withdrawal shall become effective on the first day of the month following the expiration of a period of six months after the date of receipt of such notification by the Secretary General.

Article 26

1. In relation to a State which has in matters of custody two or more systems of law of territorial application:
   (a) reference to the law of a person's habitual residence or to the law of a person's nationality shall be construed as referring to the system of law determined by the rules in force in that State or, if there are no such rules, to the system of law with which the person concerned is most closely connected;
   (b) reference to the State of origin or to the State addressed shall be construed as referring, as the case may be, to the territorial unit where the decision was given or to the territorial unit where recognition or enforcement of the decision or restoration of custody is requested.
2. Paragraph 1(a) of this Article also applies *mutatis mutandis* to States which have in matters of custody two or more systems of law of personal application.

Article 27

1. Any State may, at the time of signature or when depositing its instrument of ratification, acceptance, approval or accession, declare that it avails itself of one or more of the reservations provided for in paragraph 3 of Article 6, Article 17 and Article 18 of this Convention. No other reservation may be made.
2. Any Contracting State which has made a reservation under the preceding paragraph may wholly or partly withdraw it by means of a notification addressed to the Secretary General of the Council of Europe. The withdrawal shall take effect on the date of receipt of such notification by the Secretary General.

Article 28

At the end of the third year following the date of entry into force of this Convention and, on his own initiative, at any time after this date, the Secretary General of the Council of Europe shall invite the representatives of the central authorities appointed by the Contracting States to meet in order to study and to facilitate the functioning of the Convention. Any Member State of the Council of Europe not being a party to the Convention may be represented by an observer. A report shall be prepared on the work of each of these meetings and forwarded to the Committee of Ministers of the Council of Europe for information.

Article 29

1. Any Party may at any time denounce this Convention by means of a notification addressed to the Secretary General of the Council of Europe.
2. Such denunciation shall become effective on the first day of the month following the expiration of a period of six months after the date of receipt of the notification by the Secretary General.

Article 30

The Secretary General of the Council of Europe shall notify the Member States of the Council and any State which has acceded to this Convention, of:—

(a) any signature;
(b) the deposit of any instrument of ratification, acceptance, approval or accession;
(c) any date of entry into force of this Convention in accordance with Articles 22, 23, 24 and 25;
(d) any other act, notification or communication relating to this Convention.

In witness whereof the undersigned, being duly authorised thereto, have signed this Convention.

Done at Luxembourg, this 20th day of May 1980, in English and French, both texts being equally authentic, in a single copy which shall be deposited in the archives of the Council of Europe. The Secretary General of the Council of Europe shall transmit certified copies to each Member State of the Council of Europe and to any State invited to accede to this Convention.

Children and Immigration

CHILDREN AND IMMIGRATION

EUROPEAN LAW

Rights regarding freedom of movement of persons and dependent children are afforded under the Treaty of Rome 1959 (the EEC Treaty) as amended by the Single European Act 1987 and the Treaty on European Union 1993. Treaties, Directives and Regulations made under it and decisions of the European Court of Justice (ECJ) are enforceable in European Union countries by reason of the European Communities Act 1972. The Treaty of Rome gave powers to the then EEC and its member states to enter agreements with other states which are binding in Community Law. The most important agreements entered into are the Turkish Association Agreement 1960 and the recent Hungarian, Czech, Polish and Slovak Agreements. Under the European Economic Area Agreement the same freedom of movement extends to EU nationals and those from Norway and Liechtenstein. The view of the Commission under Article 7(a) of the EEC Treaty is that a third country national has the right to move within the internal market but lacks rights to assume residence and employment there.

British Commonwealth citizens must often obtain visas to visit other EU states. The Schengen Agreement, which has not been ratified by the UK, allows such freedom of movement within such signatory states. Under Article 8(a) of the EEC Treaty as amended by the Treaty on European Union, it is stated that 'every citizen shall have the right to move and reside freely within the territory of the Member States, subject to the limitations and conditions laid down in this Treaty and by the measures adopted to give it effect'. Different views remain as to the limitations of this Treaty. An EU national could move to and reside within the territory of the member state. The national would not have to be seeking work, though it might be that the ECJ will yet state that certain implementing measures should be applied to some aspect of movement for EU nationals

Under Title VI of the Treaty on European Union, common interest between states is expected on asylum policy, crossing of external borders of states and immigration policy generally and such policy regarding nationals of third countries. In June 1990 the Dublin Convention for determining the state responsible for considering asylum applications was signed. Even by 1993 only half the states expected to sign it have indeed signed it. It is not Community law and grants few if any enforceable rights or legitimate expectations. The External Frontiers Convention, conceived at the same time, has had even less success! As such, the Commission itself has proposed such a Convention for approval by the Council and adoption by member states under Articles of the Treaty of the European Union. Measures may yet be adopted by the European Union without the ECJ having jurisdiction over them, though some measures may be adopted under the EU with ECJ competence, providing some consistency in interpretation.

Member states give effect to EC law by the enactment of national measures implementing Community obligations; national courts can interpret general legislation; Community law is often directly applicable. It should not be forgotten that the ECJ has established the award of damages where states fail to implement a Directive. Even where states rely upon matters of public policy, security or health as reasons not to implement, the ECJ has ruled that it is not a bar to direct effectiveness of such expected provisions. Under Article 189 of the Treaty of Rome Regulations are binding in their entirety and take direct effect in each member state with member states being expected to assume Community Law.

CHILDREN AS DEPENDANTS OF:

I. EEA Nationals

Nationals of states that are themselves parties to the EEA Agreement have free movement rights. Companies with registered offices within the Community will be treated like a natural person who is a national of a Community state. Such Companies also have the right of establishment in another member state if a person has nationality of a member state which depends upon each state's own law, with free movement being reduced between states if respective nationality law is changed. Some have the nationality of more than one state and such dual nationality cannot fetter rights under Community law. Where a person returns to their home state from another part of the EU or EAA and was thereby exercising Community and national rights of entry, dependant family members may not be treated less favourably than is required by Community law.

2. Non-Nationals

Non-nationals are excluded from the Treaty, though exceptions are considered, namely:

a. family members and dependants of qualified persons;
b. directors and employees of companies constituted in one member state, carrying out work in another; and
c. persons who are stateless or refugees, acknowledged in one state but who have entered the territory of another; they might possess accrued social security rights but may lack freedom of movement

3. Workers

The ECJ established that the term 'worker' has a Community meaning attributed to it rather than distinguishable interpretations of individual countries. It is thought the term does not relate to the self-employed, only the employed. Remuneration through payment seems to be the kernel of being employed, whether in a training capacity or something more established. 'Worker' relates to job-seeker and someone in between employment. Interpretation of the terms should not be limited restrictively nor should motive for assuming employment in a state be called into question.

4. Workers within other areas of community law

Independent considerations relate to the free movement of workers in industries such as steel and coal. The Euratom and the European Coal and Steel Community Treaty offer separate provisions. The EC Treaty cannot affect the ECSC Treaty or resile from the Euratom Treaty. Workers have a right to enter and reside along with state nationals who have free movement and can remain after retirement, with family dependants being considered positively.

5. The self-employed

Articles 52 and 59 of the EC Treaty avoid restrictions on those wishing to be self-employed within business or to provide and/or receive services in another state. A self-employed person wishing to offer a service in another state can only do so if they are established in providing such service in a first state before moving to a second state to offer such service by way of self-employment. In addition through Directive 73/148 the recipients of such services can enter another state territory to receive such service.

6. Students

Fee-paying students may gain entry to another state as recipients of services. EC workers and self-employed dependants have the right of access to general and vocational education. A right of residence exists under Directive 93/96 at a recognised establishment if the principal purpose is to follow a vocational training course. Such students cannot seek grants, must be covered by health insurance and avoid becoming a financial burden on the state. They can in addition be joined by a spouse and/or a child.

7. The self-sufficient

The self-sufficient who have enough money and as such will be independent of state assistance can assume residence with a child provided there is proper provision for total financial independence, including especially health insurance. The retired can similarly stay on so long as they are already in receipt of invalidity or early retirement benefits or benefits generally of a long-term nature that will avoid dependence upon the state.

8. The family

Rights of freedom of movement extend to the spouse and other family members. Such exercise of familial rights is dependent upon Community rights but is broadly the same as the primary person's right to enter and remain in another state: if he or she has it, it will extend to his or her family. Therefore the following may benefit, namely:

a. the spouse;
b. children under 21 or dependent upon their parents;
c. dependant grandchildren;
d. non-dependant grandchildren under 21; and
e. dependant relatives.

'Children' includes natural and adopted children and probably a child who 'resides' with the principal or spouse under a court order. Regulations and Directives emphasise that member states should permit admissions of family members who do not come within the strict term if there is dependence. Community law does not consider how the couple met and lacks any sort of 'primary purpose' test. Article 10 of the Regulation does not require the spouse of a worker to live in the other state permanently, only that accommodation used was normal for the purpose of accommodating the family, with Article 11 giving family members the right to assume any activity through the member state concerned. A separated spouse will continue to enjoy rights until the moment of a final decree of divorce at least.

Children of migrant workers keep their rights under Community law even if the EEA national parent leaves, where they have already entered the education system of a state at the time the parent exercised Treaty rights. It may well be, however, that the spouse of the principal upon his departure cannot remain in a state to look after the child who retains the right to complete whatever educational course it is continuing to attend.

Where the principal dies whilst living in a state, the spouse can retain rights where:

a. the deceased resided in the state into which they immigrated for two continuous years before death;
b. the death was from an accident at work or an occupational disease; and
c. the surviving spouse lost the nationality of the state of immigration upon mariage to the deceased.

INTERNATIONAL ASPECTS

Countries are bound by the principles of customary international law and those treaties entered into and ratified pursuant to their sovereignty. Both the 1951 Convention Relating to Refugees and the UN Convention Against Torture of 1981 require signatory states not to expel persons whose deportation might lead them into situations of ill-treatment.

EUROPEAN CONVENTION ON HUMAN RIGHTS

Article 3

'No one shall be subjected to torture or to inhuman or degrading treatment or punishment'

Problems regarding persons gaining entry to states may be degrading, especially if there is a racially discriminatory context as within Article 14, as well as deportation to states that lack human rights considerations. The European Commission on Human Rights provides that treatment of a person is degrading where it lowers him in rank, position, reputation or character, whether in his own eyes or those of other people. It does not refer to physical acts only, with acts of racial discrimination also amounting to degrading treatment. Discrimination by use of language could also be deemed to affront human dignity, amounting to degrading treatment. Where deportation would expose an asylum seeker to a real risk of ill-treatment then explusion is not recommended by any means!

Article 5(1)

'Everyone has the right to liberty and security of persons. No one shall be deprived of his liberty save in the following cases in accordance with the procedure prescribed by law: the lawful arrest or detention of a person to prevent his effecting an unauthorised entry into the country or of a person against whom action is being taken with a view to deportation or extradition.'

Whilst Article 5 does not include the right to freedom of movement, it subjects the power of arrest and detention to the rule of law.

Article 8

'everyone has the right to respect for private and family life, his home and his correspondence'

The exclusion of a person from a state where his family members live can raise an Article 8 issue. The European Commission has indicated a likely violation where a couple cannot attain residence in a state where one has nationality. Similarly, if obstacles exist regarding the establishment of family life in a particular state this too might be a ground for alleging violation. In *Berrehah v. Netherlands* (1988 11 EHRR 322) a violation was held where there was a refusal to grant a residence permit to a Moroccan father whose marriage to a Dutch woman had collapsed. He had a close relationship with his child. Cohabitation was said not to be a precondition of family life and the refusal to grant the residence permit was an inteference with the relationship between father and child. In *Fadele v. UK* (Human Rights Case Digest 1990) the Commission held a case to be admissible under Article 8 where a Nigerian father with a poor immigration history had been refused admission to the UK to look after his UK-born children after their mother had died in a car crash.

A breach may well also occur where contact rights are violated through deportation. In *K v. Finland* (App 1982/92 (1993) 16 EHRR CD 47), a Jamaican rapist was only deported for two years because of family connections through a wife and child. In *Gul v. Switzerland* (Human Rights Digest 1994) a child could not join his parents in Switzerland and in *Ahmut v. Netherlands* (Human Rights Digest 1994) a child could not join his divorced Moroccan father in the Netherlands.

In addition, children lacking a right of abode in a state who as they grow older, receive sentences as a result of criminal conduct may face deportation. In *Moustaquim v. Belgium* (1991 13 EHRR 802) the court held there was no Article 8 violation where a boy who had lived in Belgium since the age of one was to be deported, though in *Beijoudi v. France* (1992 14 EHRR 801) the court held that deportation was such a violation.

Family life usually means a close relationship between persons without distinguishing between married and non-married family, and a belief that a cohabiting couple leading a normal family life are married is enough, even if the marriage is invalid or has not been fully established (*Abdulaziz, Cabales and Blakandali v. UK,* 1985 7 EHRR 471).

In *Mohammed Alam v. UK* (1967 *The Times*) the Commission admitted an application by a father over the refusal to admit his thirteen-year-old son, though in *Harbahjan Singh v. UK* (1967, *The Times*) an applicant adult living apart from his father could not show that there was family life under Article 8. In *Berrehah* (1988 EHRR 322) a close relationship between father and daughter was family life under Article 8.

A relationship that does not assume a familial one might nevertheless be a private one, as cohabiting couples and those who foster do indeed form a family and enjoy family life. Gay couples have not found favour with the Commission, though a child dependant upon a gay parent might assist an application

Article 12

'men and women of marriageable age have the right to marry and found a family according to the national laws governing the exercise of this right'

The Commission has concluded that factors that justify interference with family life also apply to the right to marry.

The Dublin Convention –
Convention Determining the State Responsible for Examining Applications for Asylum lodged in one of the Member States of the European Communities

Signed in Dublin on 15 June 1990

Having regard to the objective, fixed by the European Council meeting in Strasbourg on 8 and 9 December 1989, of the harrnonisation of their asylum policies;

Determined, in keeping with their common humanitarian tradition, to guarantee adequate protection to refugees in accordance with the terms of the Geneva Convention of 28 July 1951, as amended by the New York Protocol of 31 January 1967 relating to the Status of Refugees, hereinafter referred to as the 'Geneva Convention' and the 'New York Protocol' respectively;

Considering the joint objective of an area without internal frontiers in which the free movement of persons shall, in particular, be ensured, in accordance with the provisions of the Treaty establishing the European Economic Community, as amended by the Single European Act;

Aware of the need, in pursuit of this objective, to take measures to avoid any situations arising, with the result that applicants for asylum are left in doubt for too long as regards the likely outcome of their applications and concerned to provide all applicants for asylum with a guarantee that their applications will be examined by one of the member states and to ensure that applicants for asylum are not referred successively from one member state to another without any of these states acknowledging itself to be competent to examine the application for asylum;

Desiring to continue the dialogue with the United Nations High Commissioner for Refugees in order to achieve the above objectives;

Determined to co-operate closely in the application of this Convention through various means, including exchanges of information.

[The representatives of the member states of the EEC]...

Have agreed as follows:*

Article 1

1. For the purposes of this Convention:
   (a) Alien means: any person other than a national of a member state;
   (b) Application for asylum means: a request whereby an alien seeks from a member state protection under the Geneva Convention by claiming refugee status within the meaning of Article 1 of the Geneva Convention, as amended by the New York Protocol;
   (c) Applicant for asylum means: an alien who has made an application for asylum in respect of which a final decision has not yet been taken;
   (d) Examination of an application for asylum means: all the measures for examination, decisions or rulings given by the competent authorities on an application for asylum, except for procedures to determine the

* Denmark has not yet acceded to the Convention

state responsible for examining the application for asylum pursuant to this Convention;

(e) Residence permit means: any authorization issued by the authorities of a member state authorizing an alien to stay in its territory, with the exception of visas and 'stay permits' issued during examination of an application for a residence permit or for asylum.

(f) Entry visa means: authorization or decision by a member state to enable an alien to enter its territory, subject to the other entry conditions being fulfilled;

(g) Transit visa means: authorization or decision by a member state to enable an alien to transit through its territory or pass through the transit zone of a port or airport, subject to the other transit conditions being fulfilled.

2. The nature of the visa shall be assessed in the light of the definitions set out in paragraph 1, points (f) and (g).

Article 2

The member states reaffirm their obligations under the Geneva Convention, as amended by the New York Protocol, with no geographic restriction of the scope of these instruments, and their commitment to co-operating with the services of the United Nations High Commissioner for Refugees in applying these instruments.

Article 3

1. Member states undertake to examine the application of any alien who applies at the border or in their territory to any one of them for asylum.
2. That application shall be examined by a single member state, which shall be determined in accordance with the criteria defined in this Convention. The criteria set out in Articles 4 to 8 shall apply in the order in which they appear.
3. That application shall be examined by that state in accordance with its national laws and its international obligations.
4. Each member state shall have the right to examine an application for asylum submitted to it by an alien, even if such examination is not its responsibility under the criteria defined in this Convention, provided that the applicant for asylum agrees thereto.

   The member state responsible under the above criteria is then relieved of its obligations, which are transferred to the member state which expressed the wish to examine the application. The latter state shall inform the member state responsible under the said criteria if the application has been referred to it.
5. Any member state shall retain the right, pursuant to its national laws, to send an applicant for asylum to a third state, in compliance with the provisions of the Geneva Convention, as amended by the New York Protocol.
6. The process of determining the member state responsible for examining the application for asylum under this Convention shall start as soon as an application for asylum is first lodged with a member state.
7. An applicant for asylum who is present in another member state and there lodges an application for asylum after withdrawing his or her application during the process of determining the state responsible shall be taken back,

under the conditions laid down in Article 13, by the member state with which that application for asylum was lodged, with a view to completing the process of determining the state responsible for examining the application for asylum.

This obligation shall cease to apply if the applicant for asylum has since left the territory of the member states for a period of at least three months or has obtained from a member state a residence permit valid for more than three months.

Article 4

Where the applicant for asylum has a member of his family who has been recognized as having refugee status within the meaning of the Geneva Convention, as amended by the New York Protocol, in a member state and is legally resident there, that state shall be responsible for examining the application, provided that the persons concerned so desire.

The family member in question may not be other than the spouse of the applicant for asylum or his or her unmarried child who is a minor of under eighteen years, or his or her father or mother where the applicant for asylum is himself or herself an unmarried child who is a minor of under eighteen years.

Article 5

1. Where the applicant for asylum is in possession of a valid residence permit, the member state which issued the permit shall be responsible for examining the application for asylum.
2. Where the applicant for asylum is in possession of a valid visa, the member state which issued the visa shall be responsible for examining the application for asylum, except in the following situations:
   (a) if the visa was issued on the written authorization of another member state, that state shall be responsible for examining the application for asylum. Where a member state first consults the central authority of another member state, inter alia for security reasons, the agreement of the latter shall not constitute written authorization within the meaning of this provision.
   (b) where the applicant for asylum is in possession of a transit visa and lodges his application in another member state in which he is not subject to a visa requirement, that state shall be responsible for examining the application for asylum.
   c) where the applicant for asylum is in possession of a transit visa and lodges his application in the state which issued him or her with the visa and which has received written confirmation from the diplomatic or consular authorities of the member state of destination that the alien for whom the visa requirement was waived fulfilled the conditions for entry into that state, the latter shall be responsible for examining the application for asylum.
3. Where the applicant for asylum is in possession of more than one valid residence permit or visa issued by different member states, the responsibility for examining the application for asylum shall be assumed by the member states in the following order:

(a) the state which issued the residence permit conferring the right to the longest period of residency or, where the periods of validity of all the permits are identical, the state which issued the residence permit having the latest expiry date;
(b) the state which issued the visa having the latest expiry date where the various visas are of the same type;
(c) where visas are of different kinds, the state which issued the visa having the longest period of validity, or where the periods of validity are identical, the state which issued the visa having the latest expiry date. This provision shall not apply where the applicant is in possession of one or more transit visas, issued on presentation of an entry visa for another member state. In that case, that member state shall be responsible.

4. Where the applicant for asylum is in possession only of one or more residence permits which have expired less than two years previously or one or more visas which have expired less than six months previously and enabled him or her actually to enter the territory of a member state, the provisions of paragraphs 1, 2 and 3 of this Article shall apply for such time as the alien has not left the territory of the member states.

   Where the applicant for asylum is in possession of one or more residence permits which have expired more than two years previously or one or more visas which have expired more than six months previously and enabled him or her to enter the territory of a member state and where an alien has not left Community territory, the member state in which the application is lodged shall be responsible.

Article 6

When it can be proved that an applicant for asylum has irregularly crossed the border into a member state by land, sea or air, having come from a non-member state of the European Communities, the member state thus entered shall be responsible for examining the application for asylum.

That state shall cease to be responsible, however, if it is proved that the applicant has been living in the member state where the application for asylum was made at least six months before making this application for asylum. In that case it is the latter member state which is responsible for examining the application for asylum.

Article 7

1. The responsibility for examining an application for asylum shall be incumbent upon the member state responsible for controlling the entry of the alien into the territory of the member states, except where, after legally entering a member state in which the need for him or her to have a visa is waived, the alien lodges his or her application for asylum in another member state in which the need for him or her to have a visa for entry into the territory is also waived. In this case, the latter state shall be responsible for examining the application for asylum.
2. Pending the entry into force of an agreement between member states on arrangements for crossing external borders, the member state which authorizes transit without a visa through the transit zone of its airports shall not be regarded as responsible for control on entry, in respect of travellers who do not leave the transit zone.

3. Where the application for asylum is made in transit in an airport of a member state, that state shall be responsible for examination.

Article 8

Where no member state responsible for examining the application for asylum can be designated on the basis of the other criteria listed in this Convention, the first member state with which the application for asylum is lodged shall be responsible for examining it.

Article 9

Any member state, even when it is not responsible under the criteria laid out in this Convention, may, for humanitarian reasons, based in particular on family or cultural grounds, examine an application for asylum at the request of another member state, provided that the applicant so desires.

If the member state thus approached accedes to the request, responsibility for examining the application shall be transferred to it.

Article 10

1. The member state responsible for examining an application for asylum according to the criteria set out in this Convention shall be obliged to:
   (a) Take charge under the conditions laid down in Article 11 of an applicant who has lodged an application for asylum in a different member state.
   (b) Complete the examination of the application for asylum.
   (c) Re-admit or take back under the conditions laid down in Article 13 an applicant whose application is under examination and who is irregularly in another member state.
   (d) Take back, under the conditions laid down in Article 13, an applicant who has withdrawn the application under examination and lodged an application in another member state.
   (e) Take back, under the conditions laid down in Article 13, an alien whose application it has rejected and who is illegally in another member state.
2. If a member state issues to the applicant a residence permit valid for more than three months, the obligations specified in paragraph 1, points (a) to (e) shall be transferred to that member state.
3. The obligations specified in paragraph 1, points (a) to (d) shall cease to apply if the alien concerned has left the territory of the member states for a period of at least three months.
4. The obligations specified in paragraph 1, points (d) and (e) shall cease to apply if the state responsible for examining the application for asylum, following the withdrawal or rejection of the application, takes and enforces the necessary measures for the alien to return to his country of origin or to another country which he may lawfully enter.

Article 11

1. If a member state with which an application for asylum has been lodged considers that another member state is responsible for examining the application, it may, as quickly as possible and in any case within the six months following the date on which the application was lodged, call upon the other member state to take charge of the applicant.

If the request that charge be taken is not made within the six-month time limit, responsibility for examining the application for asylum shall rest with the state in which the application was lodged.

2. The request that charge be taken shall contain indications enabling the authorities of that other state to ascertain whether it is responsible on the basis of the criteria laid down in this Convention.
3. The state responsible in accordance with those criteria shall be determined on the basis of the situation obtaining when the applicant for asylum first lodged his application with a member state.
4. The member state shall pronounce judgment on the request within three months of receipt of the claim. Failure to act within that period shall be tantamount to accepting the claim.
5. Transfer of the applicant for asylum from the member state where the application was lodged to the member state responsible must take place not later than one month after acceptance of the request to take charge or one month after the conclusion of any proceedings initiated by the alien challenging the transfer decision if the proceedings are suspensory.

(6) Measures taken under Article 18 may subsequently determine the details of the process by which applicants shall be taken in charge.

Article 12

Where an application for asylum is lodged with the competent authorities of a member state by an applicant who is on the territory of another member state, the determination of the member state responsible for examining the application for asylum shall be made by the member state on whose territory the applicant is. The latter member state shall be informed without delay by the member state which received the application and shall then, for the purpose of applying this Convention, be regarded as the member state with which the application for asylum was lodged.

Article 13

1. An applicant for asylum shall be taken back in the cases provided for in Article 3(7) and in Article 10 as follows:
   (a) the request for the applicant to be taken back must provide indications enabling the state with which the request is lodged to ascertain that it is responsible in accordance with Article 3(7) and with Article 10;
   (b) the state called upon to take back the applicant shall give an answer to the request within eight days of the matter being referred to it. Should it acknowledge responsibility, it shall then take back the applicant for asylum as quickly as possible and at the latest one month after it agrees to do so.
2. Measures taken under Article 18 may at a later date set out the details of the procedure for taking the applicant back.

Article 14

1. Member states shall conduct mutual exchanges with regard to:
   - national legislative or regulatory measures or practices applicable in the field of asylum;

- statistical data on monthly arrivals of applicants for asylum, and their breakdown by nationality. Such information shall be forwarded quarterly through the General Secretariat of the Council of the European Communities, which shall see that it is circulated to the member states and the Commission of the European Communities and to the United Nations High Commissioner for Refugees.

2. The member states may conduct mutual exchanges with regard to:
   - general information on new trends in applications for asylum;
   - general information on the situation in the countries of origin or of provenance of applicants for asylum.
3. If the member state providing the information referred to in paragraph 2 wants it to be kept confidential, the other member states shall comply with this wish.

Article 15

1. Each member state shall communicate to any member state that so requests such information on individual cases as is necessary for:
   - determining the member state which is responsible for examining the application for asylum;
   - examining the application for asylum;
   - implementing any obligation arising under this Convention.
2. This information may only cover:
   - personal details of the applicant, and, where appropriate, the members of his family (full name – where appropriate, former name –, nick-names or pseudonyms, nationality – present and former –, date and place of birth);
   - identity and travel papers (references, validity, date of issue, issuing authority, place of issue, etc);
   - other information necessary for establishing the identity of the applicant;
   - places of residence and routes travelled;
   - residence permits or visas issued by a member state;
   - the place where the application was lodged;
   - the date any previous application for asylum was lodged, the date the present application was lodged, the stage reached in the proceedings and the decision taken, if any.
3. Furthermore, one member state may request another member state to let it know on what grounds the applicant for asylum bases his or her application and, where applicable, the grounds for any decisions taken concerning the applicant. It is for the member state from which the information is requested to decide whether or not to impart it. In any event, communication of the information requested shall be subject to the approval of the applicant for asylum.
4. This exchange of information shall be effected at the request of a member state and may only take place between authorities the designation of which by each member state has been communicated to the Committee provided for under Article 18.
5. The information exchanged may only be used for the purposes set out in paragraph 1. In each member state such information may only be communicated to the authorities and courts and tribunals entrusted with:

- determining the member state which is responsible for examining the application for asylum;
- examining the application for asylum;
- implementing any obligation arising under this Convention.

6. The member state that forwards the information shall ensure that it is accurate and up-to-date.

   If it appears that this member state has supplied information which is inaccurate or which should not have been forwarded, the recipient member state, shall be immediately informed thereof. They shall be obliged to correct such information or to have it erased.

[1097] *Article 16*

1. Any member state may submit to the Committee referred to in Article 18 proposals for revision of this Convention in order to eliminate difficulties in the application thereof.
2. If it proves necessary to revise or amend this Convention pursuant to the achievement of the objectives set out in Article 8a of the Treaty establishing the European Economic Community, such achievement being linked in particular to the establishment of a harmonised asylum and a common visa policy, the member state holding the Presidency of the Council of the European Communities shall organize a meeting of the Committee referred to in Article 18.
3. Any revision of this Convention or amendment hereto shall be adopted by the Committee referred to in Article 18. They shall enter into force in accordance with the provisions of Article 22.

[1098] *Article 17*

1. If a member state experiences major difficulties as a result of a substantial change in the circumstances obtaining on conclusion of this Convention, the state in question may bring the matter before the Committee referred to in Article 18 so that the latter may put to the member states measured to deal with the situation or adopt such revisions or amendments to this Convention as appear necessary, which shall enter into force as provided for in Article 16(3).
2. If, after six months, the situation mentioned in paragraph 1 still obtains, the Committee, acting in accordance with Article 18(2), may authorize the member state affected by that change to suspend temporarily the application of the provisions of this Convention, without such suspension being allowed to impede the achievement of the objectives mentioned in Article 8a of the Treaty establishing the European Economic Treaty or contravene other international obligations of the member states.
3. During the period of suspension, the Committee shall continue its discussions with a view to revising the provisions of this Convention, unless it has already reached an agreement.

Article 18

1. A Committee shall be set up comprising one representative of the Government of each member state.

The Committee shall be chaired by the member state holding the Presidency of the Council of the European Communities.

The Commission of the European Communities may participate in the discussions of the Committee and the working parties referred to in paragraph 4.

2. The Committee shall examine, at the request of one or more member states, any question of a general nature concerning the application or interpretation of this Convention.

   The Committee shall determine the measures referred to in Article 11(6) and Article 13(2) and shall give the authorization referred to in Article 17(2).

   The Committee shall adopt decisions revising or amending the Convention pursuant to Articles 16 and 17.

3. The Committee shall take its decisions unanimously, except where it is acting pursuant to Article 17(2), in which case it shall take its decisions by a majority of two-thirds of the votes of its members.

4. The Committee shall determine its rules of procedure and may set up working parties.

   The Secretariat of the Committee and of the working parties shall be provided by the General Secretariat of the Council of the European Communities.

Article 19

As regards the Kingdom of Denmark, the provisions of this Convention shall not apply to the Faroe Islands nor to Greenland unless a declaration to the contrary is made by the Kingdom of Denmark. Such a declaration may be made at any time by a communication to the Government of Ireland which shall inform the Governments of the other member states thereof.

Article 22

1. This Convention shall be subject to ratification, acceptance or approval. The instruments of ratification, acceptance or approval shall be deposited with the Government of Ireland.

2. The Government of Ireland shall notify the Governments of the other member states of the deposit of the instruments of ratification, acceptance or approval.

3. This Convention shall enter into force on the first day of the third month following the deposit of the instrument of ratification, acceptance or approval by the last signatory state to take this step.

   The state with which the instruments of ratification, acceptance or approval are deposited shall notify the member states of the date of entry into force of this Convention.

Children and Intercountry Adoption

HAGUE CONVENTION ON INTERCOUNTRY ADOPTION 1993

Children who are permanently or temporarily deprived of family life are entitled, pursuant to Article 20(1) of the Convention on the Rights of the Child, to protection from the State and alternative care must be assured for such children, including adoption and fostering. The two Declarations on the Rights of the Child omit reference to adoption or fostering and whilst a child might have a right to 'existing family life', human rights jurisprudence might suggest a child does not have a right to 'family life' per se.

In 1950 a European seminar took place on intercountry adoption under the UN regarding adoptions between European States, with further studies in 1953 and 1960. In 1965 The Hague Convention on Jurisdiction, Applicable Law and Recognition of Decrees Relating to Adoption was adopted, with the European Convention on the Adoption of Children taking place in 1967 and the American Convention on the Conflict of Laws Concerning the Adoption of Minors in 1984.

The purpose of The Hague Convention on Intercountry Adoption is to unify procedures regarding the adoption of children globally. Certain states require the adoption of a foreign child in accordance with their domestic legal process, despite the child having been adopted in his foreign state and having been given leave to remove to the receiving country. The Convention seeks to prevent duplication of procedures and to ensure that the procedure of the receiving state and the sending state work together. Article 23 permits the recognition of an adoption certified by the competent authority of the state of adoption as having been made in accordance with the Convention.

Article 4 requires the consent of the natural parents to the adoption, with Article 5 ensuring the authorisation of the child entering and remaining permanently within the receiving country. As with child abduction applications under the Hague Convention on the Civil Aspects of International Child Abduction 1980 a Central Authority in each state will liaise between the sending and receiving state regarding issues such as:

- consent of the natural parents;
- leave to remove from the sending country; and
- immigration clearance in the receiving country.

Under Article 14 prospective adoptive applicants who are habitually resident in a state must firstly apply to their Central Authority if they wish to adopt a child from abroad. Article 17 states that any adoption will only proceed where both

Central Authorities agree, and only then will there be authorisation for the child to enter the receiving country, whose immigration will also be dealt with by the Central Authorities under Article 18. Under Article 21 provision exists to withdraw a child where placement is not in its best interest.

Hague Convention on Protection of Children and Co-operation in Respect of Intercountry Adoption 1993

The States signatory to the present Convention,

Recognising that the child, for the full and harmonious development of his or her personality, should grow up in a family environment, in an atmosphere of happiness, love and understanding,

Recalling that each State should take, as a matter of priority, appropriate measures to enable the child to remain in the care of his or her family of origin,

Recognising that intercountry adoption may offer the advantage of a permanent family to a child for whom a suitable family cannot be found in his or her State of origin,

Convinced of the necessity to take measures to ensure that intercountry adoptions are made in the best interests of the child and with respect for his or her fundamental rights, and to prevent the abduction, the sale of, or traffic in children,

Desiring to establish common provisions to this effect, taking into account the principles set forth in international instruments, in particular the *United Nations Convention on the Rights of the Child*, of 20 November 1989, and the United Nations Declaration on Social and Legal Principles relating to the Protection and Welfare of Children, with Special Reference to Foster Placement and Adoption Nationally and Internationally (General Assembly Resolution 41/85, of 3 December 1986),

Have agreed upon the following provisions–

CHAPTER 1
SCOPE OF THE CONVENTION

Article 1

The objects of the present Convention are –

(a) to establish safeguards to ensure that intercountry adoptions take place in the best interests of the child and with respect for his or her fundamental rights as recognised in international law;

(b) to establish a system of co-operation amongst Contracting States to ensure that those safeguards are respected and thereby prevent the abduction, the sale of, or traffic in children;

(c) to secure the recognition in Contracting States of adoptions made in accordance with the Convention.

Article 2

(1) The Convention shall apply where a child habitually resident in one Contracting State ('the State of origin') has been, is being, or is to be moved to another Contracting State ('the receiving State') either after his or her adoption in the State of origin by spouses or a person habitually resident in the receiving State, or for the purposes of such an adoption in the receiving State or in the State of origin.

(2) The Convention covers only adoptions which create a permanent parent–child relationship.

Article 3

The Convention ceases to apply if the agreements mentioned in Article 17, sub-paragraph (c), have not been given before the child attains the age of eighteen years.

CHAPTER 11
REQUIREMENTS FOR INTERCOUNTRY ADOPTIONS

Article 4

An adoption within the scope of the Convention shall take place only if the competent authorities of the State of origin –

(a) have established that the child is adoptable;

(b) have determined, after possibilities for placement of the child within the State of origin have been given due consideration, that an intercountry adoption is in the child's best interests;

(c) have ensured that

  (1) the persons, institutions and authorities whose consent is necessary for adoption, have been counselled as may be necessary and duly informed of the effects of their consent, in particular whether or not an adoption will result in the termination of the legal relationship between the child and his or her family of origin,

  (2) such persons, institutions and authorities have given their consent freely, in the required legal form, and expressed or evidenced in writing,

  (3) the consents have not been induced by payment or compensation of any kind and have not been withdrawn, and

  (4) the consent of the mother, where required, has been given only after the birth of the child; and

(d) have ensured, having regard to the age and degree of maturity of the child, that

  (1) he or she has been counselled and duly informed of the effects of the adoption and of his or her consent to the adoption, where such consent is required,

  (2) consideration has been given to the child's wishes and opinions,

  (3) the child's consent to the adoption, where such consent is required, has been given freely, in the required legal form, and expressed or evidenced in writing, and

  (4) such consent has not been induced by payment or compensation of any kind.

Article 5

An adoption within the scope of the Convention shall take place only if the competent authorities of the receiving State –

(a) have determined that the prospective adoptive parents are eligible and suited to adopt;

(b) have ensured that the prospective adoptive parents have been counselled as may be necessary; and

(c) have determined that the child is or will be authorised to enter and reside permanently in that State.

CHAPTER III
CENTRAL AUTHORITIES AND ACCREDITED BODIES

Article 6

1. A Contracting State shall designate a Central Authority to discharge the duties which are imposed by the Convention upon such authorities.
2. Federal States, States with more than one system of law or States having autonomous territorial units shall be free to appoint more than one Central Authority and to specify the territorial or personal extent of their functions. Where a State has appointed more than one Central Authority, it shall designate the Central Authority to which any communication may be addressed for transmission to the appropriate Central Authority within that State.

Article 7

1. Central Authorities shall co-operate with each other and promote co-operation amongst the competent authorities in their States to protect children and to achieve the other objects to the Convention.
2. They shall take directly all appropriate measures to
   (a) provide information as to the laws of their States concerning adoption and other general information, such as statistics and standard forms;
   (b) keep one another informed about the operation of the Convention and, as far as possible, eliminate any obstacles to its application.

Article 8

Central Authorities shall take, directly or through public authorities, all appropriate measures to prevent improper financial or other gain in connection with an adoption and to deter all practices contrary to the objects of the Convention.

Article 9

Central Authorities shall take, directly or through public authorities or other bodies duly accredited in their State, all appropriate measures, in particular to –

(a) collect, preserve and exchange information about the situation of the child and the prospective adoptive parents, so far as is necessary to complete the adoption;
(b) facilitate, follow and expedite proceedings with a view to obtaining the adoption;
(c) promote the development of adoption counselling and post-adoption services in their States;
(d) provide each other with general evaluation reports about experience with intercountry adoption;
(e) reply, in so far as is permitted by the law of their State, to justified requests from other Central Authorities or public authorities for information about a particular adoption situation.

Article 10

Accreditation shall only be granted to and maintained by bodies demonstrating their competence to carry out properly the tasks with which they may be entrusted.

Article 11

An accredited body shall –

(a) pursue only non-profit objectives according to such conditions and within such limits as may be established by the competent authorities of the State of accreditation;

(b) be directed and staffed by persons qualified by their ethical standards and by training or experience to work in the field of intercountry adoption; and

(c) be subject to supervision by competent authorities of that State as to its composition, operation and financial situation.

Article 12

A body accredited in one Contracting State may act in another Contracting State only if the competent authorities of both States have authorised it to do so.

Article 13

The designation of the Central Authorities and, where appropriate, the extent of their functions, as well as the names and addresses of the accredited bodies shall be communicated by each Contracting State to the Permanent Bureau of the Hague Conference on Private International Law.

CHAPTER IV
PROCEDURAL REQUIREMENTS IN INTERCOUNTRY ADOPTION

Article 14

Persons habitually resident in a Contracting State, who wish to adopt a child habitually resident in another Contracting State, shall apply to the Central Authority in the State of their habitual residence.

Article 15

1. If the Central Authority of the receiving State is satisfied that the applicants are eligible and suited to adopt, it shall prepare a report including information about their identity, eligibility and suitability to adopt, background, family and medical history, social environment, reasons for adoption, ability to undertake and intercountry adoption, as well as the characteristics of the children for whom they would be qualified to care.
2. It shall transmit the report to the Central Authority of the State of origin.

Article 16

1. If the Central Authority of the State of origin is satisfied that the child is adoptable, it shall –

(a) prepare a report including information about his or her identity, adoptability, background, social environment, family history, medical history including that of the child's family, and any special needs of the child;
(b) give due consideration to the child's upbringing and to his or her ethnic, religious and cultural background;
(c) ensure that consents have been obtained in accordance with Article 4; and
(d) determine, on the basis in particular of the reports relating to the child and the prospective adoptive parents, whether the envisaged placement is in the best interests of the child.

2. It shall transmit to the Central Authority of the receiving State its report on the child, proof that the necessary consents have been obtained and the reasons for its determination on the placement, taking care not to reveal the identity of the mother and the father if, in the State of origin, these identities may not be disclosed.

Article 17

Any decision in the State of origin that a child should be entrusted to prospective adoptive parents may only be made if –
(a) the Central Authority of that State has ensured that the prospective adoptive parents agree;
(b) the Central Authority of the receiving State has approved such decision, where such approval is required by the law of that State or by the Central Authority of the State of origin;
(c) the Central Authorities of both States have agreed that the adoption may proceed; and
(d) it has been determined, in accordance with Article 5, that the prospective adoptive parents are eligible and suited to adopt and that the child is or will be authorised to enter and reside permanently in the receiving State.

Article 18

The Central Authorities of both States shall take all necessary steps to obtain permission for the child to leave the State of origin and to enter and reside permanently in the receiving State.

Article 19

1. The transfer of the child to the receiving State may only be carried out if the requirements of Article 17 have been satisfied.
2. The Central Authorities of both States shall ensure that this transfer takes place in secure and appropriate circumstances and, if possible, in the company of the adoptive or prospective adoptive parents.
3. If the transfer of the child does not take place, the reports referred to in Articles 15 and 16 are to be sent back to the authorities who forwarded them.

Article 20

The Central Authorities shall keep each other informed about the adoption process and the measures taken to complete it, as well as about the progress of the placement if a probationary period is required.

Article 21

1. Where the adoption is to take place after the transfer of the child to the receiving State and it appears to the Central Authority of that State that the continued placement of the child with the prospective adoptive parents is not in the child's best interests, such Central Authority shall take the measures necessary to protect the child, in particular –
   (a) to cause the child to be withdrawn from the prospective adoptive parents and to arrange temporary care;
   (b) in consultation with the Central Authority of the State of origin, to arrange without delay a new placement of the child with a view to adoption or, if this is not appropriate, to arrange alternative long term care; an adoption shall not take place until the Central Authority of the State of origin has been duly informed concerning the new prospective adoptive parents;
   (c) as a last resort, to arrange the return of the child, if his or her interests so require.
2. Having regard in particular to the age and degree of maturity of the child, he or she shall be consulted and, where appropriate, his or consent obtained in relation to measures to be taken under this Article.

Article 22

1. The functions of a Central Authority under this Chapter may be performed by public authorities or by bodies accredited under Chapter III, to the extent permitted by the law of its State.
2. Any Contracting State may declare to the depositary of the Convention that the functions of the Central Authority under Articles 15 to 21 may be performed in that State, to the extent permitted by the law and subject to the supervision of the competent authorities of that State, also by bodies or persons who –
   (a) meet the requirements of integrity, professional competence, experience and accountability of that State; and
   (b) are qualified by their ethical standards and by training or experience to work in the field of intercountry adoption.
3. A Contracting State which makes the declaration provided for in paragraph 2 shall keep the Permanent Bureau of the Hague Conference on Private International Law informed of the names and addresses of these bodies and persons.
4. Any Contracting State may declare to the depositary of the Convention that adoptions of children habitually resident in its territory may only take place if the functions of the Central Authorities are performed in accordance with paragraph 1.
5. Notwithstanding any declaration made under paragraph 2, the reports provided for in Articles 15 and 16 shall, in every case, be prepared under the responsibility of the Central Authority or other authorities or bodies in accordance with paragraph 1.

CHAPTER V
RECOGNITION AND EFFECTS OF THE ADOPTION

Article 23

1. An adoption certified by the competent authority of the State of the adoption as having been made in accordance with the Convention shall be recognised by operation of law in the other Contracting States. The certificate shall specify when and by whom the agreements under Article 17, sub-paragraph (c), were given.
2. Each Contracting State shall, at the time of signature, ratification, acceptance, approval or accession, notify the depositary of the Convention of the identity and the functions of the authority or the authorities which, in that State, are competent to make the certification. It shall also notify the depositary of any modification in the designation of these authorities.

Article 24

The recognition of an adoption may be refused in a Contracting State only if the adoption is manifestly contrary to its public policy, taking into account the best interests of the child.

Article 25

Any Contracting State may declare to the depositary of the Convention that it will not be bound under this Convention to recognise adoptions made in accordance with an agreement concluded by application of Article 39, paragraph 2.

Article 26

1. The recognition of an adoption includes recognition of
   (a) the legal parent–child relationship between the child and his or her adoptive parents;
   (b) parental responsibility of the adoptive parents for the child;
   (c) the termination of a pre-existing legal relationship between the child and his or her mother and father, if the adoption has this effect in the Contracting State where it was made.
2. In the case of an adoption having the effect of terminating a pre-existing legal parent–child relationship, the child shall enjoy in the receiving State, and in any other Contracting State where the adoption is recognised, rights equivalent to those resulting from adoptions having this effect in each such State.
3. The preceding paragraphs shall not prejudice the application of any provision more favourable for the child, in force in the Contracting State which recognises the adoption.

Article 27

1. Where an adoption granted in the State of origin does not have the effect of terminating a pre-existing legal parent–child relationship, it may, in the receiving State which recognises the adoption under the Convention, be converted into an adoption having such an effect –
   (a) if the law of the receiving State so permits; and

(b) if the consents referred to in Article 4, sub-paragraphs (c) and (d), have been or are given for the purpose of such an adoption.

2. Article 23 applies to the decision converting the adoption.

CHAPTER VI
GENERAL PROVISIONS

Article 28

The Convention does not affect any law of a State of origin which requires that the adoption of a child habitually resident within that State take place in that State or which prohibits the child's placement in, or transfer to, the receiving State prior to adoption.

Article 29

There shall be no contact between the prospective adoptive parents and the child's parents or any other person who has care of the child until the requirements of Article 4, sub-paragraphs (a) to (c), and Article 5, sub-paragraph (a), have been met, unless the adoption takes place within a family or unless the contact is in compliance with the conditions established by the competent authority of the State of origin.

Article 30

1. The competent authorities of a Contracting State shall ensure that information held by them concerning the child's origin, in particular information concerning the identity of his or her parents, as well as the medical history, is preserved.
2. They shall ensure that the child or his or her representative has access to such information, under appropriate guidance, in so far as is permitted by the law of that State.

Article 31

Without prejudice to Article 30, personal data gathered or transmitted under the Convention, especially data referred to in Articles 15 and 16, shall be used only for the purposes for which they were gathered or transmitted.

Article 32

1. No one shall derive improper financial or other gain from an activity related to an intercountry adoption.
2. Only costs and expenses, including reasonable professional fees of persons involved in the adoption, may be charged or paid.
3. The directors, administrators and employees of bodies involved in an adoption shall not receive remuneration which is unreasonably high in relation to services rendered.

Article 33

A competent authority which finds that any provision of the Convention has not been respected or that there is a serious risk that it may not be respected, shall immediately inform the Central Authority of its State. This Central Authority shall be responsible for ensuring that appropriate measures are taken.

Article 34

If the competent authority of the State of destination of a document so requests, a translation certified as being in conformity with the original must be furnished. Unless otherwise provided, the costs of such translation are to be borne by the prospective adoptive parents.

Article 35

The competent authorities of the Contracting States shall act expeditiously in the process of adoption.

Article 36

In relation to a State which has two or more systems of law with regard to adoption applicable in different territorial units –

(a) any reference to habitual residence in that State shall be construed as referring to habitual residence in a territorial unit of that State;
(b) any reference to the law of that State shall be construed as referring to the law in force in the relevant territorial unit;
(c) any reference to the competent authorities or to the public authorities of that State shall be construed as referring to those authorised to act in the relevant territorial unit;
(d) any reference to the accredited bodies of that State shall be construed as referring to bodies accredited in the relevant territorial unit.

Article 37

In relation to a State which with regard to adoption has two or more systems of law applicable to different categories of persons, any reference to the law of that State shall be construed as referring to the legal system specified by the law of that State.

Article 38

A State within which different territorial units have their own rules of law in respect of adoption shall not be bound to apply the Convention where a State with a unified system of law would not be bound to do so.

Article 39

1. The Convention does not affect any international instrument to which Contracting States are Parties and which contains provisions on matters governed by the Convention, unless a contrary declaration is made by the States Parties to such instrument.
2. Any Contracting State may enter into agreements with one or more other Contracting States, with a view to improving the application of the Convention in their mutual relations. These agreements may derogate only from the provisions of Articles 14 to 16 and 18 to 21. The States which have concluded such an agreement shall transmit a copy to the depositary of the Convention.

Article 40

No reservation to the Convention shall be permitted.

Article 41

The Convention shall apply in every case where an application pursuant to Article 14 has been received after the Convention has entered into force in the receiving State and the State of origin.

Article 42

The Secretary General of the Hague Conference on Private International Law shall at regular intervals convene a Special Commission in order to review the practical operation of the Convention.

CHAPTER VII
FINAL CLAUSES

Article 43

1. The Convention shall be open for signature by the States which were Members of the Hague Conference on Private International Law at the time of its Seventeenth Session and by the other States which participated in that Session.
2. It shall be ratified, accepted or approved and the instrument of ratification, acceptance or approval shall be deposited with the Ministry of Foreign Affairs of the Kingdom of the Netherlands, depositary of the Convention.

Article 44

1. Any other State may accede to the Convention after it has entered into force in accordance with Article 46, paragraph 1.
2. The instrument of accession shall be deposited with the depositary.
3. Such accession shall have effect only as regards the relations between the acceding State and those Contracting States which have not raised an objection to its accession in the six months after the receipt of the notification referred to in sub-paragraph (b) of Article 48. Such an objection may also be raised by States at the time when they ratify, accept or approve the Convention after an accession. Any such objection shall be notified to the depositary.

Article 45

1. If a State has two or more territorial units in which different systems of law are applicable in relation to matters dealt with in the Convention, it may at the time of signature, ratification, acceptance, approval or accession declare that this Convention shall extend to all its territorial units or only to one or more of them and may modify this declaration by submitting another declaration at any time.
2. Any such declaration shall be notified to the depositary and shall state expressly the territorial units to which the Convention applies.
3. If a State makes no declaration under this Article, the Convention is to extend to all territorial units of that State.

Article 46

1. The Convention shall enter into force on the first day of the month following the expiration of three months after the deposit of the third instrument of ratification, acceptance or approval referred to in Article 43.
2. Thereafter the Convention shall enter into force –
   (a) for each State ratifying, accepting or approving it subsequently, or acceding to it, on the first day of the month following the expiration of three months after the deposit of its instrument of ratification, acceptance, approval or accession;
   (b) for a territorial unit to which the Convention has been extended in conformity with Article 45, on the first day of the month following the expiration of three months after the notification referred to in that Article.

Article 47

1. A State Party to the Convention may denounce it by a notification in writing addressed to the depositary.
2. The denunciation takes effect on the first day of the month following the expiration of twelve months after the notification is received by the depositary. Where a longer period for the denunciation to take effect is specified in the notification, the denunciation takes effect upon the expiration of such longer period after the notification is received by the depositary.

Article 48

The depositary shall notify the States Members of the Hague Conference on Private International Law, the other States which participated in the Seventeenth Session and the States which have acceded in accordance with Article 44, of the following –

(a) the signatures, ratifications, acceptances and approvals referred to in Article 43;
(b) the accessions and objections raised to accessions referred to in Article 44;
(c) the date on which the Convention enters into force in accordance with Article 46;
(d) the declarations and designations referred to in Articles 22, 23, 25 and 45;
(e) the agreements referred to in Article 39;
(f) the denunciations referred to in Article 47.

Inter-American Convention on Conflict of Laws Concerning the Adoption of Minors 1984

The Governments of the Member States of the Organization of American States, desirous of concluding a convention on conflict of laws concerning the adoption of minors, have agreed as follows:

Article 1

This Convention shall apply to the adoption of minors in the form of full adoption, adoptive legitimation and other similar institutions that confer on the adoptee a legally established filiation, when the domicile of the adopter (or of the adopters) is in one State Party and the habitual residence of the adoptee is in another State Party.

Article 2

When signing, ratifying or acceding to this Convention, any State Party may declare that it applies to any other form of international adoption of minors.

Article 3

The law of the habitual residence of the minor shall govern capacity, consent, and other requirements for adoption, as well as those procedures and formalities that are necessary for creating the relationship.

Article 4

The law of the domicile of the adopter (or adopters) shall govern:
(a) The capacity to be an adopter;
(b) The age and marital status requirement to be met by an adopter;
(c) The consent of an adopter's spouse, if required, and
(d) The other requirements for being an adopter.
If, however, the requirements of the law of the adopter (or adopters) are manifestly less strict than those of the law of the adoptee's habitual residence, the law of the adoptee shall govern.

Article 5

Adoption that are in conformity with this Convention shall produce their effects unconditionally in the State Parties, and the exception of the unknown institution may not be invoked.

Article 6

The requirements of publication and registration of adoption shall be subject to the law of the State in which they are to be satisfied.

The particular features and type of adoption shall be stated in the registration.

Article 7

Where called for, the secrecy of the adoption shall be guaranteed. However, whenever possible, medical background information on the minor and on the birth parents, if it is known, shall be communicated to the legally appropriate person, without mention of their name or of other data whereby they may be identified.

Article 8

In adoptions governed by this Convention, the authorities granting the adoption may require the adopter (or adopters) to provide evidence of this physical, moral, psychological and economic capacity, through public or private institutions, the specific purpose is to protect minors. These institutions must be specifically authorized by some State or by some international organization.

The institutions that certify the capacity referred to above shall undertake to report to the authority granting the adoption on the conditions under which the adoption has developed over a period of one year. To this end, the authority granting the adoption shall inform the certifying institution that the adoption has been granted.

Article 9

In case of full adoption, adoptive legitimation, and similar institutions:

(a) The relations between the adopter (or adopters) and the adoptee, including support relations, and the relations between the adoptee and the family of the adopter (or adopters), shall be governed by the same law as would govern the relations between the adopter (or adopters) and his legitimate family;

(b) Ties between the adoptee and his family of origin shall be considered dissolved. However, impediments to marriage shall continue.

Article 10

In the case of adoptions other than full adoption. adoptive legitimation, and similar institutions, relations between the adopter (or adopters) and the adoptee shall be governed by the law of the domicile of the adopter (or adopters).

The relations between the adoptee and his family of origin shall be governed by the law of his habitual residence at the time of adoption.

Article 11

The rights of succession of the adoptee or the adopter (or adopters) shall be governed by the rules applicable to the respective successions.

In case of full adoption, adoptive legitimation, and similar institutions, the adoptee, and the adopter (or adopters) and the family thereof, shall have the same rights of succession as those of legitimate family members.

Article 12

Adoptions referred to in Article 1 are irrevocable. Revocation of adoptions referred to in Article 2 shall be governed by the law of the habitual residence of the adoptee at the time of adoption.

Article 13

Where it is permitted, conversion of simple adoption into full adoption, adoptive legitimation, or similar institutions shall be governed, at the choice of the petitioner, by the law of the habitual residence of the adoptee at the time of the adoption, or by that of the State in which the adopter (or adopters) has his domicile at the time the conversion is requested.

If the adoptee is more than 14 years of age, his consent shall be required.

Article 14

Annulment of the adoption shall be governed by the law under which it was granted. An annulment shall be decreed only by judicial authorities, and the interests of the minor shall be protected in accordance with Article 19 of this Convention.

Article 15

The authorities of the State of the habitual residence of the adoptee shall be competent to grant the adoptions referred to in this Convention.

Article 16

The judges of the State where the adoptee was habitually resident at the time the adoption was granted shall be competent to decide on annulment or revocation of the adoption.

The authorities of the State of habitual residence of the adoptee at the time of the adoptions; those of the States of domicile of the adopter (or adopters); or those of the State of domicile of the adoptee, if he has a domicile of his own at the time the conversion is requested, shall be competent, at the option of the petitioner, to decide on the conversion, where it is permitted, of simple adoption into full adoption, adoptive legitimation, or similar institutions.

Article 17

The judges of the State of the domicile of the adopter (or adopters) shall be competent to rule on matters concerning the relations between the adoptee and the adopter (or adopters) and the family thereof until the adoptee has domicile of his own.

As soon as the adoptee has his own domicile, the judge of the domicile the adoptee or that of the adopter (or adopters) shall, at the option of the petitioner, have jurisdiction.

Article 18

The authorities of a State Party may refuse to apply the law declared applicable under this Convention when the law is manifestly contrary to public policy (*ordre public*).

Article 19

The terms of this Convention and the laws applicable under it shall be interpreted consistently and in favor of the validity of the adoption and the best interests of the adoptee.

Article 20

A State Party may at any time declare that this Convention applies to adoptions of minors habitually resident in it by persons also habitually resident in it when, in the opinion of the authority concerned, the circumstances of a given case indicate that the adopter (or adopters) plans to establish his domicile in another State Party after the adoption has been granted.

Article 21

This Convention shall be open for signature by the Member States of the Organization of American States.

Article 22

This Convention is subject to ratification. The instruments of ratification shall be deposited with the General Secretariat of the Organization of American States.

Article 23

This Convention shall remain open for accession by any other State. The instruments of accession shall be deposited with the General Secretariat of the Organization of American States.

Article 24

Each State may, at the time of signature, ratification or accession, make reservations to this Convention, provided that each reservation concerns one or more specific provisions.

Article 25

Adoptions granted according to domestic law when the adoptee and the adopter (or adopters) have their domicile or habitual residence in the same State Party shall produce their effects unconditionally in the other States Parties, without prejudice to their being governed by the law of the new domicile of the adopter (or adopters).

Article 26

This Convention shall enter into force on the thirtieth day following the date of deposit of the second instrument of ratification.

For each State ratifying or acceding to the Convention after the deposit of the second instrument of ratification, the Convention shall enter into force on the thirtieth day after deposit by such State of its instrument of ratification or accession.

Article 27

If a State Party has two or more territorial units in which different systems of law apply in relation to the matters dealt with in this Convention, it may, at the time of signature, ratification or accession, declare that this Convention shall extend to all its territorial units or to only one or more of them.

Such declaration may be modified by subsequent declarations, which shall expressly indicate the territorial unit or units to which the Convention applies. Such subsequent declarations shall be transmitted to the General Secretariat of the Organization of American States, and shall become effective thirty days after the date of their receipt.

Article 28

This Convention shall remain in force indefinitely, but any of the States Parties may denounce it. The instrument of denunciation shall be deposited with the General Secretariat of the Organization of American States. After one year from the date of deposit of the instrument of denunciation, the Convention shall no longer be in effect for the denouncing State, but shall remain in effect for the other States Parties.

Article 29

The original instrument of this Convention, the English, French, Portuguese and Spanish texts of which are equally authentic, shall be deposited with the General Secretariat of the Organization of American States, which shall forward an authenticated copy of its text to the Secretariat of the United Nations for registration and publication in accordance with Article 102 of its Charter. The General Secretariat of the Organization of American states shall notify the Member States of that Organization and the States that have acceded to the Convention of the signatures, deposits of instruments of ratification, accession and denunciation as well as of reservations, if any. It shall also transmit the declarations provided for in Article 2, 20, and 27 of this Convention.

IN WITNESS WHEREOF, the undersigned Plenipotentiaries, being duly authorized thereto by their respective Governments, have signed this Convention.

DONE AT LA PAZ, Republic of Bolivia, this twenty-fourth day of May, one thousand nine hundred and eighty-four.

Children and Maintenance

THE BRUSSELS AND LUGANO CONVENTIONS ON CHILD MAINTENANCE: ORDERS, RECOVERY AND RECIPROCAL ENFORCEMENT

Where a court of a state has made a maintenance order, such maintenance order can be registered and enforced in another state signatory of the relevant Convention. There exist a number of International Conventions in this arena, namely:

1. The Brussels Convention on Jurisdiction and the Enforcement of Judgments in Civil and Commercial Matters 1968.
2. The Lugano Convention on Jurisdiction and the Enforcement of Judgments in Civil and Commercial Matters 1988.
3. The United Nations Convention on Recovery Abroad of Maintenance 1956.
4. The Hague Convention on the Recognition and Enforcement of Decisions Relating to Maintenance Obligations.

The Brussels Convention

The Brussels Convention was acknowledged among the then members of the European Community with the subsequent accession of other member states raising an expectation of their adherence to the Convention. It was concluded pursuant to Article 220 of the Treaty of Rome. Questions of the Convention's interpretation should be made according to the principles laid down by any relevant decision of the European Court of Justice. The Convention considers its own scope, its jurisdiction and the methods of dealing with relevant judgments. In *Hoffman v. Krieg* (1988 ECR 645) a German judgment ordered an estranged husband to pay his wife maintenance, as it assumed a marriage existed between them, but such a judgment was found irreconcilable with a Dutch decree that had already dissolved the marriage.

The Lugano Convention

The Lugano Convention 1988 was concluded between the then members of the European Union and the members of the European Free Trade Area. The principles attributed to a judgment of any contracting Lugano state should be considered by any other contracting state in determining its issues. The judgment seeking to be registered and enforced must firstly have been given by a court of a contracting state, must fall within the scope of the Convention and for the purpose of child maintenance cases will do so by reason of being a 'civil' matter.

Even if a judgment was delivered by a contracting state, the petitioned contracting state where the judgment is sought to be registered can still reconsider the scope of the Convention when the issue came before the first foreign court, though under Article 26 of the Brussels Convention 'a judgement shall be recognised in the other contracting states without any special procedure being required', which also applies to the Lugano Convention.

Defences exist to registration and enforcement. Foreign judgments cannot be reviewed upon an application to register and enforce in any detail, though the following will be considered as a Defence:

1. if an appeal is pending in the original state;
2. if the exercise of the original state's jurisdiction is contrary to the provisions governing jurisdiction in matters of exclusive jurisdiction pursuant to Article 16;
3. if recognition is contrary to public policy;
4. if judgment was given in default of appearance by reason of the Defendant not being served under Article 27(2).
5. if a judgment is irreconcilable with a judgment given in a dispute between the same parties in a state in which recognition is sought; and
6. if a judgment is irreconcilable and contains mutually exclusive legal consequences.

The foreign judgment must be enforceable in the state of origin.

The Hague Convention on the Recognition and Enforcement of Decisions Relating to Maintenance Obligations

A maintenance decision or settlement made in one contracting state may be recognised and enforced in another where it was a decision made by a judicial or administrative authority in respect of a maintenance obligation arising from a relationship of family, parentage or affinity, including pursuant to Art 1, towards a child who is not legitimate. It applies to a decision in respect of periodical payments or a lump sum, provided the latter is for support. The judicial authority in the state of origin has authority:

1. if, when procedings were begun, the maintenance debtor or creditor was habitually resident in the state of origin or both were nationals of the state of origin;
2. the Defendant submitted to the jurisdiction; and
3. the maintenance is due by reason of divorce, legal separation or nullity proceedings in that state.

Defences to such recognition and enforcement exist where:

1. they are incompatible with public policy;
2. the original decision was obtained by fraud;
3. proceedings between the same parties on the same grounds are pending before an authority in the state addressed and they were instituted there first; and
4. the decision is incompatible with a decision rendered between the same parties and having the same purpose, either in the state addressed or another state, provided the latter decision fulfils the conditions necessary for its recognition and enforcement in the state addressed.

Convention on Jurisdiction and the Enforcement of Judgments in Civil and Commercial Matters

PREAMBLE

The High Contracting Parties to the Treaty establishing the European Economic Community.

Desiring to implement the provisions of Article 220 of that Treaty by virtue of which they undertook to secure the simplification of formalities governing the reciprocal recognition and enforcement of judgments of courts or tribunals;

Anxious to strengthen in the Community the legal protection of persons therein established;

Considering that it is necessary for this purpose to determine the international jurisdiction of their courts, to facilitate recognition and to introduce an expeditious procedure for securing the enforcement of judgments, authentic instruments and court settlements;

Have decided to conclude this Convention and to this end have designated as their Plenipotentiaries:

(Designations of Plenipotentiaries of the original six Contracting States)

Who, meeting within the Council, having exchanged their Full Powers, found in good and due form,

Have agreed as follows:

TITLE I

SCOPE

Article I

This Convention shall apply in civil and commercial matters whatever the nature of the court or tribunal. It shall not extend, in particular, to revenue, customs or administrative matters.

The Convention shall not apply to:

(1) the status or legal capacity of natural persons, rights in property arising out of a matrimonial relationship, wills and succession;

(2) bankruptcy, proceedings relating to the winding-up of insolvent companies or other legal persons, judicial arrangements, compositions and analogous proceedings;

(3) social security;

(4) arbitration.

[SCHEDULE 1 Section 2(2)

TEXT OF 1968 CONVENTION, AS AMENDED

ARRANGEMENT OF PROVISIONS

Convention on Jurisdiction and the Enforcement of Judgments in Civil and Commercial Matters

PREAMBLE

The High Contracting Parties to the Treaty establishing the European Economic Community,

Desiring to implement the provisions of Article 220 of that Treaty by virtue of which they undertook to secure the simplification of formalities governing the reciprocal recognition and enforcement of judgments of courts or tribunals;

Anxious to strengthen in the Community the legal protection of persons therein established;

Considering that it is necessary for this purpose to determine the international jurisdiction of their courts, to facilitate recognition and to introduce an expeditious procedure for securing the enforcement of judgments, authentic instruments and court settlements;

Have decided to conclude this Convention and to this end have designated as their Plenipotentiaries:

(Designations of Plenipotentiaries of the original six Contracting States)

Who, meeting within the Council, having exchanged their Full Powers, found in good and due form.

Have agreed as follows:]

TITLE I

SCOPE

Article 1

This Convention shall apply in civil and commercial matters whatever the nature of the court or tribunal. It shall not extend, in particular, to revenue, customs or administrative matters.

The Convention shall not apply to:

(1) the status or legal capacity of natural persons, rights in property arising out of a matrimonial relationship, wills and succession;

(2) bankruptcy proceedings relating to the winding-up of insolvent companies or other legal persons, judicial arrangements, compositions and analogous proceedings;

(3) social security;

(4) arbitration.

Note. The whole of this Schedule was substituted by Civil Jurisdiction and Judgments Act 1982 (Amendment) Order 1989, SI 1989 No 1346, art 9(1), Sch 1.

The whole of this Schedule was again substituted by Civil Jurisdiction and Judgments Act 1982 (Amendment) Order 1990, SI 1990 No 2591. art 12(1). Sch 1. as from 1 December 1991. The text of this Article remains unchanged.

TITLE II

JURISDICTION

Section 1
General provisions

Article 2

Subject to the provisions of this Convention, persons domiciled in a Contracting State, shall, whatever their nationality, be sued in the courts of that State.

Persons who are not nationals of the State in which they are domiciled shall be governed by the rules of jurisdiction applicable to nationals of that State.

Article 3

Persons domiciled in a Contracting State may be sued in the courts of another Contracting State only by virtue of the rules set out in Sections 2 to 6 of this Title.

In particular the following provisions shall not be applicable as against them:

- *in Belgium:* *Article 15 of the civil code (Code civil – Burgerlijk Wetboek) and Article 638 of the Judicial code (Code judiciaire – Gerechtelijk Wetboek);*
- *in Denmark:* *Article 248(2) of the law on civil procedure (Lov om rettens pleje) and Chapter 3, Article 3 of the Greenland law on civil procedure (Lov for Grønland om rettens pleje);*

– *in the Federal Republic of Germany:*	*Article 23 of the code of civil procedure (Zivil prozessordnung);*
– *in France:*	*Articles 14 and 15 of the civil code (Code civil);*
– *in Ireland:*	*the rules which enable jurisdiction to be founded on the document instituting the proceedings having been served on the defendant during his temporary presence in Ireland:*
– *in Italy:*	*Article 2 and Article 4, Nos 1 and 2 of the code of civil procedure (Codice di procedura civile);*
– *in Luxembourg:*	*Articles 14 and 15 of the civil code (Code civil);*
– *in the Netherlands:*	*Article 126(3) and Article 127 of the code of civil procedure (Wetboek van Burgerlijke Rechtsvordering);*
– *in the United Kingdom:*	*the rules which enable jurisdiction to be founded on:* (a) *the document instituting the proceedings having been served on the defendant during his temporary presence in the United Kingdom; or* (b) *the presence within the United Kingdom of property belonging to the defendant; or* (c) *the seizure by the plaintiff of property situated in the United Kingdom.*

Article 4

If the defendant is not domiciled in a Contracting State, the jurisdiction of the courts of each Contracting State shall, subject to the provisions of Article 16, be determined by the law of that State.

As against such a defendant any person domiciled in a Contracting State may whatever his nationality, avail himself in that State of the rules of jurisdiction there in force, and in particular those specified in the second paragraph of Article 3, in the same way as the nationals of that State.

Section 2
Special jurisdiction

Article 5

A person domiciled in a Contracting State may, in another Contracting State, be sued:

(2) in matters relating to maintenance, in the courts for the place where the maintenance creditor is domiciled or habitually resident or, if the matter is ancillary to proceedings concerning the status of a person, in the court which, according to its own law, has jurisdiction to entertain those proceedings, unless that jurisdiction is based solely on the nationality of one of the parties;

Article 6

A person domiciled in a Contracting State may also be sued:

(1) where he is one of a number of defendants, in the courts for the place where any one of them is domiciled;

(2) as a third party in an action on a warranty or guarantee or in any other third party proceedings, in the court seised of the original proceedings, unless these were instituted solely with the object of removing him from the jurisdiction of the court which would be competent in his case;

(3) on a counterclaim arising from the same contract or facts on which the original claim was based, in the court in which the original claim is pending.

Section 5
Exclusive jurisdiction

Article 16

The following courts shall have exclusive jurisdiction, regardless of domicile:

(5) in proceedings concerned with the enforcement of judgments, the courts of the Contracting State in which the judgment has been or is to be enforced.

Section 6
Prorogation of jurisdiction

Article 18

Apart from jurisdiction, derived from other provisions of this Convention, a court of a Contracting State before whom a defendant enters an appearance shall have jurisdiction. This rule shall not apply where appearance was entered solely to contest the jurisdiction, or where another court has exclusive jurisdiction by virtue of Article 16.

Section 7
Examination as to jurisdiction and admissibility

Article 19

Where a court of a Contracting State is seised of a claim which is principally concerned with a matter over which the courts of another Contracting State have exclusive jurisdiction by virtue of Article 16, it shall declare of its own motion that it has no jurisdiction.

Article 20

Where a defendant domiciled in one Contracting State is sued in a court of another Contracting State and does not enter an appearance, the court shall declare of its own motion that it has no jurisdiction unless its jurisdiction is derived from the provisions of this Convention.

The court shall stay the proceedings so long as it is not shown that the defendant has been able to receive the document instituting the proceedings or an equivalent document in sufficient time to enable him to arrange for his defence, or that all necessary steps have been taken to this end.

The provisions of the foregoing paragraph shall be replaced by those of Article 15 of the Hague Convention of 15 November 1965 on the service abroad of judicial and extrajudicial documents in civil or commercial matters, if the document instituting the proceedings or notice thereof had to be transmitted abroad in accordance with that Convention.

Section 8
Lis pendens–related actions

Article 21

Where proceedings involving the same cause of action and between the same parties are brought in the courts of different Contracting States, any court other than the court first seised shall of its own motion decline jurisdiction in favour of that court.

A court which would be required to decline jurisdiction may stay its proceedings if the jurisdiction of the other court is contested.

Article 22

Where related actions are brought in the courts of different Contracting States, any court other than the court first seised may, while the actions are pending at first instance, stay its proceedings.

A court other than the court first seised may also, on the application of one of the parties, decline jurisdiction if the law of that court permits the consolidation of related actions and the court first seised has jurisdiction over both actions.

For the purposes of this Article, actions are deemed to be related where they are so closely connected that it is expedient to hear and determine them together to avoid the risk of irreconcilable judgments resulting from separate proceedings.

Article 23

Where actions come within the exclusive jurisdiction of several courts, any court other than the court first seised shall decline jurisdiction in favour of that court.

Section 9
Provisional, including protective, measures

Article 24

Application may be made to the courts of a Contracting State for such provisional, including protective, measures as may be available under the law of that State, even if under this Convention, the courts of another Contracting State have jurisdiction as to the substance of the matter.

TITLE II

JURISDICTION

Section 1
General provisions

Article 2

Subject to the provisions of this Convention, persons domiciled in a Contracting State shall, whatever their nationality, be sued in the courts of that State.

Persons who are not nationals of the State in which they are domiciled shall be governed by the rules of jurisdiction applicable to nationals of that State.

Article 3

Persons domiciled in a Contracting State may be sued in the courts of another Contracting State only by virtue of the rules set out in Sections 2 to 6 of this Title.

In particular the following provisions shall not be applicable as against them

- in Belgium: Article 15 of the civil code (Code civil–Burgerlijk Wetboek) and Article 638 of the judicial code (Code judiciaire–Gerechtelijk Wetboek),
- *in Denmark: Article 248(2) of the law on civil procedure (Lov om rettens pleje) and Chapter 3, Article 3 of the Greenland law on civil procedure (Lov for Grønland om rettens pleje),*

[- in Denmark: Article 246(2) and (3) of the law on civil procedure (Lov om rettenspleje),]

- in the Federal Republic of Germany: Article 23 of the code of civil procedure (Zivilprozeßordnung),
- in Greece: Article 40 of the code of civil procedure (Κωδικας Πολιτικης Δικομιας,
- in France: Articles 14 and 15 of the civil code (Code civil),
- in Ireland: the rules which enable jurisdiction to be founded on the document instituting the proceedings having been served on the defendant during his temporary presence in Ireland,
- in Italy: Articles 2 and 4, nos 1 and 2 of the code of civil procedure (Codice di procedura civile),
- in Luxembourg: Articles 14 and 15 of the civil code (Code civil),
- in the Netherlands: Articles 126(3) and 127 of the code of civil procedure (Wetboek van Burgerlijke Rechtsvordering),

[- in Portugal: Article 65(1)(c), article 65(2) and Article 65A(c) of the code of civil procedure (Córdigo de Processo Civil) and Article 11 of the code of labour procedure (Córdigo de Processo de Trabaiho),]

- in the United Kingdom: the rules which enable jurisdiction to be founded on:
  (a) the document instituting the proceedings having been served on the defendant during his temporary presence in the United Kingdom; or
  (b) the presence within the United Kingdom of property belonging to the defendant; or
  (c) the seizure by the plaintiff of property situated in the United Kingdom.

Note. The text of art 3 remains unchanged, except for the substitution of the entry relating to Denmark and the addition of the entry relating to Portugal.

Article 4

If the defendant is not domiciled in a Contracting State, the jurisdiction of the courts of each Contracting State shall, subject to the provisions of Article 16, be determined by the law of that State.

As against such a defendant, any person domiciled in a Contracting State may, whatever his nationality, avail himself in that State of the rules of jurisdiction there in force, and in particular those specified in the second paragraph of Article 3, in the same way as the nationals of that State.

Section 2
Special jurisdiction

Article 5

A person domiciled in a Contracting State may, in another Contracting State, be sued –

2. In matters relating to maintenance, in the courts for the place where the maintenance creditor is domiciled or habitually resident or, if the matter is ancillary to proceedings concerning the status of a person, in the court which, according to its own law, has jurisdiction to entertain those proceedings, unless that jurisdiction is based solely on the nationality of one of the parties.

Article 6

A person domiciled in a Contracting State may also be sued –

1. Where he is one of a number of defendants, in the courts for the place where any one of them is domiciled.
2. As a third party in an action on a warranty or guarantee or in any other third party proceedings, in the court seised of the original proceedings, unless these were instituted solely with the object of removing him from the jurisdiction of the court which would be competent in his case.
3. On a counter-claim arising from the same contract or facts on which the original claim was based, in the court in which the original claim is pending.

[4. In matters relating to a contract, if the action may be combined with an action against the same defendant in matters relating to rights in rem in immovable property, in the court of the Contracting State in which the property is situated.]

Note. The text of art 6 remains unchanged, except for the addition in square brackets.

Section 5
Exclusive jurisdiction

Article 16

The following courts shall have exclusive jurisdiction, regardless of domicile:

5. In proceedings concerned with the enforcement of judgments, the courts of the Contracting State in which the judgment has been or is to be enforced.

Section 6
Prorogation of jurisdiction

Article 18

Apart from jurisdiction derived from other provisions of this Convention, a court of a Contracting State before whom a defendant enters an appearance shall have jurisdiction. This rule shall not apply where appearance was entered solely to contest the jurisdiction, or where another court has exclusive jurisdiction by virtue of Article 16.

Section 7
Examination as to jurisdiction and admissibility

Article 19

Where a court of a Contracting State is seised of a claim which is principally concerned with a matter over which the courts of another Contracting State have exclusive jurisdiction by virtue of Article 16, it shall declare of its own motion that it has no jurisdiction.

Article 20

Where a defendant domiciled in one Contracting State is sued in a court of another Contracting State and does not enter an appearance, the court shall declare

Article 30

A court of a Contracting State in which recognition is sought of a judgment given in another Contracting State may stay the proceedings if an ordinary appeal against the judgment has been lodged.

A court of a Contracting State in which recognition is sought of a judgment given in Ireland or the United Kingdom may stay the proceedings if enforcement is suspended in the State in which the judgment was given by reason of an appeal.

Section 2
Enforcement

Article 31

A judgment given in a Contracting State and enforceable in that State shall be enforced in another Contracting State when, on the application of any interested party, the order for its enforcement has been issued there.

However, in the United Kingdom, such a judgment shall be enforced in England and Wales, in Scotland or in Northern Ireland when, on the application of any interested party, it has been registered for enforcement in that part of the United Kingdom.

Article 32

The application shall be submitted:

- *in Belgium, to the tribunal de premiere instance or rechtbank van eerste aanleg;*
- *in Denmark, to the underret;*
- *in the Federal Republic of Germany, to the presiding judge of a chamber of the Landgericht;*
- *in France, to the presiding judge of the tribunal de grande instance;*
- *in Ireland, to the High Court;*
- *in Italy, to the corte d'appello;*
- *in Luxembourg, to the presiding judge of the tribunal d'arrondissement;*
- *in the Netherlands, to the presiding judge of the arrondissementsrechtbank;*
- *in the United Kingdom.*
    1. *in England and Wales, to the High Court of Justice, or in the case of a maintenance judgment to the Magistrates' Court on transmission by the Secretary of State;*

2. *in Scotland. to the Court of Session, or in the case of a maintenance judgment to the Sheriff Court on transmission by the Secretary of State;*
3. *in Northern Ireland, to the High Court of Justice, or in the case of a maintenance judgment to the Magistrates' Court on transmission by the Secretary of State.*

The jurisdiction of local courts shall be determined by reference to the place of domicile of the party against whom enforcement is sought. If he is not domiciled in the State in which enforcement is sought, it shall be determined by reference to the place of enforcement.

Article 33

The procedure for making the application shall be governed by the law of the State in which enforcement is sought.

The applicant must give an address for service of process within the area of jurisdiction of the court applied to. However, if the law of the State in which enforcement is sought does not provide for the furnishing of such an address, the applicant shall appoint a representative ad litem.

The documents referred to in Articles 46 and 47 shall be attached to the application.

Article 34

The court applied to shall give its decision without delay; the party against whom enforcement is sought shall not at this stage of the proceedings be entitled to make any submissions on the application.

The application may be refused only for one of the reasons specified in Articles 27 and 28. Under no circumstances may the foreign judgment be reviewed as to its substance.

Article 35

The appropriate officer of the court shall without delay bring the decision given on the application to the notice of the applicant in accordance with the procedure laid down by the law of the State in which enforcement is sought.

Article 36

If enforcement is authorised, the party against whom enforcement is sought may appeal against the decision within one month of service thereof.

If that party is domiciled in a Contracting State other than that in which the decision authorising enforcement was given, the time for appealing shall be two months and shall run from the date of service, either on him in person or at his residence. No extension of time may be granted on account of distance.

Article 37

An appeal against the decision authorising enforcement shall be lodged in accordance with the rules governing procedure in contentious matters:

- *in Belgium, with the tribunal de premiere instance or rechtbank van eerste aanleg;*
- *in Denmark, with the landsret;*
- *in the Federal Republic of Germany, with the Oberlandesgericht;*
- *in France, with the cour d'appel;*
- *in Ireland, with the High Court;*
- *in Italy, with the corte d'appello;*
- *in Luxembourg, with the Cour supérieure de justice sitting as a court of civil appeal;*

- *in the Netherlands, with the arrondissementsrechtbank;*
- *in the United Kingdom:*
  1. *in England and Wales, with the High Court of Justice, or in the case of a maintenance judgment with the Magistrates' Court;*
  2. *in Scotland, with the Court of Session, or in the case of a maintenance judgment with the Sheriff Court;*
  3. *in Northern Ireland, with the High Court of Justice, or in the case of a maintenance judgment with the Magistrates' Court.*

The judgment given on the appeal may be contested only:

- *in Belgium, Greece, France, Italy, Luxembourg and the Netherlands by an appeal in cassation:*
- *in Denmark, by an appeal to the højesteret, with the leave of the Minister of Justice;*
- *in the Federal Republic of Germany, by a Rechtsbeschwerde;*
- *in Ireland, by an appeal on a point of law to the Supreme Court;*
- *in the United Kingdom, by a single further appeal on a point of law.*

Article 38

The court with which the appeal under the first paragraph of Article 37 is lodged may, on the application of the appellant, stay the proceedings if an ordinary appeal has been lodged against the judgment in the State in which that judgment was given or if the time for such an appeal has not yet expired; in the latter case, the court may specify the time within which such an appeal is to be lodged.

Where the judgment was given in Ireland or the United Kingdom, any form of appeal available in the State in which it was given shall be treated as an ordinary appeal for the purposes of the first paragraph.

The court may also make enforcement conditional on the provision of such security as it shall determine.

Article 39

During the time specified for an appeal pursuant to Article 36 and until any such appeal has been determined, no measures of enforcement may be taken other than protective measures taken against the property of the party against whom enforcement is sought.

The decision authorising enforcement shall carry with it the power to proceed to any such protective measures.

Article 40

If the application for enforcement is refused, the applicant may appeal:

- *in Belgium, to the cour d'appel or hof van beroep;*
- *in Denmark, to the landsret;*
- *in the Federal Republic of Germany to the Oberlandesgericht;*
- *in France, to the cour d'appel;*
- *in Ireland, to the High Court;*
- *in Italy, to the corte d'appello;*
- *in Luxembourg, to the Cour supérieure de justice sitting as a court of civil appeal;*
- *in the Netherlands, to the gerechtshof;*
- *in the United Kingdom:*

1. *in England and Wales, to the High Court of Justice, or in the case of a maintenance judgment to the Magistrates' Court;*
2. *in Scotland, to the Court of Session, or in the case of a maintenance judgment to the Sheriff Court;*
3. *in Northern Ireland, to the High Court of Justice, or in the case of a maintenance judgment to the Magistrates' Court.*

The party against whom enforcement is sought shall be summoned to appear before the appellate court. If he fails to appear the provisions of the second and third paragraphs of Article 20 shall apply even where he is not domiciled in any of the Contracting States.

Article 41

A judgment given on an appeal provided for in Article 40 may be contested only:

- *in Belgium, Greece, France, Italy, Luxembourg and the Netherlands, by an appeal in cassation;*
- *in Denmark, by an appeal to the højesteret, with the leave of the Minister of Justice;*
- *in the Federal Republic of Germany, by a Rechtsbeschwerde;*
- *in Ireland, by an appeal on a point of law to the Supreme Court;*
- *in the United Kingdom, by a single further appeal on a point of law.*

Article 42

Where a foreign judgment has been given in respect of several matters and enforcement cannot be authorised for all of them, the court shall authorise enforcement for one or more of them.

An applicant may request partial enforcement of a judgment.

Article 43

A foreign judgment which orders a periodic payment by way of a penalty shall be enforceable in the State in which enforcement is sought only if the amount of the payment has been finally determined by the courts of the State in which the judgment was given.

Article 44

An applicant who, in the State in which the judgment was given, has benefited from complete or partial legal aid or exemption from costs or expenses. shall be entitled, in the procedures provided for in Articles 32 to 35, to benefit from the most favourable legal aid or the most extensive exemption from costs or expenses provided for by the law of the State addressed.

However an applicant who requests the enforcement of a decision given by an administrative authority in Denmark in respect of a maintenance order may, in the State addressed, claim the benefits referred to in the first paragraph if he presents a statement from the Danish Ministry of Justice to the effect that he fulfils the economic requirements to qualify for the grant of complete or partial legal aid or exemption from costs or expenses.

Article 45

No security, bond or deposit, however described, shall be required of a party who in one Contracting State applies for enforcement of a judgment given in another

Contracting State on the ground that he is a foreign national or that he is not domiciled or resident in the State in which enforcement is sought.

Section 3
Common provisions

Article 46

A party seeking recognition or applying for enforcement of a judgment shall produce:

1. *a copy of the judgment which satisfies the conditions necessary to establish its authenticity;*
2. *in the case of a judgment given in default, the original or a certified true copy of the document which establishes that the party in default was served with the document instituting the proceedings or with an equivalent document.*

Article 47

A party applying for enforcement shall also produce:

1. *documents which establish that, according to the law of the State in which it has been given, the judgment is enforceable and has been served;*
2. *where appropriate, a document showing that the applicant is in receipt of legal aid in the State in which the judgment was given.*

Article 48

If the documents specified in Article 46(2) and Article 47(2) are not produced, the court may specify a time for their production, accept equivalent documents or, if it considers that it has sufficient information before it, dispense with their production.

If the court so requires, a translation of the documents shall be produced; the translation shall be certified by a person qualified to do so in one of the Contracting States.

Article 49

No legalisation or other similar formality shall be required in respect of the documents referred to in Articles 46 or 47 or the second paragraph of Article 48, or in respect of a document appointing a representative ad litem.

TITLE III

RECOGNITION AND ENFORCEMENT

Article 25

For the purposes of this Convention, 'judgment' means any judgment given by a court or tribunal of a Contracting State, whatever the judgment may be called, including a decree, order, decision or writ of execution, as well as the determination of costs or expenses by an officer of the court.

Section 1
Recognition

Article 26

A judgment given in a Contracting State shall be recognized in the other Contracting States without any special procedure being required.

Any interested party who raises the recognition of a judgment as the principal issue in a dispute may, in accordance with the procedures provided for in Sections 2 and 3 of this Title, apply for a decision that the judgment be recognized.

If the outcome of proceedings in a court of a Contracting State depends on the determination of an incidental question of recognition that court shall have jurisdiction over that question.

Article 27

A judgment shall not be recognized –

1. If such recognition is contrary to public policy in the State in which recognition is sought.
2. Where it was given in default of appearance, if the defendant was not duly served with the document which instituted the proceedings or with an equivalent document in sufficient time to enable him to arrange for his defence.
3. If the judgment is irreconcilable with a judgment given in a dispute between the same parties in the State in which recognition is sought.
4. If the court of the State of origin, in order to arrive at its judgment, has decided a preliminary question concerning the status or legal capacity of natural persons, rights in property arising out of a matrimonial relationship, wills or succession in way that conflicts with a rule of the private international law of the State in which the recognition is sought, unless the same result would have been reached by the application of the rules of private international law of that State.
5. If the judgment is irreconcilable with an earlier judgment given in a non-contracting State involving the same cause of action and between the same parties, provided that this latter judgment fulfils the conditions necessary for its recognition in the state addressed.

Article 28

Moreover, a judgment shall not be recognized if it conflicts with the provisions of Sections 3, 4 or 5 of Title II, or in a case provided for in Article 59.

In its examination of the grounds of jurisdiction referred to in the foregoing paragraph, the court or authority applied to shall be bound by the findings of fact on which the court of the State of origin based its jurisdiction.

Subject to the provisions of the first paragraph, the jurisdiction of the court of the State of origin may not be reviewed; the test of public policy referred to in point 1 of Article 27 may not be applied to the rules relating to jurisdiction.

Article 29

Under no circumstances may a foreign judgment be reviewed as to its substance.

Article 30

A court of a Contracting State in which recognition is sought of a judgment given in another Contracting State may stay the proceedings if an ordinary appeal against the judgment has been lodged.

A court of a Contracting State in which recognition is sought of a judgment given in Ireland or the United Kingdom may stay the proceedings if enforcement is suspended in the State in which the judgment was given by reason of an appeal.

[A court of a Contracting State in which recognition is sought of a judgment given in another Contracting State may stay the proceedings if an ordinary appeal against the judgment has been lodged.

A court of a Contracting State in which recognition is sought of a judgment given in Ireland or the United Kingdom may stay the proceedings if enforcement is suspended in the State of origin, by reason of an appeal.]

Note. The text of the new art 30 reads as substituted in square brackets above; see the note to art 1 (p2850).

Section 2
Enforcement

Article 31

A judgment given in a Contracting State and enforceable in that State shall be enforced in another Contracting State when, on the application of any interested party, the order for its enforcement has been issued there.

However, in the United Kingdom, such a judgment shall be enforced in England and Wales, in Scotland, or in Northern Ireland when, on the application of any interested party, it has been registered for enforcement in that part of the United Kingdom.

[A judgment given in a Contracting State and enforceable in that State shall be enforced in another Contracting State when, on the application of any interested party, it has been declared enforceable there.

However, in the United Kingdom, such a judgment shall be enforced in England and Wales, in Scotland, or in Northern Ireland when, on the application of any interested party, it has been registered for enforcement in that part of the United Kingdom.]

Note. The text of the new art 31 reads as in square brackets; see the note to art 1 (p 2850).

Article 32

The application shall be submitted:

- *in Belgium, to the tribunal de première instance or rechtbank van eerste aanleg;*
- *in Denmark, to the underret;*
- *in the Federal Republic of Germany, to the presiding judge of a chamber of the Landgericht;*
- *in Greece, to the Μονομελεζ Πρωτοδικειο;*
- *in France, to the presiding judge of the tribunal de grande instance;*
- *in Ireland, to the High Court;*
- *in Italy, to the corte d'appello;*
- *in Luxembourg, to the presiding judge of the tribunal d'arrondissement;*
- *in the Netherlands, to the presiding judge of the arrondissementsrechtbank;*
- *in the United Kingdom;*
    - *(1) in England and Wales, to the High Court of Justice, or in the case of a maintenance judgment to the Magistrates' Court on transmission by the Secretary of State;*
    - *(2) in Scotland, to the Court of Session, or in the case of a maintenance judgment to the Sheriff Court on transmission by the Secretary of State;*

(3) in Northern Ireland, to the High Court of Justice, or in the case of a maintenance judgment to the Magistrates' Court on transmission by the Secretary of State.

The jurisdiction of local courts shall be determined by reference to the place of domicile of the party against whom enforcement is sought. If he is not domiciled in the State in which enforcement is sought, it shall be determined by reference to the place of enforcement.

[1. The application shall be submitted –

– in Belgium, to the tribunal de première instance or rechtbank van eerste aanleg,
– in Denmark, to the byret,
– in the Federal Republic of Germany, to the presiding judge of a chamber of the Landgericht.
– in Greece, to the Μονουελεζ Πρωτοδικειο;
– in Spain, to the Juzgado de Primer Instancia,
– in France, to the presiding judge of the tribunal de grande instance,
– in Ireland, to the High Court,
– in Italy, to the corte d'appello,
– in Luxembourg, to the presiding judge of the tribunal d'arrondissement,
– in the Netherlands, to the presiding judge of the arrondissementsrechtbank,
– in Portugal, to the Tribunal Judicial de Circulo,
– in the United Kingdom –
  (a) in England and Wales, to the High Court of Justice, or in the case of maintenance judgment to the Magistrates' Court on transmission by the Secretary of State;
  (b) in Scotland, to the Court of Session, or in the case of a maintenance judgment to the Sheriff Court on transmission by the Secretary of State;
  (c) in Northern Ireland, to the High Court of Justice, or in the case of a maintenance judgment to the Magistrates' Court on transmission by the Secretary of State.

2. The jurisdiction of local courts shall be determined by reference to the place of domicile of the party against whom enforcement is sought. If he is not domiciled in the State in which enforcement is sought, it shall be determined by reference to the place of enforcement.]

Note. The text of the new art 32 reads as in square brackets above; see the note to art 1 (p 2850).

Article 33

The procedure for making the application shall be governed by the law of the State in which enforcement is sought.

The applicant must give an address for service of process within the area of jurisdiction of the court applied to. However, if the law of the State in which enforcement is sought does not provide for the furnishing of such an address, the applicant shall appoint a representative ad litem.

The documents referred to in Articles 46 and 47 shall be attached to the application.

Article 34

The court applied to shall give its decision without delay; the party against whom enforcement is sought shall not at this stage of the proceedings be entitled to make any submissions on the application.

The application may be refused only for one of the reasons specified in Articles 27 and 28.

Under no circumstances may the foreign judgment be reviewed as to its substance.

Article 35

The appropriate officer of the court shall without delay bring the decision given on the application to the notice of the applicant in accordance with the procedure laid down by the law of the State in which enforcement is sought.

Article 36

If enforcement is authorized, the party against whom enforcement is sought may appeal against the decision within one month of service thereof.

If that party is domiciled in a Contracting State other than that in which the decision authorizing enforcement was given, the time for appealing shall be two months and shall run from the date of service, either on him in person or at his residence. No extension of time may he granted on account of distance.

Article 37

An appeal against the decision authorizing enforcement shall be lodged in accordance with the rules governing procedure in contentious matters:

- *in Belgium, with the tribunal de première instance or rechtbank van eerste aanleg;*
- *in Denmark, with the landsret;*
- *in the Federal Republic of Germany, with the Oberlandesgericht:*
- *in Greece, with the Εψετειο;*
- *in France, with the cour d'appel;*
- *in Ireland, with the High Court;*
- *in Italy, with the corte d'appello;*
- *in Luxembourg, with the Cour supérieure de justice sitting as a court of civil appeal;*
- *in the Netherlands, with the arrondissementsrechtbank;*
- *in the United Kingdom;*
  - *(1) in England and Wales, with the High Court of Justice or in the case of a maintenance judgment with the Magistrates' Court;*
  - *(2) in Scotland, with the Court of Session, or in the case of a maintenance judgment with the Sheriff Court;*
  - *(3) in Northern Ireland, with the High Court of Justice, or in the case of a maintenance judgment with the Magistrates' Court.*

The judgment given on the appeal may be contested only:

- *in Belgium, Greece, France, Italy, Luxembourg and the Netherlands, by an appeal on cassation;*
- *in Denmark, by an appeal to the højesteret, with the leave of the Minister of justice;*
- *in the Federal Republic of Germany, by a Rechtsbeschwerde;*

- *in Ireland, by an appeal on a point of law to the Supreme Court;*
- *in the United Kingdom, by a single further appeal on a point of law.*

[1. An appeal against the decision authorizing enforcement shall be lodged in accordance with the rules governing procedure in contentious matters –

- in Belgium, with the tribunal de première instance or rechtbank van eerste aanleg,
- in Denmark, with the landsret,
- in the Federal Republic of Germany, with the Oberlandesgericht,
- in Greece, with the Εφετειο,
- in Spain, with the Audiencia Provincial,
- in France, with the cour d'appel,
- in Ireland, with the High Court,
- in Italy, with the corte d'appello,
- in Luxembourg, with the Cour supérieure de justice sitting as a court of civil appeal,
- in the Netherlands, with the arrondissementsrechtbank,
- in Portugal, with the Tribunal de Relação.
- in the United Kingdom –
  (a) in England and Wales, with the High Court of Justice, or in the case of a maintenance judgment with the Magistrates' Court;
  (b) in Scotland, with the Court of Session, or in the case of a maintenance judgment with the Sheriff Court;
  (c) in Northern Ireland, with the High Court of Justice, or in the case of a maintenance judgment with the Magistrates' Court.

2. The judgment given on the appeal may be contested only –

- in Belgium, Greece, Spain, France, Italy, Luxembourg and in the Netherlands, by an appeal in cassation,
- in Denmark, by an appeal to the højesteret, with the leave of the Minister of Justice,
- in the Federal Republic of Germany, by a Rechtsbeschwerde,
- in Ireland, by an appeal on a point of law to the Supreme Court,
- in Portugal, by an appeal on a point of law,
- in the United Kingdom, by a single further appeal on a point of law.]

Note. The text of the new art 37 reads as in square brackets above; see the note to art 1 (p 2850).

Article 38

The court with which the appeal under the first paragraph of Article 37 is lodged may, on the application of the appellant, stay the proceedings if an ordinary appeal has been lodged against the judgment in the State in which that judgment was given or if the time for such an appeal has not yet expired; in the latter case, the court may specify the time within which such an appeal is to be lodged.

Where the judgment was given in Ireland or the United Kingdom, any form of appeal available in the State in which it was given shall be treated as an ordinary appeal for the purposes of the first paragraph.

The court may also make enforcement conditional on the provision of such security as it shall determine

[The court with which the appeal under Article 37(1) is lodged may, on the application of the appellant, stay the proceedings if an ordinary appeal has been lodged against the judgment in the State of origin or if the time for such an appeal has not yet expired; in the latter case, the court may specify the time within which such an appeal is to be lodged.

Where the judgment was given in Ireland or the United Kingdom, any form of appeal available in the State of origin shall be treated as an ordinary appeal for the purposes of the first paragraph.

The court may also make enforcement conditional on the provision of such security as it shall determine.]

Note. The text of art 38 reads as in square brackets above; see the note to art 1 (p 2850).

Article 39

During the time specified for an appeal pursuant to Article 36 and until any such appeal has been determined, no measures of enforcement may be taken other than protective measures taken against the property of the party against whom enforcement is sought.

The decision authorizing enforcement shall carry with it the power to proceed to any such protective measures.

Article 40

If the application for enforcement is refused, the applicant may appeal;

- *in Belgium, to the cour d'appel or hof van beroep;*
- *in Denmark, to the landsret;*
- *in the Federal Republic of Germany, to the Oberlandesgericht;*
- *in Greece, to the Εψετειο;*
- *in France, to the cour d'appel;*
- *in Ireland, to the High Court;*
- *in Italy, to the corte d'appello;*
- *in Luxembourg, to the Cour supérieure de justice sitting as a court of civil appeal;*
- *in the Netherlands, to the gerechtshof;*
- *in the United Kingdom;*
  - *(1) in England and Wales, to the High Court of Justice, or in the case of a maintenance judgment to the Magistrates Court;*
  - *(2) in Scotland, to the Court of Session, or in the case of a maintenance judgment to the Sheriff Court;*
  - *(3) in Northern Ireland, to the High Court of Justice, or in the case of a maintenance judgment to the Magistrates Court.*

The party against whom enforcement is sought shall be summoned to appear before the appellate court. If he fails to appear, the provisions of the second and third paragraphs of Article 20 shall apply even where he is not domiciled in any of the Contracting States.

[1. If the application for enforcement is refused, the applicant may appeal –

- in Belgium, to the cour d'appel or hof van beroep,
- in Denmark, to the landsret,
- in the Federal Republic of Germany, to the Oberlandesgericht,
- in Greece, to the Εψετειο,
- in Spain, to the Audiencia Provincial,
- in France, to the cour d'appel,
- in Ireland, to the High Court,

- in Italy, to the corte d'appello,
- in Luxembourg, to the Cour supérieure de justice sitting as a court of civil appeal,
- in the Netherlands, to the gerechtshof,
- in Portugal, to the Tribunal da Relação,
- in the United Kingdom –
  - (a) in England and Wales, to the High Court of Justice, or in the case of a maintenance judgment to the Magistrates' Court;
  - (b) in Scotland, to the Court of Session, or in the case of a maintenance judgment to the Sheriff Court;
  - (c) in Northern Ireland, to the High Court of Justice, or in the case of a maintenance judgment to the Magistrates' Court.

2. The party against whom enforcement is sought shall be summoned to appear before the appellate court. If he fails to appear, the provisions of the second and third paragraphs of Article 20 shall apply even where he is not domiciled in any of the Contracting States.]

Note. The text of art 40 reads as in square brackets above; see the note to art I (p 2850).

Article 41

A judgment given on an appeal provided for in Article 40 may be contested only:
- *in Belgium, Greece, France, Italy, Luxembourg and in the Netherlands, by an appeal in cassation;*
- *in Denmark, by an appeal to the højesteret, with the leave of the Minister of justice;*
- *in the Federal Republic of Germany by a Rechtsbeschwerde;*
- *in Ireland, by an appeal on a point of law to the Supreme Court;*
- *in the United Kingdom, by a single further appeal on a point of law.*

[A judgment given on appeal provided for in Article 40 may be contested only –
- in Belgium, Greece, Spain, France, Italy, Luxembourg and in the Netherlands, by an appeal on cassation.
- in Denmark, by an appeal to the højesteret, with the leave of the Minister of Justice,
- in the Federal Republic of Germany, by a Rechtsbeschwerde,
- in Ireland, by an appeal on a point of law to the Supreme Court,
- in Portugal, by an appeal on a point of law,
- in the United Kingdom, by a single further appeal on a point of law.]

Note. The text of art 41 reads as in square brackets above; see the note to art 1 (p 2850).

Article 42

Where a foreign judgment has been given in respect of several matters and enforcement cannot be authorized for all of them, the court shall authorize enforcement for one or more of them.

An applicant may request partial enforcement of a judgment.

Article 43

A foreign judgment which orders a periodic payment by way of a penalty shall be enforceable in the State in which enforcement is sought only if the amount of the payment has been finally determined by the courts of the State in which the judgment was given.

[A foreign judgment which orders a periodic payment by way of a penalty shall be enforceable in the State in which enforcement is sought only if the amount of the payment has been finally determined by the courts of the State of origin.]

Note. The text of art 43 reads as in square brackets above, see the note to art 1 (p 2850).

Article 44

An applicant who, in the State of origin has benefited from complete or partial legal aid or exemption from costs or expenses, shall be entitled, in the procedures provided for in Articles 32 to 35, to benefit from the most favourable legal aid or the most extensive exemption from costs or expenses provided for by the law of the State addressed.

However, an applicant who requests the enforcement of a decision given by an administrative authority in Denmark in respect of a maintenance order may, in the State addressed, claim the benefits referred to in the first paragraph if he presents a statement from the Danish Ministry of Justice to the effect that he fulfils the economic requirements to qualify for the grant of complete or partial legal aid or exemption from costs or expenses.

Article 45

No security, bond or deposit, however described, shall be required of a party who in one Contracting State applies for enforcement of a judgment given in another Contracting State on the ground that he is a foreign national or that he is not domiciled or resident in the State in which enforcement is sought.

Section 3
Common provisions

Article 46

A party seeking recognition or applying for enforcement of a judgment shall produce –

1. a copy of the judgment which satisfies the conditions necessary to establish its authenticity;
2. in the case of a judgment given in default, the original or a certified true copy of the document which establishes that the party in default was served with the document instituting the proceedings or with an equivalent document.

Article 47

A party applying for enforcement shall also produce:

1. *documents which establish that, according to the law of the State in which it has been given, the judgment is enforceable and has been served;*
2. *where appropriate, a document showing that the applicant is in receipt of legal aid in the State in which the judgment was given.*

[A party applying for enforcement shall also produce –

1. documents which establish that, according to the law of the State of origin the judgment is enforceable and has been served;

2. where appropriate, a document showing that the applicant is in receipt of legal aid in the State of origin.]

Note. The text of art 47 reads as in square brackets above: see the note to art 1 (p 2850).

Article 48

If the documents specified in point 2 of Articles 46 and 47 are not produced, the court may specify a time for their production, accept equivalent documents or, if it considers that it has sufficient information before it, dispense with their production.

If the court so requires, a translation of the documents shall be produced; the translation shall be certified by a person qualified to do so in one of the Contracting States.

Article 49

No legalization or other similar formality shall be required in respect of the documents referred to in Articles 46 or 47 or the second paragraph of Article 48, or in respect of a document appointing a representative ad litem.]

TITLE IV

AUTHENTIC INSTRUMENTS AND COURT SETTLEMENTS

Article 50

A document which has been formally drawn up or registered as an authentic instrument and is enforceable in one Contracting State shall, in another Contracting State, have an order for its enforcement issued there, on application made in accordance with the procedures provided for in Article 31 et seq. The application may be refused only if enforcement of the instrument is contrary to public policy in the State in which enforcement is sought.

The instrument produced must satisfy the conditions necessary to establish its authenticity in the State of origin.

The provisions of Section 3 of Title III shall apply as appropriate.

Article 51

A settlement which has been approved by a court in the course of proceedings and is enforceable in the State in which it was concluded shall be enforceable in the State in which enforcement is sought under the same conditions as authentic instruments.

[TITLE IV

AUTHENTIC INSTRUMENTS AND COURT SETTLEMENTS

Article 50

A document which has been formally drawn up or registered as an authentic instrument and is enforceable in one Contracting State shall, in another Contracting State, have an order for its enforcement issued there, on application made in accordance with the procedures provided for in Article 31 et seq. The application may be refused only if enforcement of the instrument is contrary to public policy in the State in which enforcement is sought.

The instrument produced must satisfy the conditions necessary to establish its authenticity in the State of origin.

The provisions of Section 3 of Title III shall apply as appropriate.

[A document which has been formally drawn up or registered as an authentic instrument and is enforceable in one Contracting State shall, in another Contracting State, be declared enforceable there, on application made in accordance with the procedures provided for in Article 31 et seq. The application may be refused only if enforcement of the instrument is contrary to public policy in the State addressed.

The instrument produced must satisfy the conditions necessary to establish its authenticity in the State of origin.

The provisions of Section 3 of Title III shall apply as appropriate.]

Note. The text of art 50 reads as in square brackets above; see the note to art 1 (p 2850).

Article 51

A settlement which has been approved by a court in the course of proceedings and is enforceable in the State in which it was concluded shall be enforceable in the State in which enforcement is sought under the same conditions as authentic instruments.

[A settlement which has been approved by a court in the course of proceedings and is enforceable in the State in which it was concluded shall be enforceable in the State addressed under the same conditions as authentic instruments.]]

Note. The text of art 51 reads as in square brackets above; see the note to art 1 (p 2850).

TITLE V

GENERAL PROVISIONS

Article 52

In order to determine whether a party is domiciled in the Contracting State whose courts are seised of the matter, the court shall apply its internal law.

If a party is not domiciled in the State whose courts are seised of the matter, then, in order to determine whether the party is domiciled in another Contracting State, the court shall apply the law of that State.

The domicile of a party shall, however, be determined in accordance with his national law if, by that law, his domicile depends on that of another person or on the seat of an authority.

[In order to determine whether a party is domiciled in the Contracting State whose courts are seised of a matter, the Court shall apply its internal law.

If a party is not domiciled in the State whose courts are seised of the matter then, in order to determine whether the party is domiciled in another Contracting State, the court shall apply the law of that State.]

Note. The text of art 52 reads as in square brackets above; the note to art 1 (p 2850).

TITLE VI

TRANSITIONAL PROVISIONS

Article 54

The provisions of this Convention shall apply only to legal proceedings instituted and to documents formally drawn up or registered as authentic instruments after its entry into force

However, judgments given after the date of entry into force of this Convention in proceedings instituted before that date shall be recognised and enforced in accordance with the provisions of Title III if jurisdiction was founded upon rules which accorded with those provided for either in Title II of this Convention or in a convention concluded between the State of origin and the State addressed which was in force when the proceedings were instituted.

[**TITLE VI**

TRANSITIONAL PROVISIONS

Article 54

The provisions of this Convention shall apply only to legal proceedings instituted and documents formally drawn up or registered as authentic instruments after its entry into force.

However, judgments given after the date of entry into force of this Convention in proceedings instituted before that date shall be recognised and enforced in accordance with the provisions of Title III if jurisdiction was founded upon rules which accorded with those provided for either in Title II of this Convention or in a convention concluded between the State of origin and the State addressed which was in force when the proceedings were instituted.

[The provisions of the Convention shall apply only to legal proceedings instituted and to documents formally drawn up or registered as authentic instruments after its entry into force in the State of origin and, where recognition or enforcement of a judgment or authentic instruments is sought, in the State addressed.

However, judgments given after the date of entry into force of this Convention between the State of origin and the State addressed in proceedings instituted before that date shall be recognized and enforced in accordance with the provisions of Title III if jurisdiction was founded upon rules which accorded with those provided for either in Title II of this Convention or in a convention concluded between the State of origin and the State addressed which was in force when the proceedings were instituted.

If the parties to a dispute concerning a contract had agreed in writing before 1st June 1988 for Ireland or before 1st January 1987 for the United Kingdom that the contract was to be governed by the law of Ireland or of a part of the United Kingdom, the courts of Ireland or of that part of the United Kingdom shall retain the right to exercise jurisdiction in the dispute.]

Note. The text of art 54 reads as in square brackets above; see the note to art 1 (p 2850).

Article 54A

[For a period of three years from 1st November 1986 for Denmark and from 1st June 1988 for Ireland, jurisdiction in maritime matters shall be determined in these States not only in accordance with the provisions of Title II, but also in accordance with the provisions of paragraphs 1 to 6 following. However, upon the entry into force of the International Convention relating to the arrest of sea-going ships, signed at Brussels on 10th May 1952, for one of these States, these provisions shall cease to have effect for that State.

1. A person who is domiciled in a Contracting State may be sued in the Courts of one of the States mentioned above in respect of a maritime claim if the ship to which the claim relates or any other ship owned by him has been arrested by judicial process within the territory of the latter State to secure the claim, or could have been so arrested there but bail or other security has been given, and either –
   (a) the claimant is domiciled in the latter State, or
   (b) the claim arose in the latter State, or
   (c) the claim concerns the voyage during which the arrest was made or could have been made, or
   (d) the claim arises out of a collision or out of damage caused by a ship to another ship or to goods or persons on board either ship, either by the execution or non-execution of a manoeuvre or by the non-observance of regulations, or
   (e) the claim is for salvage, or
   (f) the claim is in respect of a mortgage or hypothecation of the ship arrested.
2. A claimant may arrest either the particular ship to which the maritime claim relates, or any other ship which is owned by the person who was, at the time when the maritime claim arose, the owner of the particular ship. However, only the particular ship to which the maritime claim relates may be arrested in respect of the maritime claims set out in (5)(o), (p) or (q) of this Article.
3. Ships shall be deemed to be in the same ownership when all the shares therein are owned by the same person or persons.
4. When in the case of a charter by demise of a ship the charterer alone is liable in respect of a maritime claim relating to that ship, the claimant may arrest that ship or any other ship owned by the charterer, but no other ship owned by the owner may be arrested in respect of such claim. The same shall apply to any case in which a person other than the owner of a ship is liable in respect of a maritime claim relating to that ship.
5. The expression 'maritime claim' means a claim arising out of one or more of the following –
   (a) damage caused by any ship either in collision or otherwise;
   (b) loss of life or personal injury caused by any ship or occurring in connection with the operation on any ship;
   (c) salvage;
   (d) agreement relating to the use of hire of any ship whether by charter-party or otherwise;
   (e) agreement relating to the carriage of goods in any ship whether by charterparty or otherwise;
   (f) loss of or damage to goods including baggage carried in any ship;

(g) general average;
(h) bottomry;
(i) towage;
(j) pilotage;
(k) goods or materials wherever supplied to a ship for her operation or maintenance;
(l) construction, repair or equipment of any ship or dock charges and dues;
(m) wages of master, officers or crew;
(n) master's disbursements, including disbursements made by shippers, charterers or agents on behalf of a ship or her owner;
(o) dispute as to the title to or ownership of any ship;
(p) disputes between co-owners of any ship as to the ownership, possession, employment or earnings of that ship;
(q) the mortgage or hypothecation of any ship.

6. In Denmark, the expression 'arrest' shall be deemed as regards the maritime claims referred to in 5(o) and (p) of this Article, to include a 'forbud', where that is the only procedure allowed in respect of such a claim under Articles 646 to 653 of the law on civil procedure (lov om rettens pleje).]]

Note. This article is inserted on the substitution of the whole Schedule, as noted to art 1 (p2850).

TITLE VII

RELATIONSHIP TO OTHER CONVENTIONS

Article 55

Subject to the provisions of the second paragraph of Article 54, and of Article 56, this Convention shall, for the States which are parties to it, supersede the following conventions concluded between two or more of them:

- *the Convention between Belgium and France on Jurisdiction and the Validity and Enforcement of Judgments, Arbitration Awards and Authentic Instruments, signed at Paris on 8 July 1899;*
- *the Convention between Belgium and the Netherlands on Jurisdiction, Bankruptcy and the Validity and Enforcement of Judgments, Arbitration Awards and Authentic Instruments, signed at Brussels on 28 March 1925;*
- *the Convention between France and Italy on the Enforcement of Judgments in Civil and Commercial Matters, signed at Rome on 3 June 1930;*
- *the Convention between the United Kingdom and the French Republic providing for the Reciprocal Enforcement of Judgments in Civil and Commercial Matters, with Protocol, signed at Paris on 18 January 1934;*
- *the Convention between the United Kingdom and the Kingdom of Belgium providing for the Reciprocal Enforcement of Judgments in Civil and Commercial Matters, with Protocol, signed at Brussels on 2 May 1934;*
- *the Convention between Germany and Italy on the Recognition and Enforcement of Judgments in Civil and Commercial matters, signed at Rome on 9 March 1936;*
- *the Convention between the Federal Republic of Germany and the Kingdom of Belgium on the Mutual Recognition and Enforcement of Judgments*

Arbitration Awards and Authentic Instruments in Civil and Commercial Matters signed at Bonn on 30 June 1958:
- *the Convention between the Kingdom of the Netherlands and the Italian Republic on the Recognition and Enforcement of Judgments in Civil and Commercial Matters, signed at Rome on 17 April 1959;*
- *the Convention between the United Kingdom and the Federal Republic of Germany for the Reciprocal Recognition and Enforcement of Judgments in Civil and Commercial Matters, signed at Bonn on 14 July 1960;*
- *the Convention between the Kingdom of Belgium and the Italian Republic on the Recognition and Enforcement of Judgments and other Enforceable Instruments in Civil and Commercial Matters, signed at Rome on 6 April 1962:*
- *the Convention between the Kingdom of the Netherlands and the Federal Republic of Germany on the Mutual Recognition and Enforcement of Judgments and other Enforceable Instruments in Civil and Commercial Matters, signed at The Hague on 30 August 1962;*
- *the Convention between the United Kingdom and the Republic of Italy for the Reciprocal Recognition and Enforcement of Judgments in Civil and Commercial Matters, signed at Rome on 7 February 1964, with amending Protocol signed at Rome on 14 July 1970;*
- *the Convention between the United Kingdom and the Kingdom of the Netherlands providing for the Reciprocal Recognition and Enforcement of Judgments in Civil Matters, signed at The Hague on 17 November 1967,*

and, in so far as it is in force:
- *the Treaty between Belgium, the Netherlands and Luxembourg on Jurisdiction, Bankruptcy and the Validity and Enforcement of Judgments, Arbitration Awards and Authentic Instruments, signed at Brussels on 24 November 1961.*

Article 56

The Treaty and the conventions referred to in Article 55 shall continue to have effect in relation to matters to which this Convention does not apply.

They shall continue to have effect in respect of judgments given and documents formally drawn up or registered as authentic instruments before the entry into force of this Convention.

Article 57

This Convention shall not affect any conventions to which the Contracting States are or will be parties and which, in relation to particular matters, govern jurisdiction or the recognition or enforcement of judgments.

This Convention shall not affect the application of provisions which, in relation to particular matters, govern jurisdiction or the recognition or enforcement of judgments and which are or will be contained in acts of the institutions of the European communities or in national laws harmonised in implementation of such acts.

(Article 25(2) of the Accession Convention provides:

'With a view to its uniform interpretation, paragraph 1 of Article 57 shall be applied in the following manner –

(a) The 1968 Convention as amended shall not prevent a court of a Contracting State which is a party to a convention on a particular matter from assuming

jurisdiction in accordance with that convention, even where the defendant is domiciled in another Contracting State which is not a party to that convention. The court shall, in any event, apply Article 20 of the 1968 Convention as amended.

(b) A judgment given in a Contracting State in the exercise of jurisdiction provided for in a convention on a particular matter shall be recognized and enforced in the other Contracting State in accordance with the 1968 Convention as amended.

Where a convention on a particular matter to which both the State of origin and the State addressed are parties lays down conditions for the recognition or enforcement of judgments, those conditions shall apply. In any event, the provisions of the 1968 Convention as amended which concern the procedure for recognition and enforcement of judgments may be applied.)

Article 58

This Convention shall not affect the rights granted to Swiss nationals by the Convention concluded on 15th June 1869 between France and the Swiss Confederation on Jurisdiction and the Enforcement of Judgments in Civil Matters

Article 59

This Convention shall not prevent a Contracting State from assuming, in a convention on the recognition and enforcement of judgments, an obligation towards a third State not to recognise judgments given in other Contracting States against defendants domiciled or habitually resident in the third State where, in cases provided for in Article 4, the judgment could only be founded on a ground of jurisdiction specified in the second paragraph of Article 3.

However a Contracting State may not assume an obligation towards a third State not to recognise a judgment given in another Contracting State by a court basing its jurisdiction on the presence within that State of property belonging to the defendant, or the seizure by the plaintiff of property situated there:

(1) if the action is brought to assert or declare proprietary or possessory rights in that property, seeks to obtain authority to dispose of it, or arises from another issue relating to such property, or

(2) if the property constitutes the security for a debt which is the subject-matter of the action.

[TITLE VII

RELATIONSHIP TO OTHER CONVENTIONS

Article 55

Subject to the provisions of the second paragraph of Article 54, and of Article 56, this Convention shall, for the States which are parties to it, supersede the following conventions concluded between two or more of them:

- the Convention between Belgium and France on jurisdiction and the validity and enforcement of judgments, arbitration awards and authentic instruments, signed at Paris on 8 July 1899;
- the Convention between Belgium and the Netherlands on jurisdiction bankruptcy, and the validity and enforcement of judgments, arbitration awards and authentic instruments, signed at Brussels on 28 March 1925;

- the Convention between France and Italy on the enforcement of judgments in civil and commercial matters, signed at Rome on 3 June 1930;
- the Convention between the United Kingdom and the French Republic providing for the reciprocal enforcement of judgments in civil and commercial matters, with Protocol, signed at Paris on 18 January 1934;
- the Convention between the United Kingdom and the Kingdom of Belgium providing for the reciprocal enforcement of judgments in civil and commercial matters, with Protocol, signed at Brussels on 2 May 1934;
- the Convention between Germany and Italy on the recognition and enforcement of judgments in civil and commercial matters, signed at Rome on 9 March 1936;
- the Convention between the Federal Republic of Germany and the Kingdom of Belgium on the mutual recognition and enforcement, of judgments, arbitration awards and authentic instruments in civil and commercial matters, signed at Bonn on 30 June 1958:
- the Convention between the Kingdom of the Netherlands and the Italian Republic on the recognition and enforcement of judgments in civil and commercial matters, signed at Rome on 17 April 1959:
- the Convention between the United Kingdom and the Federal Republic of Germany for the reciprocal recognition and enforcement of judgments in civil and commercial matters, signed at Bonn on 14 July 1960:
- the Convention between the Kingdom of Greece and the Federal Republic of Germany for the reciprocal recognition and enforcement of judgments, settlements and authentic instruments in civil and commercial matters, signed in Athens on 4th November 1961.
- the Convention between the Kingdom of Belgium and the Italian Republic on the recognition and enforcement of judgments and other enforceable instruments in civil and commercial matters, signed at Rome on 6 April 1962;
- the Convention between the Kingdom of the Netherlands and the Federal Republic of Germany on the mutual recognition and enforcement of judgments and other enforceable instruments in civil and commercial matters, signed at The Hague on 30 August 1962;
- the Convention between the United Kingdom and the Republic of Italy for the reciprocal recognition and enforcement of judgments in civil and commercial matters, signed at Rome on 7 February 1964, with amending Protocol signed at Rome on 14 July 1970;
- the Convention between the United Kingdom and the Kingdom of the Netherlands providing for the reciprocal recognition and enforcement of judgments in civil matters, signed at The Hague on 17 November 1967,

[- the Convention between Spain and France on the recognition and enforcement of judgment arbitration awards in civil and commercial matters, signed at Paris on 28th May 1969,
- the Convention between Spain and Italy regarding legal aid and the recognition and enforcement of judgments in civil and commercial matters, signed at Madrid on 22nd May 1973.
- the Convention between Spain and the Federal Republic of Germany on the recognition and enforcement of judgments, settlements and enforceable authentic instruments in civil and commercial matters, signed at Bonn on 14th November 1983.]

and, in so far as it is in force –

– the Treaty between Belgium, the Netherlands and Luxembourg on jurisdiction, bankruptcy, and the validity and enforcement of judgments, arbitration awards and authentic instruments, signed at Brussels on 24 November 1961.

Note. The text of art 55 remains unchanged. except for the entries added in square brackets; see the note to art 1 (p 2850).

Article 56

The Treaty and the conventions referred to in Article 55 shall continue to have effect in relation to matters to which this Convention does not apply.

They shall continue to have effect in respect of judgments given and documents formally drawn up or registered as authentic instruments before the entry into force of this Convention.

Article 57

This Convention shall not affect any conventions to which the Contracting States are or will be parties and which, in relation to particular matters, govern jurisdiction or the recognition or enforcement of judgments.

This Convention shall not affect the application of provisions which, in relation to particular matters, govern jurisdiction or the recognition or enforcement of judgments and which are or will be contained in acts of the Institutions of the European Communities or in national laws harmonised in implementation of such acts.

[1. This Convention shall not affect any conventions to which the Contracting States are or will be parties and which in relation to particular matters, govern jurisdiction or the recognition or enforcement of judgments.

2. With a view to its uniform interpretation, paragraph 1 shall be applied in the following manner –
   (a) This Convention shall not prevent a court of a Contracting State which is a party to a convention on a particular matter from assuming jurisdiction in accordance with that Convention, even where the defendant is domiciled in another Contracting State which is not a party to that Convention. The court hearing the action shall, in any event, apply Article 20 of this Convention;
   (b) judgments given in a Contracting State by a court in the exercise of jurisdiction provided for in a convention on a particular matter shall be recognized and enforced in the other Contracting State in accordance with this Convention.

   Where a convention on a particular matter to which both the State of origin and the State addressed are parties lays down conditions for the recognition or enforcement of judgments, those conditions shall apply. In any event, the provisions of this Convention which concern the procedure for recognition and enforcement of judgments may be applied.

3. This Convention shall not affect the application of provisions which, in relation to particular matters, govern jurisdiction or the recognition or enforcement of judgments and which are or will be contained in acts of the institutions of the European Communities or in national laws harmonized in implementation of such acts.]

Note. The text of art 57 reads as in square brackets; see the note to art 1 (p 2850).

Article 58

This Convention shall not affect the rights granted to Swiss nationals by the Convention concluded on 15th June 1869 between France and the Swiss Confederation on Jurisdiction and the Enforcement of Judgments in Civil Matters

[Until such time as the Convention on jurisdiction and the enforcement of judgments in civil and commercial matters, signed at Lugano on 16th September 1988, takes effect with regard to France and the Swiss Confederation, this Convention shall not affect the rights granted to Swiss nationals by the Convention between France and the Swiss Confederation on jurisdiction and enforcement of judgments in civil matters, signed at Paris on 15th June 1869.]

Note. The text of art 58 reads as in square brackets: see the note to art 1 (p 2850).

Article 59

This Convention shall not prevent a contracting State from assuming, in a convention on the recognition and enforcement of judgments, an obligation towards a third State not to recognise judgments given in other Contracting States against defendants domiciled or habitually resident in the third State where, in cases provided for in Article 4, the judgment could only be founded on a ground of jurisdiction specified in the second paragraph of Article 3.

However a Contracting State may not assume an obligation towards a third State not to recognise a judgment given in another Contracting State by a court basing its jurisdiction on the presence within that State of property belonging to the defendant, or the seizure by the plaintiff of property situated there:

1. *if the action is brought to assert or declare proprietary or possessory rights in that property, seeks to obtain authority to dispose of it, or arises from another issue relating to such property, or*
2. *if the property constitutes the security for a debt which is the subject-matter of the action.*

[This Convention shall not prevent a Contracting State from assuming, in a convention on the recognition and enforcement of judgments, an obligation towards a third State not to recognize judgments given in other Contracting States against defendants domiciled or habitually resident in the third State where, in cases provided for in Article 4, the judgment could only be founded on a ground of jurisdiction specified in the second paragraph of Article 3.

However, a Contracting State may not assume an obligation towards a third State not to recognize a judgment given in another Contracting State by a court basing its jurisdiction on the presence within that State of property belonging to the defendant, or the seizure by the plaintiff of property situated there –

1. if the action is brought to assert or declare proprietary or possessory rights in that property, seeks to obtain authority to dispose of it, or arises from another issue relating to such property, or
2. if the property constitutes the security for a debt which is the subject-matter of the action.]]

Note. The text of art 59 reads as in square brackets: see the note to art 1 (p 2850).

ANNEXED PROTOCOL

Article I

Any person domiciled in Luxembourg who is sued in a court of another Contracting State pursuant to Article 5(1) may refuse to submit to the jurisdiction of that court. If the defendant does not enter an appearance the court shall declare of its own motion that it has no jurisdiction.

An agreement conferring jurisdiction, within the meaning of Article 1 shall be valid with respect to a person domiciled in Luxembourg only if that person has expressly and specifically so agreed.

Article II

Without prejudice to any more favourable provisions of national laws, persons domiciled in a Contracting State who are being prosecuted in the criminal courts of another Contracting State of which they are not nationals for an offence which was not intentionally committed may be defended by persons qualified to do so, even if they do not appear in person.

However, the court seised of the matter may order appearance in person; in the case of failure to appear, a judgment given in the civil action without the person concerned having had the opportunity to arrange for his defence need not be recognised or enforced in the other Contracting States.

Article III

In proceedings for the issue of an order for enforcement, no charge, duty or fee calculated by reference to the value of the matter in issue may be levied in the State in which enforcement is sought.

Article IV

Judicial and extrajudicial documents drawn up in one Contracting State which have to be served on persons in another Contracting State shall be transmitted in accordance with the procedures laid down in the conventions and agreements concluded between the Contracting States.

Unless the State in which service is to take place objects by declaration to the Secretary-General of the Council of the European Communities, such documents may also be sent by the appropriate public officers of the State in which the document has been drawn up directly to the appropriate public officers of the State in which the addressee is to be found. In this case the officer of the State of origin shall send a copy of the document to the officer of the State addressed who is competent to forward it to the addressee. The document shall be forwarded in the manner specified by the law of the State addressed. The forwarding shall be recorded by a certificate sent directly to the officer of the State of origin.

Article VA

In matters relating to maintenance, the expression 'court' includes the Danish administrative authorities.

Article VI

The Contracting States shall communicate to the Secretary-General of the Council of the European Communities the text of any provisions of their laws which amend either those articles of their laws mentioned in the Convention or the lists of courts specified in Section 2 of Title III of the Convention.

[ANNEXED PROTOCOL

[The High Contracting Parties have agreed upon the following provisions, which shall be annexed to the Convention.]

Article I

Any person domiciled in Luxembourg who is sued in a court of another Contracting State pursuant to Article 5(1) may refuse to submit to the jurisdiction of that court. If the defendant does not enter an appearance the court shall declare of its own motion that it has no jurisdiction.

An agreement conferring jurisdiction, within the meaning of Article 17, shall be valid with respect to a person domiciled in Luxembourg only if that person has expressly and specifically so agreed.

Article II

Without prejudice to any more favourable provisions of national laws, persons domiciled in a Contracting State who are being prosecuted in the criminal courts of another Contracting State of which they are not nationals for an offence which was not intentionally committed may be defended by persons qualified to do so, even if they do not appear in person.

However, the court seised of the matter may order appearance in person; in the case of failure to appear, a judgment given in the civil action without the person concerned having had the opportunity to arrange for his defence need not be recognized or enforced in the other Contracting States.

Article III

In proceedings for the issue of an order for enforcement, no charge, duty or fee calculated by reference to the value of the matter in issue may be levied in the State in which enforcement is sought.

Article IV

Judicial and extrajudicial documents drawn up in one Contracting State which have to be served on persons in another Contracting State shall be transmitted in accordance with the procedures laid down in the conventions and agreements concluded between the Contracting States.

Unless the State in which service is to take place objects by declaration to the Secretary-General of the Council of the European Communities, such documents may also be sent by the appropriate public officers of the State in which the document has been drawn up directly to the appropriate public officers of the State in which the addressee is to be found. In this case the officer of the State of origin shall send a copy of the document to the officer of the State applied to who is competent to forward it to the addressee. The document shall be forwarded in the manner specified by the law of the State applied to. The forwarding shall be recorded by a certificate sent directly to the officer of the State of origin.

Article V

The jurisdiction specified in Articles 6(2) and 10 in actions on a warranty or guarantee or in any other third party proceedings may not be resorted to in the Federal Republic of Germany. In that State, any person domiciled in another Contracting State may be sued in the courts in pursuance of Articles 68, 72, 73 and 74 of the code of civil procedure (Zivilprozeßordnung) concerning third-party notices.

Judgments given in the other Contracting State by virtue of point 2 of Article 6 or Article 10 shall be recognized and enforced in the Federal Republic of Germany in accordance with Title III. Any effects which judgments given in that State may have on third parties by application of Articles 68, 72, 73 and 74 of the code of civil procedure (Zivilprozeßordnung) shall also be recognized in the other Contracting States.

Article VA

In matters relating to maintenance, the expression 'court' includes the Danish administrative authorities.

Article VB

In proceedings involving a dispute between the master and a member of the crew of a sea-going ship registered in Denmark, in Greece [, in Ireland or in Portugal], concerning remuneration or other conditions of service, a court in a Contracting State shall establish whether the diplomatic or consular officer responsible for the ship has been notified of the dispute. It shall stay the proceedings so long as he has not been notified. It shall of its own motion decline jurisdiction if the officer, having been duly notified, has exercised the powers accorded to him in the matter by a consular convention, or in the absence of such a convention, has, within the time allowed, raised any objection to the exercise of such jurisdiction.

Article VC

Articles 52 and 53 of this Convention shall, when applied by Article 69(5) of the Convention for the European patent for the common market, signed at Luxembourg on 15th December 1975, to the provisions relating to 'residence' in the English text of that Convention, operate as if 'residence' in that text were the same as 'domicile' in Articles 52 and 53.

Article VD

Without prejudice to the jurisdiction of the European Patent Office under the Convention on the grant of European patents, signed at Munich on 5th October 1973, the courts of each Contracting State shall have exclusive jurisdiction, regardless of domicile, in proceedings concerned with the registration or validity of any European patent granted for that State which is not a Community patent by virtue of the provisions of Article 86 of the Convention for the European Patent for the common market, signed at Luxembourg on 15th December 1975.

Article VI

The Contracting States shall communicate to the Secretary-General of the Council of the European Communities the text of any provisions of their laws which amend either those articles of their laws mentioned in the Convention or the lists of courts specified in Section 2 of Title III of the Convention.

[(Signatures of Plenipotentiaries of the original six Contracting States)]]

Note. As to the substitution of this Schedule, see the note to art 1 (p 2850). The text of the Schedule remains unchanged, except for the words in square brackets which are inserted or substituted as noted to the above mentioned art 1.

SCHEDULE 2 Section 2(2)

TEXT OF 1971 PROTOCOL, AS AMENDED

Article 1

The Court of Justice of the European Communities shall have jurisdiction to give rulings on the interpretation of the Convention on Jurisdiction and the Enforcement of Judgments in Civil and Commercial Matters and of the Protocol annexed to that Convention, signed at Brussels on 27th September 1968, and also on the interpretation of the present Protocol.

The Court of Justice of the European Communities shall also have jurisdiction to give rulings on the interpretation of the Convention on the Accession of the Kingdom of Denmark, Ireland and the United Kingdom of Great Britain and Northern Ireland to the Convention of 27th September 1968 and to this Protocol.

Article 2

The following courts may request the Court of Justice to give preliminary rulings on questions of interpretation:

1. – *in Belgium: la Cour de Cassation – het Hof van Cassatie and le Conseil d'État – de Raad van State,*
- *in Denmark: højesteret,*
- *in the Federal Republic of Germany: die obersten Gerichtshöfe des Bundes,*
- *in France: la Cour de Cassation and le Conseil d 'État,*
- *in Ireland, the Supreme Court,*
- *in Italy: la Corte Suprema di Cassazione,*
- *in Luxembourg: la Cour supérieure de Justice when sitting as Cour de Cassation,*
- *in the Netherlands: de Hoge Raad,*
- *in the United Kingdom: the House of Lords and courts to which application has been made under the second paragraph of Article 37 or under Article 41 of the Convention.*

2. *the courts of the Contracting States when they are sitting in an appellate capacity;*

3. *in the cases provided for in Article 37 of the Convention, the courts referred to in that Article.*

Article 3

1. *Where a question of interpretation of the Convention or of one of the other instruments referred to in Article 1 is raised in a case pending before one of the courts listed in Article 2(1), that court shall, if it considers that a decision on the question is necessary to enable it to give judgment, request the Court of Justice to give a ruling thereon.*
2. *Where such a question is raised before any court referred to in Article 2(2) or (3), that court may, under the conditions laid down in paragraph (1), request the Court of Justice to give a ruling thereon.*

Article 4

1. *The competent authority of a Contracting State may request the Court of Justice to give a ruling on a question of interpretation of the Convention or of one of the other instruments referred to in Article 1 if judgments given by courts of that State conflict with the interpretation given either by the Court of Justice or in a judgment of one of the courts of another Contracting State referred to in Article 2(1) or (2). The provisions of this paragraph shall apply only to judgments which have become res judicata.*
2. *The interpretation given by the Court of Justice in response to such a request shall not affect the judgments which give rise to the request for interpretation.*
3. *The Procurators-General of the Courts of Cassation of the Contracting States, or any other authority designated by a Contracting State, shall be entitled to request the Court of Justice for a ruling on interpretation in accordance with paragraph 1).*
4. *The Registrar of the Court of Justice shall give notice of the request to the Contracting States, to the Commission and to the Council of the European Communities; they shall then be entitled within two months of the notification to submit statements of case or written observations to the Court.*
5. *No fees shall be levied or any costs or expenses awarded in respect of the proceedings provided for in this Article.*

Article 5

1. *Except where this Protocol otherwise provides, the provisions of the Treaty establishing the European Economic Community and those of the Protocol on the Statute of the Court of Justice annexed thereto, which are applicable when the Court is requested to give a preliminary ruling, shall also apply to any proceedings for the interpretation of the Convention and the other instruments referred to in Article 1.*
2. *The Rules of Procedure of the Court of Justice shall, if necessary, be adjusted and supplemented in accordance with Article 188 of the Treaty establishing the European Economic Community.*

Article 6

This Protocol shall apply to the European territories of the Contracting States, including Greenland, to the French overseas departments and territories and to Mayotte.

The Kingdom of the Netherlands may declare at the time of signing or ratifying this Protocol or at any later time, by notifying the Secretary-General of the Council of the European Communities, that this Protocol shall be applicable to the Netherlands Antilles.

Notwithstanding the first paragraph, this Protocol shall not apply to:

1. *the Faroe Islands, unless the Kingdom of Denmark makes a declaration to the contrary,*
2. *any European territory situated outside the United Kingdom for the international relations of which the United Kingdom is responsible, unless the United Kingdom makes a declaration to the contrary in respect of any such territory.*

Such declarations may be made at any time by notifying the Secretary-General of the Council of the European Communities.

[SCHEDULE 2 Section 2(2)

TEXT OF 1971 PROTOCOL, AS AMENDED

Article 1

The Court of Justice of the European Communities shall have jurisdiction to give rulings on the interpretation of the Convention on jurisdiction and the enforcement of judgments in civil and commercial matters and of the Protocol annexed to that Convention, signed at Brussels on 27th September 1968, and also on the interpretation of the present Protocol.

The Court of Justice of the European Communities shall also have jurisdiction to give rulings on the interpretation of the Convention on the accession of the Kingdom of Denmark, Ireland and the United Kingdom of Great Britain and Northern Ireland to the Convention of 27th September 1968 and to this Protocol.

The Court of Justice of the European Communities shall also have jurisdiction to give rulings on the interpretation of the Convention on the accession of the Hellenic Republic to the Convention of 27th September 1968 and to this Protocol, as adjusted by the 1978 Convention.

[The Court of Justice of the European Communities shall also have jurisdiction to give rulings on the interpretation of the Convention on the accession of the Hellenic Republic to the Convention of 27th September 1968 and to this Protocol, as adjusted by the 1978 Convention.

The Court of Justice of the European Communities shall also have jurisdiction to give rulings on the interpretation of the Convention on the accession of the Kingdom of Spain and the Portuguese Republic to the Convention of 27th September 1968 and to this Protocol, as adjusted by the 1978 Convention and the 1982 Convention.]

Article 2

The following courts may request the Court of Justice to give preliminary rulings on questions of interpretation –

1. – in Belgium: la Cour de Cassation – het Hof van Cassatie and le Conseil d'État – de Raad van State,
   – in Denmark: højesteret,

- in the Federal Republic of Germany: die obersten Gerichtshöfe des Bundes,
- in Greece: the αμωτατα δικαοτηπια
[– in Spain: el Tribunal Supremo,]
- in France: la Cour de Cassation and le Conseil d'État,
- in Ireland: the Supreme Court,
- in Italy: la Corte Suprema di Cassazione,
- in Luxembourg: la Cour supérieure de Justice when sitting as Cour de Cassation,
- in the Netherlands: de Hoge Raad,
[– in Portugal: o Supremo Tribunal de Justiça and o Supremo Tribunal Adminstrativo,]
- in the United Kingdom: the House of Lords and courts to which application has been made under the second paragraph of Article 37 or under Article 41 of the Convention.

2. The courts of the Contracting States when they are sitting in an appellate capacity.
3. In the cases provided for in Article 37 of the Convention, the courts referred to in that Article.

Article 3

1. Where a question of interpretation of the Convention or of one of the other instruments referred to in Article 1 is raised in a case pending before one of the courts listed in point 1 of Article 2, that court shall, if it considers that a decision on the question is necessary to enable it to give judgment, request the Court of Justice to give a ruling thereon.
2. Where such a question is raised before any court referred to in point 2 or 3 of Article 2, that court may, under the conditions laid down in paragraph 1, request the Court of Justice to give a ruling thereon.

Article 4

1. The competent authority of a Contracting State may request the Court of Justice to give a ruling on a question of interpretation of the Convention or of one of the other instruments referred to in Article 1 if judgments given by courts of that State conflict with the interpretation given either by the Court of Justice or in a judgment of one of the courts of another Contracting State referred to in point 1 or 2 of Article 12. The provisions of this paragraph shall apply only to judgments which have become res judicata.
2. The interpretation given by the Court of Justice in response to such a request shall not affect the judgments which gave rise to the request for interpretation.
3. The Procurators-General of the Courts of Cassation of the Contracting States, or any other authority designated by a Contracting State, shall be entitled to request the Court of Justice for a ruling on interpretation in accordance with paragraph 1.
4. The Registrar of the Court of Justice shall give notice of the request to the Contracting States, to the Commission and to the Council of the European

Communities; they shall then be entitled within two months of the notification to submit statements of case or written observations to the Court.

5. No fees shall be levied or any costs or expenses awarded in respect of the proceedings provided for in this Article.

Article 5

1. Except where this Protocol otherwise provides, the provisions of the Treaty establishing the European Economic Community and those of the Protocol on the Statute of the Court of Justice annexed thereto, which are applicable when the Court is requested to give a preliminary ruling, shall also apply to any proceedings for the interpretation of the Convention and the other instruments referred to in Article 1.
2. The Rules of Procedure of the Court of Justice shall, if necessary be adjusted and supplemented in accordance with Article 188 of the Treaty establishing the European Economic Community

Article 6

This Protocol shall apply to the European territories of the Contracting States, including Greenland, to the French overseas departments and territories, and to Mayotte.

The Kingdom of the Netherlands may declare at the time of signing or ratifying this Protocol or at any later time, by notifying the Secretary-General of the Council of the European communities, that this Protocol shall be applicable to the Netherlands Antilles.

Notwithstanding the first paragraph, this Protocol shall not apply to:

(1) the Faroe Islands, unless the Kingdom of Denmark makes a declaration to the contrary,

(2) any European territory situated outside the United Kingdom for the international relations of which the United Kingdom is responsible, unless the United Kingdom makes a declaration to the contrary in respect of any such territory.

Such declarations may be made at any time by notifying the Secretary-General of the Council of the European Communities [deleted].

Article 7

This Protocol shall be ratified by the signatory States. The instruments of ratification shall be deposited with the Secretary-General of the Council of the European Communities.

Article 8

This Protocol shall enter into force on the first day of the third month following the deposit of the instrument of ratification by the last signatory State to take this step; provided that it shall at the earliest enter into force at the same time as the Convention of 27 September 1968 on jurisdiction and the enforcement of judgments in civil and commercial matters.

Article 9

The Contracting States recognize that any State which becomes a member of the European Economic Community, and to which Article 63 of the Convention on jurisdiction and the enforcement of judgments in civil and commercial matters applies, must accept the provisions of this Protocol, subject to such adjustments as may be required.

Article 10

The Secretary-General of the Council of the European Communities shall notify the signatory States of:
(a) the deposit of each instrument of ratification;
(b) the date of entry into force of this Protocol;
(c) any designation received pursuant to Article 4;
(d) any declaration received pursuant to Article 6.
[The Secretary-General of the Council of the European Communities shall notify the signatory States of –
(a) the deposit of each instrument of ratification;
(b) the date of entry into force of this Protocol;
(c) any designation received pursuant to Article 4(3);
(d) [Deleted].]

Article 11

The Contracting States shall communicate to the Secretary-General of the Council of the European Communities the texts of any provisions of their laws which necessitate an amendment to the list of courts in point 1 of Article 2.

Article 12

This Protocol is concluded for an unlimited period.

Article 13

Any Contracting State may request the revision of this Protocol. In this event, a revision conference shall be convened by the President of the Council of the European Communities.

Article 14

This Protocol, drawn up in a single original in the Dutch, French, German and Italian languages, all four texts being equally authentic, shall be deposited in the archives of the Secretariat of the Council of the European Communities. The Secretary-General shall transmit a certified copy to the Government of each signatory State.]

Note. This Schedule substituted by Civil Jurisdiction and Judgments Act 1982 (Amendment) Order 1989. SI 1989 No 1346. art 9(2). Sch 2.

This Schedule was again substituted by Civil Jurisdiction and Judgments Act 1982 (Amendment Order 1990, SI 1990 No 2591, art 12(2), Sch 2, as from 1 December 1991. The text of the new Schedule is the text set out above with any amendments taken in as shown in square brackets.

SCHEDULE 3 Section 2(2)

TEXT OF TITLES V AND VI OF ACCESSION CONVENTION

TITLE V

TRANSITIONAL PROVISIONS

Article 34

[1. The 1968 Convention and the 1971 Protocol, with the amendments made by this Convention, shall apply only to legal proceedings instituted and to authentic instruments formally drawn up or registered after the entry into force of this Convention in the State of origin and, where recognition or enforcement of a judgment or authentic instrument is sought, in the State addressed.

2. However, as between the six Contracting States to the 1968 Convention, judgments given after the date of entry into force of this Convention in proceedings instituted before that date shall be recognised and enforced in accordance with the provisions of Title III of the 1968 Convention as amended.

3. Moreover, as between the six Contracting States to the 1968 Convention and the three States mentioned in Article 1 of this Convention, and as between those three States, judgments given after the date of entry into force of this Convention between the State of origin and the State addressed in proceedings instituted before that date shall also be recognised and enforced in accordance with the provisions of Title III of the 1968 Convention as amended if jurisdiction was founded upon rules which accorded with the provisions of Title II, as amended, or with provisions of a convention concluded between the State of origin and the State addressed which was in force when the proceedings were instituted.]

Note. The whole of this Schedule substituted by Civil Jurisdiction and Judgments Act 1982 (Amendment) Order 1990, SI 1990 No 2591, art 12(3), Sch 3, as from 1 December 199L The text of art 34 is that set out above.

[SCHEDULE 3A Section 2(2)

TEXT OF TITLES V AND VI OF 1982 ACCESSION CONVENTION

TITLE V

TRANSITIONAL PROVISIONS

Article 12

1. The 1968 Convention and the 1971 Protocol, as amended by the 1978 Convention and this Convention, shall apply only to legal proceedings instituted and to authentic instruments formally drawn up or registered after the entry into force of this Convention in the State of origin and,

where recognition or enforcement of a judgment or authentic instrument is sought, in the State addressed.

2. However, judgments given after the date of entry into force of this Convention between the State of origin and the State addressed in proceedings instituted before that date shall be recognized and enforced in accordance with the provisions of Title III of the 1968 Convention, as amended by the 1978 Convention and this Convention, if jurisdiction was founded upon rules which accorded with the provisions of Title II of the 1968 Convention, as amended, or with the provisions of a convention which was in force between the State of origin and the State addressed when the proceedings were instituted.

TITLE VI

FINAL PROVISIONS

Article 13

The Secretary-General of the Council of the European Communities shall transmit a certified copy of the 1968 Convention, of the 1971 Protocol and of the 1978 Convention in the Danish, Dutch, English, French, German, Irish and Italian languages to the Government of the Hellenic Republic.

The texts of the 1968 Convention, of the 1971 Protocol and of the 1978 Convention, drawn up in the Greek language, shall be annexed to this Convention. The texts drawn up in the Greek language shall be authentic under the same conditions as the other texts of the 1968 Convention, the 1971 Protocol and the 1978 Convention.

Article 14

This Convention shall be ratified by the signatory States. The instruments of ratification shall be deposited with the Secretary-General of the Council of the European Communities.

Article 15

This Convention shall enter into force, as between the States which have ratified it, on the first day of the third month following the deposit of the last instrument of ratification by the Hellenic Republic and those States which have put into force the 1978 Convention in accordance with Article 39 of that Convention.

It shall enter into force for each Member State which subsequently ratifies it on the first day of the third month following the deposit of its instrument of ratification.

Article 16

The Secretary-General of the Council of the European Communities shall notify the signatory States of:

(a) the deposit of each instrument of ratification;

(b) the dates of entry into force of this Convention for the Contracting States.

Article 17

This Convention, drawn up in a single original in the Danish, Dutch, English, French, German, Greek, Irish and Italian languages, all eight texts being equally authentic, shall be deposited in the archives of the General Secretariat of the Council of the European Communities. The Secretary-General shall transmit a certified copy to the Government of each signatory State.]

Note. This Schedule inserted by Civil Jurisdiction and Judgments Act 1982 (Amendment) Order 1989, SI 1989 No 1346, art 9(3), Sch 3, as from 1 October 1989.

[SCHEDULE 3B Section 2(2)

TEXT OF TITLES VI AND VII OF 1989 ACCESSION CONVENTION

TITLE VI

TRANSITIONAL PROVISIONS

Article 29

1. The 1968 Convention and the 1971 Protocol, as amended by the 1978 Convention, the 1982 Convention and this Convention, shall apply only to legal proceedings instituted and to authentic instruments formally drawn up or registered after the entry into force of this Convention in the State of origin and, where recognition or enforcement of a judgment or authentic instrument is sought, in the State addressed.
2. However, judgments given after the date of entry into force of this Convention between the State of origin and the State addressed in proceedings instituted before that date shall be recognized and enforced in accordance with the provisions of Title III of the 1968 Convention, as amended by the 1978 Convention, the 1982 Convention and this Convention, if jurisdiction was founded upon rules which accorded with the provisions of Title II of the 1968 Convention, as amended, or with the provisions of a convention which was in force between the State of origin and the State addressed when the proceedings were instituted.

TITLE VII

FINAL PROVISIONS

Article 30

1. The Secretary-General of the Council of the European Communities shall transmit a certified copy of the 1968 Convention, of the 1971 Protocol, or the 1978 Convention and of the 1982 Convention in the Danish, Dutch, English, French, German, Irish and Italian languages to the Governments of the Kingdom of Spain and of the Portuguese Republic.
2. The texts of the 1968 Convention, of the 1971 Protocol, of the 1978 Convention and of the 1982 Convention, drawn up in the Portuguese and Spanish languages, are set out in Annexes II, III, IV and V to this Convention. The texts drawn up in the Portuguese and Spanish languages shall be authentic under the same conditions as the other texts of the 1968 Convention, the 1971 Protocol, the 1978 Convention and the 1982 Convention.

Article 31

This Convention shall be ratified by the signatory States. The instruments of ratification shall be deposited with the Secretary-General of the Council of the European Communities.

Article 32

(1) This Convention shall enter into force on the first day of the third month following the date on which two signatory States, of which one is the Kingdom of Spain or the Portuguese Republic, deposit their instruments of ratification.
(2) This Convention shall take effect in relation to any other signatory State on the first day of the third month following the deposit of its instrument of ratification.

Article 33

The Secretary-General of the Council of the European Communities shall notify the signatory States of:
(a) the deposit of each instrument of ratification;
(b) the dates of entry into force of this Convention for the Contracting States.

Article 34

This Convention, drawn up in a single original in the Danish, Dutch, English, French, German, Greek, Irish, Italian, Portuguese and Spanish languages, all 10 texts being equally authentic, shall be deposited in the archives of the General Secretariat of the Council of the European Communities. The Secretary-General shall transmit a certified copy to the Government of each signatory State.]

[SCHEDULE 3C

Text of the Lugano Convention

Convention on Jurisdiction and the Enforcement of Judgments in Civil and Commercial Matters

PREAMBLE

The High Contracting Parties to this Convention,

Anxious to strengthen in their territories the legal protection of persons therein established,

Considering that it is necessary for this purpose to determine the international jurisdiction of their courts, to facilitate recognition and to introduce an expeditious procedure for securing the enforcement of judgments, authentic instruments and court settlements,

Aware of the links between them, which have been sanctioned in the economic field by the free trade agreements concluded between the European

Economic Community and the States members of the European Free Trade Association,

Taking into account the Brussels Convention of 27 September 1968 on jurisdiction and the enforcement of judgments in civil and commercial matters, as amended by the Conventions under the successive enlargements of the European Communities.

Persuaded that the extension of the principles of that Convention to the States parties to this instrument will strengthen legal and economic co-operation in Europe,

Desiring to ensure as uniform an interpretation as possible of this instrument,

Have in this spirit decided to conclude this Convention and

Have agreed as follows:

TITLE I

SCOPE

Article 1

This Convention shall apply in civil and commercial matters whatever the nature of the court or tribunal. It shall not extend, in particular. to revenue, customs or administrative matters.

The Convention shall not apply to:

1. the status or legal capacity of natural persons, rights in property arising out of a matrimonial relationship, wills and succession;
2. bankruptcy, proceedings relating to the winding-up of insolvent companies or other legal persons, judicial arrangements, compositions and analogous proceedings;
3. social security;
4. arbitration.

TITLE II

JURISDICTION

Section 1
General Provisions

Article 2

Subject to the provisions of this Convention, persons domiciled in a Contracting State shall, whatever their nationality, be sued in the courts of that State.

Persons who are not nationals of the State in which they are domiciled shall be governed by the rules of jurisdiction applicable to nationals of that State.

Article 3

Persons domiciled in a Contracting State may be sued in the courts of another Contracting State only by virtue of the rules set out in Sections 2 to 6 of this Title.

In particular the following provisions shall not be applicable as against them:

- in Belgium: Article 15 of the civil code (Code civil – Burgerlijk Wetboek) and Article 638 of the judicial code (Code judiciaire – Gerechtelijk Wetboek),

- in Denmark: Article 246(2) and (3) of the law on civil procedure (Lov om rettens pleje),
- in the Federal Republic of Germany: Article 23 of the code of civil procedure (Zivilprozeßordnung),
- in Greece: Article 40 of the code of civil procedure (Κωδικαζ πολιτικηζ δικονομιαζ),
- in France: Articles 14 and 15 of the civil code (Code civil),
- in Ireland: the rules which enable jurisdiction to be founded on the document instituting the proceedings having been served on the defendant during his temporary presence in Ireland,
- in Iceland: Article 77 of the Civil Proceedings Act (lög um međferđ einkamála (í héradi),
- in Italy: Articles 2 and 4, Nos I and 2 of the code of civil procedure (Codice di procedura civile),
- in Luxembourg: Articles 14 and 15 of the civil code (Code civil),
- in the Netherlands: Articles 126(3) and 127 of the code of civil procedure (Wetboek van Bergherlijke Rechtsvordering),
- in Norway: Section 32 of the Civil Proceedings Act (tvistemålsloven),
- in Austria: Article 99 of the Law on Court Jurisdiction (Jurisdiktionsnorm),
- in Portugal: Articles 65(1) (c), 65(2) and 65A(c) of the code of civil procedure (Codigo de Processo Civil) and Article 11 of the code of labour procedure (Código de Processo de Trabaiho),
- in Switzerland: le for du lieu du séquestre/Gerichtsstand des Arrestortes/foro del luogo del sequestro within the meaning of Article 4 of the loi fédérale sur le droit international privé/Bundesgesetz über das internationale Privatrecht/legge federale sul diritto internazionale privato,
- in Finland: the second, third and fourth sentences of Section 1 of Chapter 10 of the Code of Judicial Procedure (oikeudenkäymiskaari/rättegångs-balken),
- in Sweden: the first sentence of Section 3 of Chapter 10 of the Code of Judicial Procedure (Rättegångsbalken),
- in the United Kingdom: the rules which enable jurisdiction to be founded on:
  (a) the document instituting the proceedings having been served on the defendant during his temporary presence in the United Kingdom: or
  (b) the presence within the United Kingdom of property belonging to the defendant: or
  (c) the seizure by the plaintiff of property situated in the United Kingdom.

Article 4

If the defendant is not domiciled in a Contracting State, the jurisdiction of the courts of each Contracting State shall, subject to the provisions of Article 16, be determined by the law of that State.

As against such a defendant, any person domiciled in a Contracting State may, whatever his nationality avail himself in that State of the rules of jurisdiction there in force, and in particular those specified in the second paragraph of Article 3, in the same way as the nationals of that State.

Section 2
Special Jurisdiction

Article 5

A person domiciled in a Contracting State may, in another Contracting State, be sued:

1. in matters relating to a contract, in the courts for the place of performance of the obligation in question; in matters relating to individual contracts of employment, this place is that where the employee habitually carries out his work, or if the employee does not habitually carry out his work in any one country, this place shall be the place of business through which he was engaged;
2. in matters relating to maintenance, in the courts for the place where the maintenance creditor is domiciled or habitually resident or, if the matter is ancillary to proceedings concerning the status of a person, in the court which, according to its own law, has jurisdiction to entertain those proceedings, unless that jurisdiction is based solely on the nationality of one of the parties;
3. in matters relating to tort, delict or quasi-delict, in the courts for the place where the harmful event occurred:
4. as regards a civil claim for damages or restitution which is based on an act giving rise to criminal proceedings, in the court seised of those proceedings, to the extent that that court has jurisdiction under its own law to entertain civil proceedings;
5. as regards a dispute arising out of the operations of a branch, agency or other establishment, in the courts for the place in which the branch, agency or other establishment is situated;
6. in his capacity as senior, trustee or beneficiary of a trust created by the operation of a statute, or by a written instrument, or created orally and evidenced in writing, in the courts of the Contracting State in which the trust is domiciled;
7. as regards a dispute concerning the payment of remuneration claimed in respect of the salvage of a cargo or freight, in the court under the authority of which the cargo or freight in question:
   (a) has been arrested to secure such payment, or
   (b) could have been so arrested, but bail or other security has been given; provided that this provision shall apply only if it is claimed that the defendant has an interest in the cargo or freight or had such an interest at the time of salvage.

Article 6

A person domiciled in a Contracting State may also be sued:

1. where he is one of a number of defendants, in the courts for the place where any one of them is domiciled;
2. as a third party in an action on a warranty or guarantee or in any other third party proceedings, in the court seised of the original proceedings, unless these were instituted solely with the object of removing him from the jurisdiction of the court which would be competent in his case;
3. on a counterclaim arising from the same contract or facts on which the original claim was based, in the court in which the original claim is pending;

4. in matters relating to a contract, if the action may be combined with an action against the same defendant in matters relating to rights *in rem* in immovable property, in the court of the Contracting State in which the property is situated.

Article 6A

Where by virtue of this Convention a court of a Contracting State has jurisdiction in actions relating to liability arising from the use of operation of a ship, that court, or any other court substituted for this purpose by the internal law of that State, shall also have jurisdiction over claims for limitation of such liability.

Section 3
Jurisdiction in Matters Relating to Insurance

Article 7

In matters relating to insurance, jurisdiction shall be determined by this Section, without prejudice to the provisions of Articles 4 and 5(5).

Article 8

An insurer domiciled in a Contracting State may be sued:

1. in the courts of the State where he is domiciled; or
2. in another Contracting State, in the courts for the place where the policy-holder is domiciled; or
3. if he is a co-insurer, in the courts of a Contracting State in which proceedings are brought against the leading insurer.

An insurer who is not domiciled in a Contracting State but has a branch, agency or other establishment in one of the Contracting States shall, in disputes arising out of the operations of the branch, agency or establishment, be deemed to be domiciled in that State.

Article 9

In respect of liability insurance or insurance of immovable property, the insurer may in addition be sued in the courts for the place where the harmful event occurred. The same applies if movable and immovable property are covered by the same insurance policy and both are adversely affected by the same contingency.

Article 10

In respect of liability insurance, the insurer may also, if the law of the court permits it, be joined in proceedings which the injured party has brought against the insured.

The provisions of Articles 7, 8 and 9 shall apply to actions brought by the injured party directly against the insurer, where such direct actions are permitted.

If the law governing such direct actions provides that the policy-holder or the insured may be joined as a party to the action, the same court shall have jurisdiction over them.

Article 11

Without prejudice to the provisions of the third paragraph of Article 10, an insurer may bring proceedings only in the courts of the Contracting State in which the defendant is domiciled, irrespective of whether he is the policy-holder, the insured or a beneficiary.

The provisions of this Section shall not affect the right to bring a counterclaim in the court in which, in accordance with this Section, the original claim is pending.

Article 12

The provisions of this Section may be departed from only by an agreement on jurisdiction:

1. which is entered into after the dispute has arisen; or
2. which allows the policy-holder, the insured or a beneficiary to bring proceedings in courts other than those indicated in this Section; or
3. which is concluded between a policy-holder and an insurer, both of whom are at the time of conclusion of the contract domiciled or habitually resident in the same Contracting State, and which has the effect of conferring jurisdiction on the courts of that State even if the harmful event were to occur abroad, provided that such an agreement is not contrary to the law of the State; or
4. which is concluded with a policy-holder who is not domiciled in a Contracting State, except insofar as the insurance is compulsory or relates to immovable Property in a Contracting State: or
5. which relates to a contract of insurance insofar as it covers one or more of the risks set out in Article 12A.

Article 12A

The following are the risks referred to in Article 12(5):

1. any loss of or damage to:
   (a) sea-going ships, installations situated offshore or on the high seas, or aircraft, arising from perils which relate to their use for commercial purposes;
   (b) goods in transit other than passengers' baggage where the transit consists of or includes carriage by such ships or aircraft;
2. any liability, other than for bodily injury to passengers or loss of or damage to their baggage;
   (a) arising out of the use or operation of ships. installations or aircraft as referred to in (1) (a) above in so far as the law of the Contracting State in which such aircraft was registered does not prohibit agreements on jurisdiction regarding insurance of such risks;
   (b) for loss or damage caused by goods in transit as described in (1) (b) above:
3. any financial loss connected with the use or operation of ships, installations or aircraft as referred to in (2)(a) above, in particular loss of freight or charter-hire;
4. any risk or interest connected with any of those referred to in (1) to (3) above.

Section 4
Jurisdiction Over Consumer Contracts

Article 13

In proceedings concerning a contract concluded by a person for a purpose which can be regarded as being outside his trade or profession, hereinafter called 'the consumer', jurisdiction shall be determined by this Section. without prejudice to the provisions of Articles 4 and 5(5), if it is:

1. a contract for the sale of goods on instalment credit terms: or
2. a contract for a loan repayable by instalments, or for any other form of credit, made to finance the sale of goods; or
3. any other contract for the supply of goods or a contract for the supply of services, and
   (a) in the State of the consumer's domicile the conclusion of the contract was preceded by a specific invitation addressed to him or by advertising, and
   b) the consumer took in that State the steps necessary for the conclusion of the contract.

Where a consumer enters into a contract with a party who is not domiciled in a Contracting State but has a branch, agency or other establishment in one of the Contracting States, that party shall, in disputes arising out of the operations of the branch, agency or establishment, be deemed to be domiciled in that State.

This Section shall not apply to contracts of transport.

Article 14

A consumer may bring proceedings against the other party to a contract either in the courts of the Contracting State in which that party is domiciled or in the courts of the Contracting State in which he is himself domiciled.

Proceedings may be brought against a consumer by the other party to the contract only in the courts of the Contracting State in which the consumer is domiciled.

These provisions shall not affect the right to bring a counterclaim in the court in which, in accordance with this Section, the original claim is pending.

Article 15

This provisions of this Section may be departed from only by an agreement:

1. which is entered into after the dispute has arisen; or
2. which allows the consumer to bring proceedings in courts other than those indicated in this Section; or
3. which is entered into by the consumer and the other party to the contract, both of whom are at the time of conclusion of the contract domiciled or habitually resident in the same Contracting State, and which confers jurisdiction on the courts of that State, provided that such an agreement is not contrary to the law of that State.

Section 5
Exclusive Jurisdiction

Article 16

The following courts shall have exclusive jurisdiction, regardless of domicile:

1. (a) in proceedings which have as their object rights *in rem* in immovable property or tenancies of immovable property, the courts of the Contracting State in which the property is situated;
   (b) however, in proceedings which have as their object tenancies of immovable property concluded for temporary private use for a maximum period of six consecutive months, the courts of the Contracting State in which the defendant is domiciled shall also have jurisdiction, provided that the tenant is a natural person and neither party is domiciled in the Contracting State in which the property is situated;
2. in proceedings which have as their object the validity of the constitution, the nullity or the dissolution of companies or other legal persons or associations of natural or legal persons, or the decisions of their organs, the courts of the Contracting State in which the company, legal person or association has its seat:
3. in proceedings which have as their object the validity of entries in public registers. the courts of the Contracting State in which the register is kept;
4. in proceedings concerned with the registration or validity of patents. trade marks, designs, or other similar rights required to be deposited or registered, the courts of the Contracting State in which the deposit or registration has been applied for, has taken place or is under the terms of an international convention deemed to have taken place;
5. in proceedings concerned with the enforcement of judgments, the courts of the Contracting State in which the judgment has been or is to be enforced.

Section 6
Prorogation of Jurisdiction

Article 17

1. If the parties, one or more of whom is domiciled in a Contracting State, have agreed that a court or the courts of a Contracting State are to have jurisdiction to settle any disputes which have arisen or which may arise in connection with a particular legal relationship, that court or those courts shall have exclusive jurisdiction. Such an agreement conferring jurisdiction shall be either:
   (a) in writing or evidenced in writing, or
   (b) in a form which accords with practices which the parties have established between themselves, or
   (c) in international trade or commerce, in a form which accords with a usage of which the parties are or ought to have been aware and which in such trade or commerce is widely known to, and regularly observed by, parties to contracts of the type involved in the particular trade or commerce concerned.

Where such an agreement is concluded by parties, none of whom is domiciled in a Contracting State, the courts of other Contracting States shall have no jurisdiction over their disputes unless the court or courts chosen have declined jurisdiction.

2. The court or courts of a Contracting State on which a trust instrument has conferred jurisdiction shall have exclusive jurisdiction in any proceedings brought against a settlor, trustee or beneficiary, if relations between these persons or their rights or obligations under the trust are involved.
3. Agreements or provisions of a trust instrument conferring jurisdiction shall have no legal force if they are contrary to the provisions of Article 12 or 15, or if the courts whose jurisdiction they purport to exclude have exclusive jurisdiction by virtue of Article 16.
4. If an agreement conferring jurisdiction was concluded for the benefit of only one of the parties, that party shall retain the right to bring proceedings in any other court which has jurisdiction by virtue of this Convention.
5. In matters relating to individual contracts of employment an agreement conferring jurisdiction shall have legal force only if it is entered into after the dispute has arisen.

Article 18

Apart from jurisdiction derived from other provisions of this Convention, a court of a Contracting State before whom a defendant enters an appearance shall have jurisdiction. This rule shall not apply where appearance was entered solely to contest the jurisdiction, or where another court has exclusive jurisdiction by virtue of Article 16.

Section 7
Examination as to Jurisdiction and Admissibility

Article 19

Where a court of a Contracting State is seised of a claim which is principally concerned with a matter over which the courts of another Contracting State have exclusive jurisdiction by virtue of Article 16, it shall declare of its own motion that it has no jurisdiction.

Article 20

Where a defendant domiciled in one Contracting State is sued in a court of another Contracting State and does not enter an appearance, the court shall declare of its own motion that it has no jurisdiction unless its jurisdiction is derived from the provisions of this Convention.

The court shall stay the proceedings so long as it is not shown that the defendant has been able to receive the document instituting the proceedings or an equivalent document in sufficient time to enable him to arrange for his defence, or that all necessary steps have been taken to this end.

The provisions of the foregoing paragraph shall be replaced by those of Article 15 of the Hague Convention of 15 November 1965 on the service abroad of judicial and extrajudicial documents in civil or commercial matters, if the document instituting the proceedings or notice thereof had to be transmitted abroad in accordance with that Convention.

Section 8
Lis pendens – Related Actions

Article 21

Where proceedings involving the same cause of action and between the same parties are brought in the courts of different Contracting States, any court other than the court first seised shall of its own motion stay its proceedings until such time as the jurisdiction of the court first seised is established.

Where the jurisdiction of the court first seised is established, any court other than the court first seised shall decline jurisdiction in favour of that court.

Article 22

Where related actions are brought in the courts of different Contracting States, any court other than the court first seised may, while the actions are pending at first instance, stay its proceedings.

A court other than the court first seised may also, on the application of one of the parties, decline jurisdiction if the law of that court permits the consolidation of related actions and the court first seised has jurisdiction over both actions.

For the purposes of this Article, actions are deemed to be related where they are so closely connected that it is expedient to hear and determine them together to avoid the risk of irreconcilable judgments resulting from separate proceedings.

Article 23

Where actions come within the exclusive jurisdiction of several courts, any court other than the court first seised shall decline jurisdiction in favour of that court.

Section 9
Provisional, Including Protective, Measures

Article 24

Application may be made to the courts of a Contracting State for such provisional, including protective, measures as may be available under the law of that State, even if, under this Convention, the courts of another Contracting State have jurisdiction as to the substance of the matter.

TITLE III

RECOGNITION AND ENFORCEMENT

Article 25

For the purposes of this Convention, 'judgment' means any judgment given by a court or tribunal of a Contracting State, whatever the judgment may be called, including a decree, order, decision or writ of execution, as well as the determination of costs or expenses by an officer of the court.

Section 1
Recognition

Article 26

A judgment given in a Contracting State shall be recognised in the other Contracting States without any special procedure being required.

Any interested party who raises the recognition of a judgment as the principal issue in a dispute may, in accordance with the procedures provided for in Sections 2 and 3 of this Title, apply for a decision that the judgment be recognised.

If the outcome of proceedings in a court of a Contracting State depends on the determination of an incidental question of recognition that court shall have jurisdiction over that question.

Article 27

A judgment shall not be recognised:

1. if such recognition is contrary to public policy in the State in which recognition is sought;
2. where it was given in default of appearance, if the defendant was not duly served with the document which instituted the proceedings or with an equivalent document in sufficient time to enable him to arrange for his defence;
3. if the judgment is irreconcilable with a judgment given in a dispute between the same parties in the State in which recognition is sought;
4. if the court of the State of origin, in order to arrive at its judgment, has decided a preliminary question concerning the status or legal capacity of natural persons, rights in property arising out of a matrimonial relationship, wills or succession in a way that conflicts with a rule of the private international law of the State in which the recognition is sought, unless the same result would have been reached by the application of the rules of private international law of that State.
5. if the judgment is irreconcilable with an earlier judgment given in a non-contracting State involving the same cause of action and between the same parties, provided that this latter judgment fulfils the conditions necessary for its recognition in the State addressed.

Article 28

Moreover, a judgment shall not be recognised if it conflicts with the provisions of Section 3, 4 or 5 of Title II or in a case provided for in Article 59.

A judgment may furthermore be refused recognition in any case provided for in Article 54B(3) or 57(4).

In its examination of the grounds of jurisdiction referred to in the foregoing paragraphs, the court or authority applied to shall be bound by the findings of fact on which the court of the State of origin based its jurisdiction.

Subject to the provisions of the first and second paragraphs, the jurisdiction of the court of the State of origin may not be reviewed; the test of public policy referred to in Article 27(1) may not be applied to the rules relating to jurisdiction.

Article 29

Under no circumstances may a foreign judgment be reviewed as to its substance.

Article 30

A court of a Contracting State in which recognition is sought of a judgment given in another Contracting State may stay the proceedings if an ordinary appeal against the judgment has been lodged.

A court of a Contracting State in which recognition is sought of a judgment given in Ireland or the United Kingdom may stay the proceedings if enforcement is suspended in the State of origin by reason of an appeal.

Section 2
Enforcement

Article 31

A judgment given in a Contracting State and enforceable in that State shall be enforced in another Contracting State when, on the application of any interested party, it has been declared enforceable there.

However, in the United Kingdom. such a judgment shall be enforced in England and Wales, in Scotland, or in Northern Ireland when, on the application of any interested party, it has been registered for enforcement in that part of the United Kingdom.

Article 32

2. The application shall be submitted:
   - in Belgium, to the tribunal de première instance or rechtbank van eerste aanleg,
   - in Denmark, to the bvret,
   - in the Federal Republic of Germany, to the presiding judge of a chamber of the Landgericht,
   - in Greece, to the μονομελεζ πρωτοδικειο,
   - in Spain, to the Juzgado de Primera Instancia,
   - in France, to the presiding judge of the tribunal de grande instance,
   - in Ireland, to the High Court,
   - in Iceland, to the héradsdómari,
   - in Italy, to the corte d'appello,
   - in Luxembourg, to the presiding judge of the tribunal d'arrondissement,
   - in the Netherlands, to the presiding judge of the arrondissements-rechtbank,
   - in Norway, to the herredsrett or byrett as namsrett,
   - in Austria, to the Landesgericht or the Kreisgericht,
   - in Portugal, to the Tribunal Judicial de Círculo,
   - in Switzerland:
     (a) in respect of judgments ordering the payment of a sum of money, to the juge de la mainlevée/Rechtsöffnungsrichter/giudice competente a pronunciare sul rigetto dell'opposizione, within the framework of the procedure governed by Articles 80 and 81 of the loi fédérale sur la poursuite pour dettes et al faillite/

Bundesgesetz über Schuldbetreibung und Konkurs/legge federale sulla esecuzione e sul fallimento;

(b) in respect of judgments ordering a performance other than the payment of a sum of money, to the juge cantonal d'exequatur compétent/zuständiger kantonaler Vollstreckungsrichter/giudice cantonale' competente a pronunciare l'exequatur,

– in Finland, to the ulosotonhaltija/överexekutor,
– in Sweden, to the Svea hovrätt,
– in the United Kingdom:

(a) in England and Wales, to the High Court of Justice, or in the case of a maintenance judgment to the Magistrates' Court on transmission by the Secretary of State;

(b) in Scotland, to the Court of Session, or in the case of a maintenance judgment to the Sheriff Court on transmission by the Secretary of State;

(c) in Northern Ireland, to the High Court of Justice, or in the case of a maintenance judgment to the Magistrates' Court on transmission by the Secretary of State.

2. The jurisdiction of local courts shall be determined by reference to the place of domicile of the party against whom enforcement is sought. If he is not domiciled in the State in which enforcement is sought, it shall be determined by reference to the place of enforcement.

Article 33

The procedure for making the application shall be governed by the law of the State in which enforcement is sought.

The applicant must give an address for service of process within the area of jurisdiction of the court applied to. However, if the law of the State in which enforcement is sought does not provide for the furnishing of such an address, the applicant shall appoint a representative *ad litem*.

The documents referred to in Articles 46 and 47 shall be attached to the application.

Article 34

The court applied to shall give its decision without delay; the party against whom enforcement is sought shall not at this stage of the proceedings be entitled to make any submissions on the application.

The application may be refused only for one of the reasons specified in Articles 27 and 28.

Under no circumstances may the foreign judgment be reviewed as to its substance.

Article 35

The appropriate officer of the court shall without delay bring the decisions given on the application to the notice of the applicant in accordance with the procedure laid down by the law of the State in which enforcement is sought.

Article 36

If enforcement is authorised, the party against whom enforcement is sought may appeal against the decision within one month of service thereof.

If that party is domiciled in a Contracting State other than that in which the decision authorising enforcement was given, the time for appealing shall be two months and shall run from the date of service, either on him in person or at his residence. No extension of time may be granted on account of distance.

Article 37

1. An appeal against the decision authorising enforcement shall be lodged in accordance with the rules governing procedure in contentious matters:
   - in Belgium, with the tribunal de première instance or rechtbank van eerste aanleg,
   - in Denmark, with the landsret,
   - in the Federal Republic of Germany, with the Oberlandesgericht,
   - in Greece, with the εψετειπ,
   - in Spain, with the Audiencia Provincial,
   - in France, with the cour d'appel.
   - in Ireland, with the High Court,
   - in Iceland, with the héradsdómari,
   - in Italy, with the corte d'appello.
   - in Luxembourg, with Cour supérieure de justice sitting as a court of civil appeal,
   - in the Netherlands, with the arrondissementsrechtbank,
   - in Norway, with the lagmannsrett,
   - in Austria, with the Landesgericht or the Kreisgericht,
   - in Portugal, with the Tribunal de Relação.
   - in Switzerland, with the tribunal cantonal/Kantonsgericht/tribunale cantonale,
   - in Finland, with the hovioikeus/hovrätt,
   - in Sweden, with the Svea hovrätt,
   - in the United Kingdom:
     (a) in England and Wales, with the High Court of Justice, or in the case of a maintenance judgment with the Magistrates' Court;
     (b) in Scotland, with the Court of Session, or in the case of a maintenance judgment with the Sheriff Court;
     (c) in Northern Ireland, with the High Court of Justice, or in the case of a maintenance judgment with the Magistrates' Court.
2. The judgment given on the appeal may be contested only:
   - in Belgium, Greece, Spain, France, Italy, Luxembourg and in the Netherlands, by an appeal in cassation,
   - in Denmark. by an appeal to the højesteret, with the leave of the Minister of Justice,
   - in the Federal Republic of Germany, by a Rechtsbeschwerde,
   - in Ireland, by an appeal on a point of law to the Supreme Court,
   - in Iceland, by an appeal to the Haestiréttur,
   - in Norway, by an appeal (kjaeremål or anke) to the Hoyesteretts Kjaeremålsutvalg or Hovesterett,

- in Austria, in the case of an appeal, by a Revisionsrekurs and, in the case of opposition proceedings, by a Berufung with the possibility of a Revision,
- in Portugal, by an appeal on a point of law,
- in Switzerland, by a recours de droit public devant le tribunal fédéral/ staatsrechtliche Beschwerde beim Bundesgericht/ricorso di diritto pubblico davanti al tribunale federale,
- in Finland, by an appeal to the korkein oikeus/högsta domstolen,
- in Sweden, by an appeal to the högsta domstolen,
- in the United Kingdom, by a single further appeal on a point of law.

Article 38

The court with which the appeal under the first paragraph of Article 37 is lodged may, on the application of the appellant, stay the proceedings if an ordinary appeal has been lodged against the judgment in the State of origin or if the time for such an appeal has not yet expired; in the latter case, the court may specify the time within which such an appeal is to be lodged.

Where the judgment was given in Ireland or the United Kingdom, any form of appeal available in the State of origin shall be treated as an ordinary appeal for the purposes of the first paragraph.

The court may also make enforcement conditional on the provision of such security as it shall determine.

Article 39

During the time specified for an appeal pursuant to Article 36 and until any such appeal has been determined, no measures of enforcement may be taken other than protective measures taken against the property of the party against whom enforcement is sought.

The decision authorising enforcement shall carry with it the power to proceed to any such protective measures.

Article 40

1. If the application for enforcement is refused, the applicant may appeal:
   - in Belgium, to the cour d'appel or hof van beroep,
   - in Denmark, to the landsret,
   - in the Federal Republic of Germany, to the Oberlandesgericht,
   - in Greece, to the εψετειπ,
   - in Spain, to the Audiencia Provincial,
   - in France, to the cour d'appel.
   - in Ireland, to the High Court,
   - in Iceland, to the héradsdómari,
   - in Italy, to the corte d'appello,
   - in Luxembourg, to the Cour supérieure de justice sitting as a court of civil appeal,
   - in the Netherlands, to the gerechtshof,
   - in Norway, to the lagmannsrett.
   - in Austria, to the Landesgericht or the Kreisgericht,
   - in Portugal, to the Tribunal de Relacão,

- in Switzerland, to the tribunal cantonal/Kantonsgericht/tribunale cantonale,
- in Finland, to the hovioikeus/hovrätt,
- in Sweden, to the Svea hovrätt,
- in the United Kingdom:
  (a) in England and Wales, to the High Court of Justice, or in the case of a maintenance judgment to the Magistrates' Court;
  (b) in Scotland, to the Court of Session, or in the case of a maintenance judgment to the Sheriff Court;
  (c) in Northern Ireland, to the High Court of Justice, or in the case of a maintenance judgment to the Magistrates' Court.

2. The party against whom enforcement is sought shall be summoned to appear before the appellate court. If he fails to appear, the provisions of the second and third paragraphs of Article 20 shall apply even where he is not domiciled in any of the Contracting States.

Article 41

A judgment given on an appeal provided for in Article 40 may be contested only:

- in Belgium, Greece, Spain, France, Italy, Luxembourg and in the Netherlands, by an appeal in cassation,
- in Denmark, by an appeal to the højesteret, with the leave of the Minister of Justice,
- in the Federal Republic of Germany, by a Rechtsbeschwerde,
- in Ireland, by an appeal on a point of law to the Supreme Court,
- in Iceland, by an appeal to the Haestiréttur,
- in Norway, by an appeal (kjaeremál or anke) to the Hoyesteretts kjaeeremålsutvalg or Hoyesterett,
- in Austria, by a Revisionsrekurs,
- in Portugal, by an appeal on a point of law,
- in Switzerland, by a recours de droit public devant le tribunal fédéral/ staatsrechtliche Beschwerde beim Bundesgericht/ricorso di diritto pubblico davanti al tribunale federale,
- in Finland, by an appeal to the korkein oikeus/högsta domstolen,
- in Sweden, by an appeal to the högsta domstolen,
- in the United Kingdom, by a single further appeal on a point of law.

Article 42

Where a foreign judgment has been given in respect of several matters and enforcement cannot be authorised for all of them, the court shall authorise enforcement for one or more of them.

An applicant may request partial enforcement of a judgement.

Article 43

A foreign judgment which orders a periodic payment by way of a penalty shall be enforceable in the State in which enforcement is sought only if the amount of the payment has been finally determined by the courts of the State of origin.

Article 44

An applicant who, in the State of origin, has benefited from complete or partial legal aid or exemption from costs or expenses, shall be entitled, in the procedures provided for in Articles 32 to 35, to benefit from the most favourable legal aid or the most extensive exemption from costs or expenses provided for by the law of the State addressed.

However, an applicant who requests the enforcement of a decision given by an administrative authority in Denmark or in Iceland in respect of a maintenance order may, in the State addressed, claim the benefits referred to in the first paragraph if he presents a statement from, respectively, the Danish Ministry of Justice or the Icelandic Ministry of Justice to the effect that he fulfils the economic requirements to qualify for the grant of complete or partial legal aid or exemption from costs or expenses.

Article 45

No security, bond or deposit, however described, shall be required of a party who in one Contracting State applies for enforcement of a judgment given in another Contracting State on the ground that he is a foreign national or that he is not domiciled or resident in the State in which enforcement is sought.

Section 3
Common Provisions

Article 46

A party seeking recognition or applying for enforcement of a judgment shall produce:

1. a copy of the judgment which satisfies the conditions necessary to establish its authenticity;
2. in the case of a judgment given in default, the original or a certified true copy of the document which establishes that the party in default was served with the document instituting the proceedings or with an equivalent document.

Article 47

A party applying for enforcement shall also produce:

1. documents which establish that, according to the law of the State of origin, the judgment is enforceable and has been served;
2. where appropriate, a document showing that the applicant is in receipt of legal aid in the State of origin.

Article 48

If the documents specified in Article 46(2) and Article 47(2) are not produced, the court may specify a time for their production, accept equivalent documents or, if it considers that it has sufficient information before it, dispense with their production.

If the court so requires, a translation of the documents shall be produced; the translation shall be certified by a person qualified to do so in one of the Contracting States.

Article 49

No legalisation or other similar formality shall be required in respect of the documents referred to in Article 46 or 47 or the second paragraph of Article 48. or in respect of a document appointing a representative *ad litem*.

TITLE IV

AUTHENTIC INSTRUMENTS AND COURT SETTLEMENTS

Article 50

A document which has been formally drawn up or registered as an authentic instrument and is enforceable in one Contracting State shall, in another Contracting State, be declared enforceable there, on application made in accordance with the procedures provided for in Articles 31 *et seq*. The application may be refused only if enforcement of the instrument is contrary to public policy in the State addressed.

The instrument produced must satisfy the conditions necessary to establish its authenticity in the State of origin.

The provisions of Section 3 of Title III shall apply as appropriate.

Article 51

A settlement which has been approved by a court in the course of proceedings and is enforceable in the State in which it was concluded shall be enforceable in the State addressed under the same conditions as authentic instruments.

TITLE V

GENERAL PROVISIONS

Article 52

In order to determine whether a party is domiciled in the Contracting State whose courts are seised of a matter, the court shall apply its internal law.

If a party is not domiciled in the State whose courts are seised of the matter, then, in order to determine whether the party is domiciled in another Contracting State, the court shall apply the law of that State.

Article 53

For the purposes of this Convention, the seat of a company or other legal person or association of natural or legal persons shall be treated as its domicile. However, in order to determine that seat, the court shall apply its rules of private international law.

In order to determine whether a trust is domiciled in the Contracting State whose courts are seised of the matter, the court shall apply its rules of private international law.

TITLE VI

TRANSITIONAL PROVISIONS

Article 54

The provisions of this Convention shall apply only to legal proceedings instituted and to documents formally drawn up or registered as authentic instruments after its entry into force in the State of origin and, where recognition or enforcement of a judgment or authentic instrument is sought, in the State addressed.

However, judgments given after the date of entry into force of this Convention between the State of origin and the State addressed in proceedings instituted before that date shall be recognised and enforced in accordance with the provisions of Title III if jurisdiction was founded upon rules which accorded with those provided for either in Title II of this Convention or in a convention concluded between the State of origin and the State addressed which was in force when the proceedings were instituted.

If the parties to a dispute concerning a contract had agreed in writing before the entry into force of this Convention that the contract was to be governed by the law of Ireland or of a part of the United Kingdom, the courts of Ireland or of that part of the United Kingdom shall retain the right to exercise jurisdiction in the dispute.

Article 54A

For a period of three years from the entry into force of this Convention for Denmark, Greece, Ireland, Iceland, Norway, Finland and Sweden, respectively, jurisdiction in maritime matters shall be determined in these States not only in accordance with the provisions of Title II, but also in accordance with the provisions of paragraphs 1 to 7 following. However, upon the entry into force of the International Convention relating to the arrest of sea-going ships, signed at Brussels on 10 May 1952, for one of these States. these provisions shall cease to have effect for that State.

1. A person who is domiciled in a Contracting State may be sued in the courts of one of the States mentioned above in respect of a maritime claim if the ship to which the claim relates or any other ship owned by him has been arrested by judicial process within the territory of the latter State to secure the claim, or could have been so arrested there but bail or other security has been given, and either:
   (a) the claimant is domiciled in the latter State; or
   (b) the claim arose in the latter State; or
   (c) the claim concerns the voyage during which the arrest was made or could have been made: or
   (d) the claim arises out of a collision or out of damage caused by a ship to another ship or to goods or persons on board either ship, either by the execution or non-execution of a manoeuvre or by the non-observance of regulations: or
   (e) the claim is for salvage; or
   (f) the claim is in respect of a mortgage or hypothecation of the ship arrested.

2. A claimant may arrest either the particular ship to which the maritime claim relates, or any other ship which is owned by the person who was, at the time when the maritime claim arose, the owner of the particular ship. However, only the particular ship to which the maritime claim relates may be arrested in respect of the maritime claims set out in 5(o), (p) or (q) of this Article.
3. Ships shall be deemed to be in the same ownership when all the shares therein are owned by the same person or persons.
4. When in the case of a charter by demise of a ship the charterer alone is liable in respect of a maritime claim relating to that ship, the claimant may arrest that ship or any other ship owned by the charterer, but no other ship owned by the owner may be arrested in respect of such claim. The same shall apply to any case in which a person other than the owner of a ship is liable in respect of a maritime claim relating to that ship.
5. The expression 'maritime claim' means a claim arising out of one or more of the following:
   (a) damage caused by any ship either in collision or otherwise;
   (b) loss of life or personal injury caused by any ship or occurring in connection with the operation of any ship;
   (c) salvage;
   (d) agreement relating to the use or hire of any ship whether by charterparty or otherwise;
   (e) agreement relating to the carriage of goods in any ship whether by charterparty or otherwise;
   (f) loss of or damage to goods including baggage carried in any ship;
   (g) general average;
   (h) bottomry;
   (i) towage;
   (j) pilotage;
   (k) goods or materials wherever supplied to a ship for her operation or maintenance;
   (1) construction, repair or equipment of any ship or dock charges and dues;
   (m) wages of masters, officers or crew;
   (n) master's disbursements, including disbursements made by shippers, charterers or agents on behalf of a ship or her owner;
   (o) dispute as to the title to or ownership of any ship;
   (p) disputes between co-owners of any ship as to the ownership, possession, employment or earnings of that ship;
   (q) the mortgage or hypothecation of any ship.
6. In Denmark, the expression 'arrest' shall be deemed, as regards the maritime claims referred to in 5(o) and (p) of this Article, to include a 'forbud', where that is the only procedure allowed in respect of such a claim under Articles 646 to 653 of the law on civil procedure (lov om rettens pleje).
7. In Iceland, the expression 'arrest' shall be deemed, as regards the maritime claims referred to in 5(o) and (p) of this Article, to include a 'logbann' where that is the only procedure allowed in respect of such a claim under Chapter III of the law on arrest and injunction (lög um kyrrsetningu og lögbann).

TITLE VII

RELATIONSHIP TO THE BRUSSELS CONVENTION AND TO OTHER CONVENTIONS

Article 54B

1. This Convention shall not prejudice the application by the Member States of the European Communities of the Convention on Jurisdiction and the Enforcement of Judgments in Civil and Commercial Matters, signed at Brussels on 27 September 1968 and the Protocol on interpretation of that Convention by the Court of Justice, signed at Luxembourg on 3 June 1971, as amended by the Conventions of Accession to the said Convention and the said Protocol by the States acceding to the European Communities, all of these Conventions and the Protocol being hereinafter referred to as the 'Brussels Convention'.
2. However, this Convention shall in any event be applied:
   (a) in matters of jurisdiction, where the defendant is domiciled in the territory of a Contracting State which is not a member of the European Communities, or where Article 16 or 17 of this Convention confers a jurisdiction on the courts of such a Contracting State;
   (b) in relation to a *lis pendens* or to related actions as provided for in Articles 21 and 22, when proceedings are instituted in a Contracting State which is not a member of the European Communities and in a Contracting State which is a member of the European Communities;
   (c) in matters of recognition and enforcement, where either the State of origin or the State addressed is not a member of the European Communities.
3. In addition to the grounds provided for in Title III recognition or enforcement may be refused if the ground of jurisdiction on which the judgment has been based differs from that resulting from this Convention and recognition or enforcement is sought against a party who is domiciled in a Contracting State which is not a member of the European Communities, unless the judgment may otherwise be recognised or enforced under any rule of law in the State addressed.

Article 55

Subject to the provisions of the second paragraph of Article 54 and of Article 56, this Convention shall, for the States which are parties to it, supersede the following conventions concluded between two or more of them:

- the Convention between the Swiss Confederation and France on jurisdiction and enforcement of judgments in civil matters, signed at Paris on 15 June 1869,
- the Treaty between the Swiss Confederation and Spain on the mutual enforcement of judgments in civil or commercial matters, signed at Madrid on 19 November 1896,
- the Convention between the Swiss Confederation and the German Reich on the recognition and enforcement of judgments and arbitration awards, signed at Berne on 2 November 1929,

- the Convention between Denmark, Finland, Iceland, Norway and Sweden on the recognition and enforcement of judgments, signed at Copenhagen on 16 March 1932,
- the Convention between the Swiss Confederation and Italy on the recognition and enforcement of judgments, signed at Rome on 3 January 1933,
- the Convention between Sweden and the Swiss Confederation on the recognition and enforcement of judgments and arbitral awards, signed at Stockholm on 15 January 1936,
- the Convention between the Kingdom of Belgium and Austria on the reciprocal recognition and enforcement of judgments and authentic instruments relating to maintenance obligations, signed at Vienna on 25 October 1957,
- the Convention between the Swiss Confederation and Belgium on the recognition and enforcement of judgments and arbitration awards, signed at Berne on 29 April 1959,
- the Convention between the Federal Republic of Germany and Austria on the reciprocal recognition and enforcement of judgments, settlements and authentic instruments in civil and commercial matters, signed at Vienna on 6 June 1959,
- the Convention between the Kingdom of Belgium and Austria on the reciprocal recognition and enforcement of judgments, arbitral awards and authentic instruments in civil and commercial matters, signed at Vienna on 1 June 1959,
- the Convention between Austria and the Swiss Confederation on the recognition and enforcement of judgments, signed at Berne on 16 December 1960,
- the Convention between Norway and the United Kingdom providing for the reciprocal recognition and enforcement of judgments in civil matters, signed at London on 12 June 1961,
- the Convention between the United Kingdom and Austria providing for the reciprocal recognition and enforcement of judgments in civil and commercial matters, signed at Vienna on 14 July 1961, with amending Protocol signed at London on 6 March 1970,
- the Convention between the Kingdom of the Netherlands and Austria on the reciprocal recognition and enforcement of judgments and authentic instruments in civil and commercial matters, signed at The Hague on 6 February 1963,
- the Convention between France and Austria on the recognition and enforcement of judgments and authentic instruments in civil and commercial matters, signed at Vienna on 15 July 1966,
- the Convention between Luxembourg and Austria on the recognition and enforcement of judgments and authentic instruments in civil and commercial matters, signed at Luxembourg on 29 July 1971,
- the Convention between Italy and Austria on the recognition and enforcement of judgments in civil and commercial matters, of judicial settlements and of authentic instruments, signed at Rome on 16 November 1971,
- the Convention between Norway and the Federal Republic of Germany on the recognition and enforcement of judgments and

enforceable documents, in civil and commercial matters, signed at Oslo on 17 June 1977,

- the Convention between Denmark, Finland, Iceland, Norway and Sweden on the recognition and enforcement of judgments in civil matters, signed at Copenhagen on 11 October 1977,
- the Convention between Austria and Sweden on the recognition and enforcement of judgments in civil matters, signed at Stockholm on 16 September 1982,
- the Convention between Austria and Spain on the recognition and enforcement of judgments, settlements and enforceable authentic instruments in civil and commercial matters, signed at Vienna on 17 February 1984,
- the Convention between Norway and Austria on the recognition and enforcement of judgments in civil matters, signed at Vienna on 21 May 1984, and
- the Convention between Finland and Austria on the recognition and enforcement of judgments in civil matters, signed at Vienna on 17 November 1986.

Article 56

The Treaty and the conventions referred to in Article 55 shall continue to have effect in relation to matters to which this Convention does not apply,

They shall continue to have effect in respect of judgments given and documents formally drawn up or registered as authentic instruments before the entry into force of this Convention.

Article 57

1. This Convention shall not affect any conventions to which the Contracting States are or will be parties and which, in relation to particular matters, govern jurisdiction or the recognition or enforcement of judgments.
2. This Convention shall not prevent a court of a Contracting State which is party to a convention referred to in the first paragraph from assuming jurisdiction in accordance with that convention, even where the defendant is domiciled in a Contracting State which is not a party to that convention. The court hearing the action shall, in any event, apply Article 20 of this Convention.
3. Judgments given in a Contracting State by a court in the exercise of jurisdiction provided for in a convention referred to in the first paragraph shall be recognised and enforced in the other Contracting States in accordance with Title III of this Convention.
4. In addition to the grounds provided for in Title III, recognition or enforcement may be refused if the State addressed is not a contracting party to a convention referred to in the first paragraph and the person against whom recognition or enforcement is sought is domiciled in that State, unless the judgment may otherwise be recognised or enforced under any rule of law in the State addressed.
5. Where a convention referred to in the first paragraph to which both the State of origin and the State addressed are parties lays down conditions for the recognition or enforcement of judgments, those conditions shall apply.

In any event, the provisions of this Convention which concern the procedures for recognition and enforcement of judgments maybe applied.

Article 58

(None)

Article 59

This Convention shall not prevent a Contracting State from assuming, in a convention on the recognition and enforcement of judgments, an obligation towards a third State not to recognise judgments given in other Contracting States against defendants domiciled or habitually resident in the third State where, in cases provided for in Article 4, the judgment could only be founded on a ground of jurisdiction specified in the second paragraph of Article 3.

However, a Contracting State may not assume an obligation towards a third State not to recognise a judgment given in another Contracting State by a court basing its jurisdiction on the presence within that State of property belonging to the defendant, or the seizure by the plaintiff of property situated there:

1. if the action is brought to assert or declare proprietary or possessors' rights in that property, seeks to obtain authority to dispose of it, or rises from another issue relating to such property, or
2. if the property constitutes the security for a debt which is the subject-matter of the action.

TITLE VIII

FINAL PROVISIONS

Article 60

The following may be parties to this Convention:

(a) States which, at the time of the opening of this Convention for signature, are members of the European Communities or of the European Free Trade Association;
(b) States which, after the opening of this Convention for signature, become members of the European Communities or of the European Free Trade Association;
(c) States invited to accede in accordance with Article 62(1) (b).

Article 61

1. This Convention shall be opened for signature by the States members of the European Communities or of the European Free Trade Association.
2. The Convention shall be submitted for ratification by the signatory States. The instruments of ratification shall be deposited with the Swiss Federal Council.
3. The Convention shall enter into force on the first day of the third month following the date on which two States, of which one is a member of the European Communities and the other a member of the European Free Trade Association, deposit their instruments of ratification.

4. The Convention shall take effect in relation to any other signatory State on the first day of the third month following the deposit of its instrument of ratification.

Article 62

1. After entering into force this Convention shall be open to accession by:
(a) the States referred to in Article 60(b);
(b) other States which have been invited to accede upon a request made by one of the Contracting States to the depositary State. The depositary State shall invite the State concerned to accede only if, after having communicated the contents of the communications that this State intends to make in accordance with Article 63, it has obtained the unanimous agreement of the signatory States and the Contracting States referred to in Article 60(a) and (b).
2. If an acceding State wishes to furnish details for the purposes of Protocol No. 1, negotiations shall be entered into to that end. A negotiating conference shall be convened by the Swiss Federal Council.
3. In respect of an acceding State, the Convention shall take effect on the first day of the third month following the deposit of its instrument of accession.
4. However, in respect of an acceding State referred to in paragraph 1(a) or (b), the Convention shall take effect only in relations between the acceding State and the Contracting States which have not made any objections to the accession before the first day of the third month following the deposit of the instrument of accession.

Article 63

Each acceding State shall, when depositing its instrument of accession, communicate the information required for the application of Articles 3, 32, 37, 40, 41 and 55 of this Convention and furnish, if need be, the details prescribed during the negotiations for the purposes of Protocol No. 1.

Article 64

1. This Convention is concluded for an initial period of five years from the date of its entry into force in accordance with Article 61(3), even in the case of States which ratify it or accede to it after that date.
2. At the end of the initial five-year period, the Convention shall be automatically renewed from year to year.
3. Upon the expiry of the initial five-year period, any Contracting State may, at any time, denounce the Convention by sending a notification to the Swiss Federal Council.
4. The denunciation shall take effect at the end of the calendar year following the expiry of a period of six months from the date of receipt by the Swiss Federal Council of the notification of denunciation.

Article 65

The following are annexed to this Convention:
- a Protocol No 1, on certain questions of jurisdiction, procedure and enforcement,
- a Protocol No 2, on the uniform interpretation of the Convention,

– a Protocol No 3, on the application of Article 57.

These Protocols shall form an integral part of the Convention.

Article 66

Any Contracting State may request the revision of this Convention. To that end, the Swiss Federal Council shall issue invitations to a revision conference within a period of six months from the date of the request for revision.

Article 67

The Swiss Federal Council shall notify the States represented at the Diplomatic Conference of Lugano and the States who have later acceded to the Convention of:

(a) the deposit of each instrument of ratification or accession;
(b) the dates of entry into force of this convention in respect of the Contracting States:
(c) any denunciation received pursuant to Article 64;
(d) any declaration received pursuant to Article 1A of Protocol No 1;
(e) any declaration received pursuant to Article lB of Protocol No 1;
(f) any declaration received pursuant to Article IV of Protocol No 1;
(g) any communication made pursuant to Article IV of Protocol No 1.

Article 68

This Convention, drawn up in a single original in the Danish, Dutch, English, Finnish, French, German, Greek, Icelandic, Irish, Italian, Norwegian, Portuguese, Spanish and Swedish languages, all fourteen texts being equally authentic, shall be deposited in the archives of the Swiss Federal Council. The Swiss Federal Council shall transmit a certified copy to the Government of each State represented at the Diplomatic Conference of Lugano and to the Government of each acceding State.

Protocol No 1
On Certain Questions of Jurisdiction, Procedure and Enforcement

The High Contracting Parties have agreed upon the following provisions, which shall be annexed to the Convention:

Article I

Any person domiciled in Luxembourg who is sued in a court of another Contracting State pursuant to Article 5(1) may refuse to submit to the jurisdiction of that court. If the defendant does not enter an appearance the court shall declare of its own motion that it has no jurisdiction.

An agreement conferring jurisdiction, within the meaning of Article 17, shall be valid with respect to a person domiciled in Luxembourg only if that person has expressly and specifically so agreed.

Article IA

1. Switzerland deserves the right to declare, at the time of depositing its instrument of ratification, that a judgment given in another Contracting State shall be neither recognised nor enforced in Switzerland if the following conditions are met:

(a) the jurisdiction of the court which has given the judgment is based only on Article 5(1) of this Convention: and
(b) the defendant was domiciled in Switzerland at the time of the introduction of the proceedings: for the purposes of this Article, a company or other legal person is considered to be domiciled in Switzerland if it has its registered seat and the effective centre of activities in Switzerland; and
(c) the defendant raises an objection to the recognition or enforcement of the judgment in Switzerland, provided that he has not waived the benefit of the declaration foreseen under this paragraph.

2. This reservation shall not apply to the extent that at the time recognition or enforcement is sought a derogation has been granted from Article 59 of the Swiss Federal Constitution. The Swiss Government shall communicate such derogations to the signatory States and the acceding States.
3. This reservation shall cease to have effect on 31 December 1999. It may be withdrawn at any time.

Article IB

Any Contracting State may, by declaration made at the time of signing or of deposit of its instrument of ratification or of accession, reserved the right, notwithstanding the provisions of Article 28, not to recognise and enforce judgments given in the other Contracting States if the jurisdiction of the court of the State of origin is based, pursuant to Article 16(1) (b), exclusively on the domicile of the defendant in the State of origin, and the property is situated in the territory of the State which entered the reservation.

Article II

Without prejudice to any more favourable provisions of national laws, persons domiciled in a Contracting State who are being prosecuted in the criminal courts of another Contracting State of which they are not nationals for an offence which was not intentionally committed may be defended by persons qualified to do so, even if they do not appear in person.

However, the court seised of the matter may order appearance in person: in the case of failure to appear, a judgment given in the civil action without the person concerned having had the opportunity to arrange for his defence need not be recognised or enforced in the other Contracting States.

Article III

In proceedings for the issue of an order for enforcement, no charge, duty or fee calculated by reference to the value of the matter in issue may be levied in the State in which enforcement is sought.

Article IV

Judicial and extrajudicial documents drawn up in one Contracting State which have to be served on persons in another Contracting State shall be transmitted in accordance with the procedures laid down in the conventions and agreements concluded between the Contracting States.

Unless the State in which service is to take place objects by declaration to the Swiss Federal Council, such documents may also be sent by the appropriate public officers of the State in which the document has been drawn up directly to the appropriate public officers of the State in which the addressee is to be found. In this case the officer of the State of origin shall send a copy of the document to the officer of the State applied to who is competent to forward it to the addressee. The document shall be forwarded in the manner specified by the law of the State applied to. The forwarding shall be recorded by a certificate sent directly to the officer of the State of origin.

Article V

The jurisdiction specified in Articles 6(2) and 10 in actions on a warranty or guarantee or in any other third party proceedings may not be resorted to in the Federal Republic of Germany, in Spain, in Austria and in Switzerland. Any person domiciled in another Contracting State may be sued in the courts:

— of the Federal Republic of Germany, pursuant to Articles 68, 72, 73 and 74 of the code of civil procedure (Zivilprozeßordnung) concerning third-party notices,
— of Spain, pursuant to Article 1482 of the civil code,
— of Austria, pursuant to Article 21 of the code of civil procedure (Zivil prozeßordnung) concerning third-party notices,
— of Switzerland, pursuant to the appropriate provisions concerning third party notices of the cantonal codes of civil procedure.

Judgments given in the other Contracting States by virtue of Article 6(2) or Article 10 shall be recognised and enforced in the Federal Republic of Germany, in Spain, in Austria and in Switzerland in accordance with Title III. Any effects which judgments given in these States may have on third parties by application of the provisions in the preceding paragraph shall also be recognised in the other Contracting States.

Article VA

In matters relating to maintenance, the expression 'court' includes the Danish, Icelandic and Norwegian administrative authorities.

In civil and commercial matters, the expression 'court' includes the Finnish ulosotonhaltija/överexekutor.

Article VB

In proceedings involving a dispute between the master and a member of the crew of a sea-going ship registered in Denmark, in Greece, in Ireland, in Iceland, in Norway, in Portugal or in Sweden concerning remuneration or other conditions of service, a court in a Contracting State shall establish whether the diplomatic or consular officer responsible for the ship has been notified of the dispute. It shall stay the proceedings so long as he has not been notified. It shall of its own motion decline jurisdiction if the officer, having been duly notified, has exercised the powers accorded to him in the matter by a consular convention, or in the absence of such a convention has, within the time allowed, raised any objection to the exercise of such jurisdiction.

Article VC

(None)

Article VD

Without prejudice to the jurisdiction of the European Patent Office under the Convention on the grant of European patents, signed at Munich on 5 October 1973, the courts of each Contracting State shall have exclusive jurisdiction, regardless of domicile, in proceedings concerned with the registration or validity of any European patent granted for that State which is not a Community patent by virtue of the provision of Article 86 of the Convention for the European patent for the common market, signed at Luxembourg on 15 December 1975.

Article VI

The Contracting States shall communicate to the Swiss Federal Council the text of any provisions of their laws which amend either those provisions of their laws mentioned in the Convention or the lists of courts specified in Section 2 of Title III.

Protocol No 2
On the Uniform Interpretation of the Convention

PREAMBLE

The High Contracting Parties,

Having regard to Article 65 of this Convention,

Considering the substantial link between this Convention and the Brussels Convention,

Considering that the Court of Justice of the European Communities by virtue of the Protocol of 3 June 1971 has jurisdiction to give rulings on the interpretation of the provisions of the Brussels Convention,

Being aware of the rulings delivered by the Court of Justice of the European Communities on the interpretation of the Brussels Convention up to the time of signature of this Convention,

Considering that the negotiations which led to the conclusion of the Convention were based on the Brussels Convention in the light of these rulings,

Desiring to prevent, in full deference to the independence of the courts, divergent interpretations and to arrive at as uniform an interpretation as possible of the provisions of the Convention, and of these provisions and those of the Brussels Convention which are substantially reproduced in this Convention,

Have agreed as follows:

Article 1

The courts of each Contracting State shall, when applying and interpreting the provisions of the Convention, pay due account to the principles laid down by any relevant decision delivered by courts of the other Contracting States concerning provisions of this Convention.

Article 2

1. The Contracting Parties agree to set up a system of exchange of information concerning judgments delivered pursuant to this Convention as well as relevant judgments under the Brussels Convention. This system shall comprise:

- transmission to a central body by the competent authorities of judgments delivered by courts of last instance and the Court of Justice of the European Communities as well as judgments of particular importance which have become final and have been delivered pursuant to this Convention or the Brussels Convention,
- classification of these judgments by the central body including, as far as necessary, the drawing-up and publication of translations and abstracts,
- communication by the central body of the relevant documents to the competent national authorities of all signatories and acceding States to the Convention and to the Commission of the European Communities.

2. The central body is the Registrar of the Court of Justice of the European Communities.

SCHEDULES

SCHEDULE 1 *Section 2(2).*

TEXT OF 1968 CONVENTION, AS AMENDED

ARRANGEMENT OF PROVISIONS

Article 3

1. A Standing Committee shall be set up for the purposes of this Protocol.
2. The Committee shall be composed of representatives appointed by each signatory and acceding State.
3. The European Communities (Commission, Court of Justice and General Secretariat of the Council) and the European Free Trade Association may attend the meetings as observers.

Article 4

1. At the request of a Contracting party the depositary of the Convention shall convene meetings of the Committee for the purpose of exchanging views on the functioning of the Convention and in particular on:
   - the development of the case-law as communicated under the first paragraph first indent of Article 2,
   - the application of Article 57 of the Convention.
2. The Committee, in the light of these exchanges, may also examine the appropriateness of starting on particular topics a revision of the Convention and make recommendations.

Protocol No 3
On the Application of Article 57

The High Contracting Parties have agreed as follows:

1. For the purposes of the Convention, provisions which, in relation to particular matters, govern jurisdiction or the recognition or enforcement of judgments and which are, or will be, contained in acts of the institutions of the European Communities shall be treated in the same way as the conventions referred to in paragraph 1 of Article 57.
2. If one Contracting State is of the opinion that a provision contained in an act of the institutions of the European Communities is incompatible with the Convention, the Contracting States shall promptly consider amending the Convention pursuant to Article 66, without prejudice to the procedure established by Protocol No 2.]

Note. This Schedule inserted by Civil Jurisdiction and Judgments Act 1991, s 1(3), Sch 1, as from 1 May 1992.

SCHEDULE 4 Section 16

TITLE II OF 1968 CONVENTION AS MODIFIED FOR ALLOCATION OF JURISDICTION WITHIN UK

Children and Marriage

Convention on Consent to Marriage, Minimum Age for Marriage and Registration of Marriages 1962

Entry into force: 9 December 1964

The Contracting States,

Desiring, in conformity with the Charter of the United Nations, to promote universal respect for, and observance of, human rights and fundamental freedoms for all, without distinction as to race, sex, language or religion,

Recalling that article 16 of the Universal Declaration of Human Rights states that:

"(1) Men and women of full age, without any limitation due to race, nationality or religion, have the right to marry and to found a family. They are entitled to equal rights as to marriage, during marriage and at its dissolution.

"(2) Marriage shall be entered into only with the free and full consent of the intending spouses.',

Recalling further that the General Assembly of the United Nations declared, by resolution 843 (IX) of 17 December 1954, that certain customs, ancient laws and practices relating to marriage and the family were inconsistent with the principles set forth in the Charter of the United Nations and in the Universal Declaration of Human Rights,

Reaffirming that all States, including those which have or assume responsibility for the administration of Non-Self-Governing and Trust Territories until their achievement of independence, should take all appropriate measures with a view to abolishing such customs, ancient laws and practices by ensuring, *inter alia*, complete freedom in the choice of a spouse, eliminating completely child marriages and the betrothal of young girls before the age of puberty, establishing appropriate penalties where necessary and establishing a civil or other register in which all marriages will be recorded,

Hereby agree as hereinafter provided:

Article 1

1. No marriage shall be legally entered into without the full and free consent of both parties, such consent to be expressed by them in person after due publicity and in the presence of the authority competent to solemnize the marriage and of witnesses, as prescribed by law.
2. Notwithstanding anything in paragraph 1 above, it shall not be necessary for one of the parties to be present when the competent authority is satisfied that the circumstances are exceptional and that the party has, before a competent authority and in such manner as may be prescribed by law, expressed and not withdrawn consent.

Article 2

States Parties to the present Convention shall take legislative action to specify a minimum age for marriage. No marriage shall be legally entered into by any person under this age, except where a competent authority has granted a dispensation as to age, for serious reasons, in the interest of the intending spouses.

Article 3

All marriages shall be registered in an appropriate official register by the competent authority.

Article 4

1. The present Convention shall, until 31 December 1963, be open for signature on behalf of all States Members of the United Nations or members of any of the specialized agencies, and of any other State invited by the General Assembly of the United Nations to become a Party to the Convention.
2. The present Convention is subject to ratification. The instruments of ratification shall be deposited with the Secretary-General of the United Nations.

Article 5

1. The present Convention shall be open for accession to all States referred to in article 4, paragraph 1.
2. Accession shall be effected by the deposit of an instrument of accession with the Secretary-General of the United Nations.

Article 6

1. The present Convention shall come into force on the ninetieth day following the date of deposit of the eighth instrument of ratification or accession.
2. For each State ratifying or acceding to the Convention after the deposit of the eighth instrument of ratification or accession, the Convention shall enter into force on the ninetieth day after deposit by such State of its instrument of ratification or accession.

Article 7

1. Any Contracting State may denounce the present Convention by written notification to the Secretary-General of the United Nations. Denunciation shall take effect one year after the date of receipt of the notification by the Secretary-General.
2. The present Convention shall cease to be in force as from the date when the denunciation which reduces the number of Parties to less than eight becomes effective.

Article 8

Any dispute which may arise between any two or more Contracting States concerning the interpretation or application of the present Convention which is not settled by negotiation shall, at the request of all the parties to the dispute, be referred to the International Court of Justice for decision, unless the parties agree to another mode of settlement.

Article 9

The Secretary-General of the United Nations shall notify all States Members of the United Nations and the non-member States contemplated in article 4, paragraph 1, of the present Convention of the following:

(a) Signatures and instruments of ratification received in accordance with article 4:
(b) Instruments of accession received in accordance with article 5;
(c) The date upon which the Convention enters into force in accordance with article 6;
(d) Notifications of denunciation received in accordance with article 7, paragraph 1;
(e) Abrogation in accordance with article 7, paragraph 2.

Article 10

1. The present Convention, of which the Chinese, English, French, Russian and Spanish texts shall be equally authentic, shall be deposited in the archives of the United Nations.
2. The Secretary-General of the United Nations shall transmit a certified copy of the Convention to all States Members of the United Nations and to the non-member contemplated in article 4, paragraph 1

Children and Human Rights

EUROPEAN CONVENTION ON HUMAN RIGHTS

The Council of Europe was formed by the Statute of the Council of Europe in 1949, Article 3 of which required members to accept the principles of the rules of law and of the enjoyment of all persons within its jurisdiction of human rights and fundamental freedoms. The Convention was itself drafted between 1949 and 1950, coming into force in 1953. The European Union is not a party to the Convention and the European Court of Justice has stated that the Union cannot accede to the Convention without a change in the Treaty of Rome. Article 1 requires each contracting party to 'secure to everyone within their jurisdiction the rights and freedoms defined in Section 1,' though there is no requirement for a state to incorporate the Convention into its domestic law. Whilst the Convention does not specifically mention children's rights, their rights have nevertheless been upheld. Under Article 14 a child has a right not to suffer discrimination by reason of age or status in the exercise of the Convention.

Under the Eleventh Protocol, the Commission and the Court itself are merged into a full-time court where Judges sit in Committees of three, in Chambers of seven and in a Grand Chamber of seventeen.

An applicant must be a person, nongovernmental organisation or a group of individuals. They must claim to be the victim of a violation of a Convention right and the violation alleged must be against a contracting party. It is not necessary for actual harm to have occurred, risk is itself sufficient to commence an application, but violations can only be complained of where they are against the state or state institutions. In *Costello-Roberts v. UK* (1993) Series A No. 247–C; 19 EHRR 192 the court held that states were responsible for corporal punishment in private schools because that state had a positive obligation under Article 2 of the First Protocol, the right to education, that could not be delegated. The subject child had a right under Article 3 not to be beaten.

The Vienna Convention has been used in the interpretation of the Convention with much weight being attached to its object and purpose. Strasbourg judgments are not binding only between parties to the application and the court is free to depart from an earlier judgment.

A distinction exists between positive and negative obligations. Article 1 requires a state to 'secure' the rights and freedoms set out in the Convention, though many Articles seek a balance to be struck in determining their own operation, with rights and freedoms being balanced against one another.

RIGHTS AND FREEDOMS GUARANTEED

The following Articles have some particular bearing in considering the rights of the child:

Article 3

The Prohibition of Torture is not capable of derogation and is not qualified. In *Tyrer v. UK* (1978) Series A, No. 26 EHRR 1 the use of birching on bare buttocks as a judicial punishment, while not inhuman, was said to be degrading. In *Costello-Roberts v. UK* (1993) Series A, No. 247–C; 19 EHRR 192 the instance of corporal punishment with a gym shoe with the pupil wearing shorts, as a disciplinary measure in an independent school was distinguished.

Article 6

The Right to a Fair Trial requires the right to a fair and public hearing within a reasonable time in determination of civil rights and obligations or of any criminal charge. A dispute, for such a trial to be permitted must involve questions of fact and law, be genuine and of a serious nature. Regarding the child especially, any dispute involving a child must ensure that its voice is heard. As such, its 'voice' need not be directly relayed by the child and indeed rarely ever is, save in exceptional circumstances, depending upon the child's own age, degree of understanding of proceedings and therefore its maturity. However, the determining issue is that its voice must at least be heard, whether through legal representation, social services, the court welfare officer or some such judicial body making representations on its behalf. This is in addition to one of the requirements of the UN Convention on the Rights of the Child. In *Bulger v. UK* (1999) ECHR, the full court determined that the UK was in breach of the Convention where charges of murder were brought against two children in an adult criminal court.

Article 8

The Right to Respect for Private and Family Life covers a wide range of issues but in *Niemitz v. Germany* (1992) 16 EHRR 97 it was said that the Court considered it neither necessary nor possible for an exhaustive definition of the notion of private life. In *Johnston v. Ireland* (1986) 9 EHRR 203 it was said that as far as positive obligations upon states were concerned, the notion of 'respect' was not clear-cut: 'the fair balance that has to be struck is between the general interest of the community and the interests of the individual, the search for which is inherent in the whole Convention' it was stated in *Cossey v. UK* (1990) 13 EHRR. In *Ahmut v. Netherlands* (1997) 24 EHRR 62 it was held that Article 8 did not guarantee a right to choose the most suitable state to develop family life, it being a case that concerned a state's obligations to grant admission to relatives. In *Stubbings v. UK* (1997) 23 EHRR 213 although Article 8 was held to impose an obligation on the state to protect a person's right to respect for private life in the context of sexual abuse suffered by a child, that obligation as discharged by criminal sanctions, did not permit the applicant to commence civil proceedings outside a six-year limitation period.

In *Burghartz v. Switzerland* (1994) 18 EHRR 101 there was discrimination under Article 8 taken with Article 14, preventing an applicant putting his own surname before that of his wife. In *Johnston v. Ireland* (1986) 9 EHRR203 a legitimate child had to be placed legally and socially akin to an illegitimate child. The illegitimate child was similarly considered in *Mark v. Belgium* (1979) 2 EHRR 330 when it was held to be disrespectful of family life and impeded the court when a State refused to recognise a mother's maternity from the moment of birth regarding a non-marital child. In *Kegan v. Ireland* (1993) EHRR 409 a father's right to family life was disrespected when he was neither aware nor consented to the adoption of his illegitimate child. Parents in public care proceedings in Scotland, UK, were denied access to documents in *McMichael v. UK* (1995) ECHR in violation of Article 8, such denial being deemed to be the prevention of parents being involved in the decision-making process. The unmarried father believed he was also being discriminated against because he lacked parental responsibility regarding the child at birth. It should be noted that the plight of the unmarried father has not eased dramatically, even with the consideration of jurisprudence from the ECHR.

In *H v. UK* (1997) 10 EHRR 95 Article 8 had keen transgressed where there had been considerable delay in a parent re-establishing contact with a child during court proceedings. In *Abdulaziz Cabales and Balkandali v. UK* (1987) EHRR 471 whatever the word 'family' meant, it had to include the relationship arising from a lawful and genuine marriage. There existed a bond amounting to 'family life' between a child and its parents from the moment of birth, as stated in *Berrehab v. Netherlands* (1989) 11 EHRR 322. However, in *XYZ v. UK* (1997) ECHR it was said that whilst family life was not limited to families based upon marriage it did not believe that X ought to be recognised as the father of Z who was a female-to-male transsexual.

In *Endricks v. Netherlands* (1983) 5 ECHR 233 contact should not be denied unless strong reasons existed, with parents being part of a child's future plans being considered in *W v. UK* (1988) 10 ECHR 29, with the attempt at reunion of child and parent being emphasised in *Johansen v. Norway* (1996) ECHR. In *Hokakenen v. Finland* (1996) ECHR the State was criticised for not doing enough where a father permitted the temporary stay of a child with maternal grandparents after the mother's death, only to find it impossible to be reunited thereafter. In *B v. UK* (1999 ECHR) the unmarried father was deemed not to have been discriminated against despite him not having the same right as a married father to trigger the Hague Convention on Child Abduction when his child was abducted.

The European Court of Human Rights has said on many occasions that the purpose of Article 8 is to protect the person against arbitrary interferences with family life, with a negative approach of non-interference being mainly adopted; but a child can expect a State to implement positive measures to ensure the respect for its private life.

THE UN CONVENTION ON THE RIGHTS OF THE CHILD

Article 5 of the UN Convention on the Rights of the Child recognises the rights and responsibilities of parents to provide direction and guidance to children, 'consistent with the evolving capacities of the child'. The 'family' is seen as the natural and fundamental group unit of society with entitlement to protection by the State.

Article 14

The Prohibition of Discrimination was considered in the *Belgian Linguistic Case* (1968) 1 EHRR 252 where the court stated that Article 14 does not prohibit different treatment where this is 'founded on an objective assessment of essentially different factual circumstances and which, being based on the public interest, strikes a fair balance between the protection of the interests of the community and respect for the rights and freedoms safeguarded by the Convention'. Under Article 2, First Protocol, Right to Education, the court held that although the first sentence of the Article was couched in negative terms, it nevertheless enshrined a right. The 'travaux preparatoires' implies that the Convention does not perhaps recognise a right to education such as to expect states to establish at their own expense, or to subsidise education of any particular type or level. The only right guarantees a person to avail himself of the means of instruction existing at a given time. The right impliedly carries a right to be educated in the national language or in one of the national languages but not in a language of choice. The Article binds all the functions of the state in the sphere of education and teaching and not just some of them.

International Covenant on Civil and Political Rights

16 December 1966

Entry into force 23 March 1976

Note The UK has ratified this Covenant, but not its optional Protocol, which confers on individuals the right to communicate complaints.

PREAMBLE

The states parties to the present Covenant,

Considering that, in accordance with the principles proclaimed in the Charter of the United Nations, recognition of the inherent dignity and of the equal and inalienable rights of all members of the human family is the foundation of freedom, justice and peace in the world,

Recognising that these rights derive from the inherent dignity of the human person,

Recognising that, in accordance with the Universal Declaration of Human Rights, the ideal of free human beings enjoying civil and political freedom and freedom from fear and want can only be achieved if conditions are created whereby everyone may enjoy his civil and political rights, as well as his economic, social and cultural rights,

Considering the obligation of states under the Charter of the United Nations to promote universal respect for, and observance of, human rights and freedoms,

Realising that the individual, having duties to other individuals and to the community to which he belongs, is under a responsibility to strive for the promotion and observance of the rights recognised in the present Covenant,

Agree upon the following articles:

PART I
[1]

Article 1

1. All peoples have the right of self-determination. By virtue of that right they freely determine their political status and freely pursue their economic, social and cultural development.
2. All peoples may, for their own ends, freely dispose of their natural wealth and resources without prejudice to any obligations arising out of international economic co-operation, based upon the principle of mutual benefit, and international law. In no case may a people be deprived of its own means of subsistence.
3. The states parties to the present Covenant, including those having responsibility for the administration of Non-Self-Governing and Trust Territories, shall promote the realization of the right of self-determination, and shall respect that right, in conformity with the provisions of the Charter of the United Nations.

PART II

1. Each state party to the present Covenant undertakes to respect and to ensure to all individuals within its territory and subject to its jurisdiction the rights recognized in the present Covenant, without distinction of any kind, such as race, colour, sex, language, religion, political or other opinion, national or social origin, property, birth or other status.
2. Where not already provided for by existing legislative or other measures, each state party to the present Covenant undertakes to take the necessary steps, in accordance with its constitutional processes and with the provisions of the present Covenant, to adopt such legislative or other measures as may be necessary to give effect to the rights recognized in the present Covenant.
3. Each state party to the present Covenant undertakes:
   (a) to ensure that any person whose rights or freedoms as herein recognised are violated shall have an effective remedy, notwithstanding that the violation has been committed by persons acting in an official capacity;
   (b) to ensure that any person claiming such a remedy shall have his right thereto determined by competent judicial, administrative or legislative authorities, or by any other competent authority provided for by the legal system of the state, and to develop the possibilities of judicial remedy;
   (c) to ensure that the competent authorities shall enforce such remedies when granted.

Article 3

The states parties to the present Covenant undertake to ensure the equal right of men and women to the enjoyment of all civil and political rights set forth in the present Covenant.

Article 4

1. In time of public emergency which threatens the life of the nation and the existence of which is officially proclaimed, the states parties to the present Covenant may take measures derogating from their obligations under the present Covenant to the extent strictly required by the exigencies of the situation, provided that such measures are not inconsistent with their other obligations under international law and do not involve discrimination solely on the ground of race, colour, sex, language, religion or social origin.
2. No derogation from articles 6, 7, 8 (paragraphs 1 and 2), 11, 15, 16 and 18 may be made under this provision.
3. Any state party to the present Covenant availing itself of the right of derogation shall immediately inform the other states parties to the present Covenant, through the intermediary of the Secretary-General of the United Nations, of the provisions from which it has derogated and of the reasons by which it was actuated. A further communication shall be made, through the same intermediary, on the date on which it terminates such derogation.

Article 5

1. Nothing in the present Covenant may be interpreted as implying for any state, group or person any right to engage in any activity or perform any act aimed at the destruction of any of the rights and freedoms recognized herein or at their limitation to a greater extent than is provided for in the present Covenant.
2. There shall be no restriction upon or derogation from any of the fundamental human rights recognized or existing in any state party to the present Covenant pursuant to law, conventions, regulations or custom on the pretext that the present Covenant does not recognize such rights or that it recognizes them to a lesser extent.

PART III

Article 6

1. Every human being has the inherent right to life. This right shall be protected by law. No one shall be arbitrarily deprived of his life.
2. In countries which have not abolished the death penalty, sentence of death may be imposed only for the most serious crimes in accordance with the law in force at the time of the commission of the crime and not contrary to the provisions of the present Covenant and to the Convention on the Prevention and Punishment of the Crime of Genocide. This penalty can only be carried out pursuant to a final judgement rendered by a competent court.
3. When deprivation of life constitutes the crime of genocide, it is understood that nothing in this article shall authorize any state party to the present Covenant to derogate in any way from any obligation assumed under the provisions of the Convention on the Prevention and Punishment of the Crime of Genocide.
4. Anyone sentenced to death shall have the right to seek pardon or commutation of the sentence. Amnesty, pardon or commutation of the sentence of death may be granted in all cases.
5. Sentence of death shall not be imposed for crimes committed by persons below eighteen years of age and shall not be carried out on pregnant women.
6. Nothing in this article shall be invoked to delay or to prevent the abolition of capital punishment by any state party to the present Covenant.

Article 7

No one shall be subjected to torture or to cruel, inhuman or degrading treatment or punishment. In particular, no one shall be subjected without his free consent to medical or scientific experimentation.

Article 8

1. No one shall be held in slavery; slavery and the slave-trade in all their forms shall be prohibited.
2. No one shall be held in servitude.
3 (a) No one shall be required to perform forced or compulsory labour;
   (b) paragraph 3 (a) shall not be held to preclude, in countries where imprisonment with hard labour may be imposed as a punishment for a

crime, the performance of hard labour in pursuance of a sentence to such punishment by a competent court;

(c) for the purpose of this paragraph the term 'forced or compulsory labour' shall not include:
   (i) any work or service, not referred to in subparagraph (b), normally required of a person who is under detention in consequence of a lawful order of a court, or of a person during conditional release from such detention;
   (ii) any service of a military character and, in countries where conscientious objection is recognised, any national service required by law of conscientious objectors;
   (iii) any service exacted in cases of emergency or calamity threatening the life or well-being of the community;
   (iv) any work or service which forms part of normal civil obligations.

Article 9

1. Everyone has the right to liberty and security of person. No one shall be subjected to arbitrary arrest or detention. No one shall be deprived of his liberty except on such grounds and in accordance with such procedure as are established by law.
2. Anyone who is arrested shall be informed, at the time of arrest, of the reasons for his arrest and shall be promptly informed of any charges against him.
3. Anyone arrested or detained on a criminal charge shall be brought promptly before a judge or other officer authorized by law to exercise judicial power and shall be entitled to trial within a reasonable time or to release. It shall not be the general rule that persons awaiting trial shall be detained in custody, but release may be subject to guarantees to appear for trial, at any other stage of the judicial proceedings, and, should occasion arise, for execution of the judgement.
4. Anyone who is deprived of his liberty by arrest or detention shall be entitled to take proceedings before a court, in order that that court may decide without delay on the lawfulness of his detention and order his release if the detention is not lawful.
5. Anyone who has been the victim of unlawful arrest or detention shall have an enforceable right to compensation.

Article 10

1. All persons deprived of their liberty shall be treated with humanity and with respect for the inherent dignity of the human person.
2. (a) Accused persons shall, save in exceptional circumstances, be segregated from convicted persons and shall be subject to separate treatment appropriate to their status as unconvicted persons;
   (b) Accused juvenile persons shall be separated from adults and brought as speedily as possible for adjudication.
3. The penitentiary system shall comprise treatment of prisoners the essential aim of which shall be their reformation and social rehabilitation. Juvenile offenders shall be segregated from adults and be accorded treatment appropriate to their age and legal status.

Article 11

No one shall be imprisoned merely on the ground of inability to fulfil a contractual obligation.

Article 12

1. Everyone lawfully within the territory of a state shall, within that territory, have the right to liberty of movement and freedom to choose his residence.
2. Everyone shall be free to leave any country, including his own.
3. The above-mentioned rights shall not be subject to any restrictions except those which are provided by law, are necessary to protect national security, public order (*ordre public*), public health or morals or the rights and freedoms of others, and are consistent with the other rights recognized in the present Covenant.
4. No one shall be arbitrarily deprived of the right to enter his own country.

Article 13

An alien lawfully in the territory of a state party to the present Covenant may be expelled therefrom only in pursuance of a decision reached in accordance with law and shall, except where compelling reasons of national security otherwise require, be allowed to submit the reasons against his expulsion and to have his case reviewed by, and be represented for the purpose before, the competent authority or a person or persons especially designated by the competent authority.

Article 14

1. All persons shall be equal before the courts and tribunals. In the determination of any criminal charge against him, or of his rights and obligations in a suit at law, everyone shall be entitled to a fair and public hearing by a competent, independent and impartial tribunal established by law. The Press and the public may be excluded from all or part of a trial for reasons of morals, public order (*ordre public*) or national security in a democratic society, or when the interest of the private lives of the parties so requires, or to the extent strictly necessary in the opinion of the court in special circumstances where publicity would prejudice the interests of justice; but any judgement rendered in a criminal case or in a suit at law shall be made public except where the interest of juvenile persons otherwise requires or the proceedings concern matrimonial disputes or the guardianship of children.
2. Everyone charged with a criminal offence shall have the right to be presumed innocent until proved guilty according to law.
3. In the determination of any criminal charge against him, everyone shall be entitled to the following minimum guarantees, in full equality:
   (a) to be informed promptly and in detail in a language which he understands of the nature and cause of the charge against him;
   (b) to have adequate time and facilities for the preparation of his defence and to communicate with counsel of his own choosing;
   (c) to be tried without undue delay;
   (d) to be tried in his presence, and to defend himself in person or through legal assistance of his own choosing; to be informed, if he does not

have legal assistance, of this right; and to have legal assistance assigned to him, in any case where the interests of justice so require, and without payment by him in any such case if he does not have sufficient means to pay for it;

(e) to examine, or have examined, the witnesses against him and to obtain the attendance and examination of witnesses on his behalf under the same conditions as witnesses against him;

(f) to have the free assistance of an interpreter if he cannot understand or speak the language used in court;

(g) not to be compelled to testify against himself or to confess guilt.

4. In the case of juvenile persons, the procedure shall be such as will take account of their age and the desirability of promoting their rehabilitation.

5. Everyone convicted of a crime shall have the right to his conviction and sentence being reviewed by a higher tribunal according to law.

6. When a person has by a final decision been convicted of a criminal offence and when subsequently his conviction has been reversed or he has been pardoned on the ground that a new or newly discovered fact shows conclusively that there has been a miscarriage of justice, the person who has suffered punishment as a result of such conviction shall be compensated according to law, unless it is proved that the non-disclosure of the unknown fact in time is wholly or partly attributable to him.

7. No one shall be liable to be tried or punished again for an offence for which he has already been finally convicted or acquitted in accordance with the law and penal procedure of each country.

Article 15

1. No one shall be held guilty of any criminal offence on account of any act or omission which did not constitute a criminal offence, under national or international law, at the time when it was committed. Nor shall a heavier penalty be imposed than the one that was applicable at the time when the criminal offence was committed. If, subsequent to the commission of the offence, provision is made by law for the imposition of a lighter penalty, the offender shall benefit thereby.

2. Nothing in this article shall prejudice the trial and punishment of any person for any act or omission which, at the time when it was committed, was criminal according to the general principles of law recognized by the community of nations.

Article 16

Everyone shall have the right to recognition everywhere as a person before the law.

Article 17

1. No one shall be subjected to arbitrary or unlawful interference with his privacy, family, home or correspondence, nor to unlawful attacks on his honour and reputation.

2. Everyone has the right to the protection of the law against such interference or attacks.

Article 18

1. Everyone shall have the right to freedom of thought, conscience and religion. This right shall include freedom to have or to adopt a religion or belief of his choice, and freedom, either individually or in community with others and in public or private, to manifest his religion or belief in worship, observance, practice and teaching.
2. No one shall be subject to coercion which would impair his freedom to have or to adopt a religion or belief of his choice.
3. Freedom to manifest one's religion or beliefs may be subject only to such limitations as are prescribed by law and are necessary to protect public safety, order, health, or morals or the fundamental rights and freedoms of others.
4. The states parties to the present Covenant undertake to have respect for the liberty of parents and, when applicable, legal guardians to ensure the religious and moral education of their children in conformity with their own convictions.

Article 19

1. Everyone shall have the right to hold opinions without interference.
2. Everyone shall have the right to freedom of expression; this right shall include freedom to seek, receive and impart information and ideas of all kinds, regardless of frontiers, either orally, in writing or in print, in the form of art, or through any other media of his choice.
3. The exercise of the rights provided for in paragraph 2 of this article carries with it special duties and responsibilities. It may therefore be subject to certain restrictions, but these shall only be such as are provided by law and are necessary:
   (a) for respect of the rights or reputations of others;
   (b) for the protection of national security or of public order (*ordre public*), or of public health or morals.

Article 20

1. Any propaganda for war shall be prohibited by law.
2. Any advocacy of national, racial or religious hatred that constitutes incitement to discrimination, hostility or violence shall be prohibited by law.

Article 21

The right of peaceful assembly shall be recognized. No restrictions may be placed on the exercise of this right other than those imposed in conformity with the law and which are necessary in a democratic society in the interests of national security or public safety, public order (*ordre public*), the protection of public health or morals or the protection of the rights and freedoms of others.

Article 22

1. Everyone shall have the right to freedom of association with others, including the right to form and join trade unions for the protection of his interests.
2. No restrictions may be placed on the exercise of this right other than those which are prescribed by law and which are necessary in a democratic society in the interests of national security or public safety, public order

(*ordre public*), the protection of public health or morals or the protection of the rights and freedoms of others. This article shall not prevent the imposition of lawful restrictions on members of the armed forces and of the police in their exercise of this right.

3. Nothing in this article shall authorize States Parties to the International Labour Organisation Convention of 1948 concerning Freedom of Association and Protection of the Right to Organise to take legislative measures which would prejudice, or to apply the law in such a manner as to prejudice, the guarantees provided for in that Convention.

Article 23

1. The family is the natural and fundamental group unit of society and is entitled to protection by society and the state.
2. The right of men and women of marriageable age to marry and to found a family shall be recognized.
3. No marriage shall be entered into without the free and full consent of the intending spouses.
4. States parties to the present Covenant shall take appropriate steps to ensure equality of rights and responsibilities of spouses as to marriage, during marriage and at its dissolution. In the case of dissolution, provision shall be made for the necessary protection of any children.

Article 24

1. Every child shall have, without any discrimination as to race, colour, sex, language, religion, national or social origin, property or birth, the right to such measures of protection as are required by his status as a minor, on the part of his family, society and the state.
2. Every child shall be registered immediately after birth and shall have a name.
3. Every child has the right to acquire a nationality.

Article 25

Every citizen shall have the right and the opportunity, without any of the distinctions mentioned in article 2 and without unreasonable restrictions:

(a) to take part in the conduct of public affairs, directly or through freely chosen representatives;
(b) to vote and to be elected at genuine periodic elections which shall be by universal and equal suffrage and shall be held by secret ballot, guaranteeing the free expression of the will of the electors;
(c) to have access, on general terms of equality, to public service in his country.

Article 26

All persons are equal before the law and are entitled without any discrimination to the equal protection of the law. In this respect, the law shall prohibit any discrimination and guarantee to all persons equal and effective protection against discrimination on any ground such as race, colour, sex, language, religion, political or other opinion, national or social origin, property, birth or other status.

Article 27

In those states in which ethnic, religious or linguistic minorities exist, persons belonging to such minorities shall not be denied the right, in community with the other members of their group, to enjoy their own culture, to profess and practise their own religion, or to use their own language.

PART IV

Article 28

1. There shall be established a Human Rights Committee (hereafter referred to in the present Covenant as the Committee). It shall consist of eighteen members and shall carry out the functions hereinafter provided.
2. The Committee shall be composed of nationals of the states parties to the present Covenant who shall be persons of high moral character and recognised competence in the field of human rights, consideration being given to the usefulness of the participation of some persons having legal experience.
3. The members of the Committee shall be elected and shall serve in their personal capacity.

Article 29

1. The members of the Committee shall be elected by secret ballot from a list of persons possessing the qualifications prescribed in article 28 and nominated for the purpose by the states parties to the present Covenant.
2. Each state party to the present Covenant may nominate not more than two persons. These persons shall be nationals of the nominating state.
3. A person shall be eligible for renomination.

Article 30

1. The initial election shall be held no later than six months after the date of the entry into force of the present Covenant.
2. At least four months before the date of each election to the Committee, other than an election to fill a vacancy declared in accordance with article 34, the Secretary-General of the United Nations shall address a written invitation to the states parties to the present Covenant to submit their nominations for membership of the Committee within three months.
3. The Secretary-General of the United Nations shall prepare a list in alphabetical order of all the persons thus nominated, with an indication of the states parties which have nominated them, and shall submit it to the states parties to the present Covenant no later than one month before the date of each election.
4. Elections of the members of the Committee shall be held at a meeting of the states parties to the present Covenant convened by the Secretary-General of the United Nations at the Headquarters of the United Nations. At that meeting, for which two thirds of the states parties to the present Covenant shall constitute a quorum, the persons elected to the Committee shall be those nominees who obtain the largest number of votes and an absolute majority of the votes of the representatives of states parties present and voting.

Article 31

1. The Committee may not include more than one national of the same state.
2. In the election of the Committee, consideration shall be given to equitable geographical distribution of membership and to the representation of the different forms of civilization and of the principal legal systems.

Article 32

1. The members of the Committee shall be elected for a term of four years. They shall be eligible for re-election if renominated. However, the terms of nine of the members elected at the first election shall expire at the end of two years; immediately after the first election, the names of these nine members shall be chosen by lot by the Chairman of the meeting referred to in article 30, paragraph 4.
2. Elections at the expiry of office shall be held in accordance with the preceding articles of this part of the present Covenant.

Article 33

1. If, in the unanimous opinion of the other members, a member of the Committee has ceased to carry out his functions for any cause other than absence of a temporary character, the Chairman of the Committee shall notify the Secretary-General of the United Nations, who shall then declare the seat of that member to be vacant.
2. In the event of the death or the resignation of a member of the Committee, the Chairman shall immediately notify the Secretary-General of the United Nations, who shall declare the seat vacant from the date of death or the date on which the resignation takes effect.

Article 34

1. When a vacancy is declared in accordance with article 33 and if the term of office of the member to be replaced does not expire within six months of the declaration of the vacancy, the Secretary-General of the United Nations shall notify each of the states parties to the present Covenant, which may within two months submit nominations in accordance with article 29 for the purpose of filling the vacancy.
2. The Secretary-General of the United Nations shall prepare a list in alphabetical order of the persons thus nominated and shall submit it to the states parties to the present Covenant. The election to fill the vacancy shall then take place in accordance with the relevant provisions of this part of the present Covenant.
3. A member of the Committee elected to fill a vacancy declared in accordance with article 33 shall hold office for the remainder of the term of the member who vacated the seat on the Committee under the provisions of that article.

Article 35

The members of the Committee shall, with the approval of the General Assembly of the United Nations, receive emoluments from United Nations resources on such terms and conditions as the General Assembly may decide, having regard to the importance of the Committee's responsibilities.

Article 36

The Secretary-General of the United Nations shall provide the necessary staff and facilities for the effective performance of the functions of the Committee under the present Covenant.

Article 37

1. The Secretary-General of the United Nations shall convene the initial meeting of the Committee at the Headquarters of the United Nations.
2. After its initial meeting, the Committee shall meet at such times as shall be provided in its rules of procedure.
3. The Committee shall normally meet at the Headquarters of the United Nations or at the United Nations Office at Geneva.

Article 38

Every member of the Committee shall, before taking up his duties, make a solemn declaration in open committee that he will perform his functions impartially and conscientiously.

Article 39

1. The Committee shall elect its officers for a term of two years. They may be re-elected.
2. The Committee shall establish its own rules of procedure, but these rules shall provide, *inter alia*, that:
   (a) twelve members shall constitute a quorum;
   (b) decisions of the Committee shall be made by a majority vote of the members present.

Article 40

1. The states parties to the present Covenant undertake to submit reports on the measures they have adopted which give effect to the rights recognized herein and on the progress made in the enjoyment of those rights:
   (a) within one year of the entry into force of the present Covenant for the states parties concerned;
   (b) thereafter whenever the Committee so requests.
2. All reports shall be submitted to the Secretary-General of the United Nations, who shall transmit them to the Committee for consideration. Reports shall indicate the factors and difficulties, if any affecting the implementation of the present Covenant.
3. The Secretary-General of the United Nations may, after consultation with the Committee, transmit to the specialized agencies concerned copies of such parts of the reports as may fall within their field of competence.
4. The Committee shall study the reports submitted by the states parties to the present Covenant. It shall transmit its reports, and such general comments as it may consider appropriate, to the states parties. The Committee may also transmit to the Economic and Social Council these comments along with the copies of the reports it has received from states parties to the present Covenant.

5. The states parties to the present Covenant may submit to the Committee observations on any comments that may be made in accordance with paragraph 4 of this article.

Article 41

1. A state party to the present Covenant may at any time declare under this article that it recognizes the competence of the Committee to receive and consider communications to the effect that a state party claims that another state party is not fulfilling its obligations under the present Covenant. Communications under this article may be received and considered only if submitted by a state party which has made a declaration recognizing in regard to itself the competence of the Committee. No communication shall be received by the Committee if it concerns a state party which has not made such a declaration. Communications received under this article shall be dealt with in accordance with the following procedure:
   (a) If a state party to the present Covenant considers that another state party is not giving effect to the provisions of the present Covenant, it may, by written communication, bring the matter to the attention of that state party. Within three months after the receipt of the communication, the receiving state shall afford the state which sent the communication an explanation or any other statement in writing clarifying the matter, which should include, to the extent possible and pertinent, reference to domestic procedures and remedies taken, pending, or available in the matter.
   (b) If the matter is not adjusted to the satisfaction of both states parties concerned within six months after the receipt by the receiving state of the initial communication, either state shall have the right to refer the matter to the Committee, by notice given to the Committee and to the other state.
   (c) The Committee shall deal with a matter referred to it only after it has ascertained that all available domestic remedies have been invoked and exhausted in the matter, in conformity with the generally recognized principles of international law. This shall not be the rule where the application of the remedies is unreasonably prolonged.
   (d) The Committee shall hold closed meetings when examining communications under this article.
   (e) Subject to the provisions of subparagraph (c), the Committee shall make available its good offices to the states parties concerned with a view to a friendly solution of the matter on the basis of respect for human rights and fundamental freedoms as recognized in the present Covenant.
   (f) In any matter referred to it, the Committee may call upon the states parties concerned, referred to in subparagraph (b), to supply any relevant information.
   (g) The states parties concerned, referred to in subparagraph (b), shall have the right to be represented when the matter is being considered in the Committee and to make submissions orally and/or in writing.
   (h) The Committee shall, within twelve months after the date of receipt of notice under subparagraph (b), submit a report:

(i) if a solution within the terms of subparagraph (e) is reached, the Committee shall confine its report to a brief statement of the facts and of the solution reached;

(ii) if a solution within the terms of subparagraph (e) is not reached, the Committee shall confine its report to a brief statement of the facts; the written submissions and record of the oral submissions made by the states parties concerned shall be attached to the report.

In every matter, the report shall be communicated to the states parties concerned.

2. The provisions of this article shall come into force when ten states parties to the present Covenant have made declarations under paragraph 1 of this article. Such declarations shall be deposited by the states parties with the Secretary-General of the United Nations, who shall transmit copies thereof to the other states parties. A declaration may be withdrawn at any time by notification to the Secretary-General. Such a withdrawal shall not prejudice the consideration of any matter which is the subject of a communication already transmitted under this article; no further communication by any state party shall be received after the notification of withdrawal of the declaration has been received by the Secretary-General, unless the state party concerned has made a new declaration.

Article 42

1. (a) If a matter referred to the Committee in accordance with article 41 is not resolved to the satisfaction of the states parties concerned, the Committee may, with the prior consent of the states parties concerned, appoint an *ad hoc* Conciliation Commission (hereinafter referred to as the Commission). The good offices of the Commission shall be made available to the states parties concerned with a view to an amicable solution of the matter on the basis of respect for the present Covenant;

(b) the Commission shall consist of five persons acceptable to the states parties concerned. If the states parties concerned fail to reach agreement within three months on all or part of the composition of the Commission, the members of the Commission concerning whom no agreement has been reached shall be elected by secret ballot by a two-thirds majority vote of the Committee from among its members.

2. The members of the Commission shall serve in their personal capacity. They shall not be nationals of the states parties concerned, or of a state not party to the present Covenant, or of a state party which has not made a declaration under article 41.

3. The Commission shall elect its own Chairman and adopt its own rules of procedure.

4. The meetings of the Commission shall normally be held at the Headquarters of the United Nations or at the United Nations Office at Geneva. However, they may be held at such other convenient places as the Commission may determine in consultation with the Secretary-General of the United Nations and the states parties concerned.

5. The secretariat provided in accordance with article 36 shall also service the commissions appointed under this article.

6. The information received and collated by the Committee shall be made available to the Commission and the Commission may call upon the states parties concerned to supply any other relevant information.
7. When the Commission has fully considered the matter, but in any event not later than twelve months after having been seized of the matter, it shall submit to the Chairman of the Committee a report for communication to the states parties concerned:
   (a) if the Commission is unable to complete its consideration of the matter within twelve months, it shall confine its report to a brief statement of the status of its consideration of the matter;
   (b) if an amicable solution to the matter on the basis of respect for human rights as recognized in the present Covenant is reached, the Commission shall confine its report to a brief statement of the facts and of the solution reached;
   (c) if a solution within the terms of subparagraph (b) is not reached, the Commission's report shall embody its findings on all questions of fact relevant to the issues between the states parties concerned, and its views on the possibilities of an amicable solution of the matter. This report shall also contain the written submissions and a record of the oral submissions made by the states parties concerned;
   (d) if the Commission's report is submitted under subparagraph (c), the states parties concerned shall, within three months of the receipt of the report, notify the Chairman of the Committee whether or not they accept the contents of the report of the Commission.
8. The provisions of this article are without prejudice to the responsibilities of the Committee under article 41.
9. The states parties concerned shall share equally all the expenses of the members of the Commission in accordance with estimates to be provided by the Secretary-General of the United Nations.
10. The Secretary-General of the United Nations shall be empowered to pay the expenses of the members of the Commission, if necessary, before reimbursement by the states parties concerned, in accordance with paragraph 9 of this article.

Article 43

The members of the Committee, and of the *ad hoc* conciliation commissions which may be appointed under article 42, shall be entitled to the facilities, privileges and immunities of experts on mission for the United Nations as laid down in the relevant sections of the Convention on the Privileges and Immunities of the United Nations.

Article 44

The provisions for the implementation of the present Covenant shall apply without prejudice to the procedures prescribed in the field of human rights by or under the constituent instruments and the conventions of the United Nations and of the specialised agencies and shall not prevent the states parties to the present Covenant from having recourse to other procedures for settling a dispute in accordance with general or special international agreements in force between them.

Article 45

The Committee shall submit to the General Assembly of the United Nations, through the Economic and Social Council, an annual report on its activities.

PART V

Article 46

Nothing in the present Covenant shall be interpreted as impairing the provisions of the Charter of the United Nations and of the constitutions of the specialised agencies which define the respective responsibilities of the various organs of the United Nations and of the specialised agencies in regard to the matters dealt with in the present Covenant.

Article 47

Nothing in the present Covenant shall be interpreted as impairing the inherent right of all peoples to enjoy and utilise fully and freely their natural wealth and resources.

PART VI

Article 48

1. The present Covenant is open for signature by any state member of the United Nations or member of any of its specialised agencies, by any state party to the Statute of the International Court of Justice, and by any other state which has been invited by the General Assembly of the United Nations to become a party to the present Covenant.
2. The present Covenant is subject to ratification. Instruments of ratification shall be deposited with the Secretary-General of the United Nations.
3. The present Covenant shall be open to accession by any state referred to in paragraph 1 of this article.
4. Accession shall be effected by the deposit of an instrument of accession with the Secretary-General of the United Nations.
5. The Secretary-General of the United Nations shall inform all states which have signed this Covenant or acceded to it of the deposit of each instrument of ratification or accession.

Article 49

1. The present Covenant shall enter into force three months after the date of the deposit with the Secretary-General of the United Nations of the thirty-fifth instrument of ratification or instrument of accession.
2. For each state ratifying the present Covenant or acceding to it after the deposit of the thirty-fifth instrument of ratification or instrument of accession, the present Covenant shall enter into force three months after the date of the deposit of its own instrument of ratification or instrument of accession.

Article 50

The provisions of the present Covenant shall extend to all parts of federal states without any limitations or exceptions.

Article 51

1. Any state party to the present Covenant may propose an amendment and file it with the Secretary-General of the United Nations. The Secretary General of the United Nations shall thereupon communicate any proposed amendments to the states parties to the present Covenant with a request that they notify him whether they favour a conference of states parties for the purpose of considering and voting upon the proposals. In the event that at least one third of the states parties favours such a conference, the Secretary-General shall convene the conference under the auspices of the United Nations. Any amendment adopted by a majority of the states parties present and voting at the conference shall be submitted to the General Assembly of the United Nations for approval.
2. Amendments shall come into force when they have been approved by the General Assembly of the United Nations and accepted by a two-thirds majority of the states parties to the present Covenant in accordance with their respective constitutional processes.
3. When amendments come into force, they shall be binding on those states parties which have accepted them, other states parties still being bound by the provisions of the present Covenant and any earlier amendment which they have accepted.

Article 52

Irrespective of the notifications made under article 48, paragraph 5, the Secretary-General of the United Nations shall inform all states referred to in paragraph 1 of the same article of the following particulars:
(a) signatures, ratifications and accessions under article 48;
(b) the date of the entry into force of the present Covenant under article 49 and the date of the entry into force of any amendments under article 51.

Article 53

1. The present Covenant, of which the Chinese, English, French, Russian and Spanish texts are equally authentic, shall be deposited in the archives of the United Nations.
2. The Secretary-General of the United Nations shall transmit certified copies of the present Covenant to all states referred to in article 48.

The European Convention on Human Rights, 1950: Section I and Relevant Protocols

The Governments signatory hereto, being Members of the Council of Europe,

Considering the Universal Declaration of Human Rights proclaimed by the General Assembly of the United Nations on 10 December 1948;

Considering that this Declaration aims at securing the universal and effective recognition and observance of the Rights therein declared;

Considering that the aim of the Council of Europe is the achievement of greater unity between its Members and that one of the methods by which the aim is to be pursued is the maintenance and further realization of Human Rights and Fundamental Freedoms;

Reaffirming their profound belief in those Fundamental Freedoms which are the foundation of justice and peace in the world and are best maintained on the one hand by an effective political democracy and on the other by a common understanding and observance of the Human Rights upon which they depend;

Being resolved, as the Governments of European countries which are likeminded and have a common heritage of political traditions, ideals, freedom and the rule of law to take the first steps for the collective enforcement of certain of the Rights stated in the Universal Declaration;

Have agreed as follows:

Article 1

The High Contracting Parties shall secure to everyone within their jurisdiction the rights and freedoms defined in Section 1 of this Convention.

SECTION 1

Article 2

1. Everyone's right to life shall be protected by law. No one shall be deprived of his life intentionally save in the execution of a sentence of a court following his conviction of a crime for which this penalty is provided by law.
2. Deprivation of life shall not be regarded as inflicted in contravention of this Article when it results from the use of force which is no more than absolutely necessary:
   (a) in defence of any person from unlawful violence;
   (b) in order to effect a lawful arrest or to prevent the escape of a person lawfully detained;
   (c) in action lawfully taken for the purpose of quelling a riot or insurrection.

Article 3

No one shall be subjected to torture or to inhuman or degrading treatment or punishment.

Article 4

1. No one shall be held in slavery or servitude.
2. No one shall be required to perform forced or compulsory labour.

3. For the purpose of this Article the term 'forced or compulsory labour' shall not include:
   (a) any work required to be done in the ordinary course of detention imposed according to the provisions of Article 5 of this Convention or during conditional release from such detention;
   (b) any service of a military character or, in case of conscientious objectors in countries where they are recognized, service exacted instead of compulsory military service;
   (c) any service exacted in case of an emergency or calamity threatening the life or well-being of the community;
   (d) any work or service which forms part of normal civic obligations.

Article 5

1. Everyone has the right to liberty and security of person. No one shall be deprived of his liberty save in the following cases and in accordance with a procedure prescribed by law;
   (a) the lawful detention of a person after conviction by a competent court;
   (b) the lawful arrest or detention of a person for non-compliance with the lawful order of a court or in order to secure the fulfilment of any obligation prescribed by law;
   (c) the lawful arrest or detention of a person effected for the purpose of bringing him before the competent legal authority on reasonable suspicion of having committed an offence or when it is reasonably considered necessary to prevent his committing an offence or fleeing after having done so;
   (d) the detention of a minor by lawful order for the purpose of educational supervision or his lawful detention for the purpose of bringing him before the competent legal authority;
   (e) the lawful detention of persons for the prevention of the spreading of infectious diseases, of persons of unsound mind, alcoholics or drug addicts, or vagrants;
   (f) the lawful arrest or detention of a person to prevent his effecting an unauthorized entry into the country or of a person against whom action is being taken with a view to deportation or extradition.
2. Everyone who is arrested shall be informed promptly, in a language which he understands, of the reasons for his arrest and of any charge against him.
3. Everyone arrested or detained in accordance with the provisions of paragraph 1 (c) of this Article shall be brought promptly before a judge or other officer authorised by law to exercise judicial power and shall be entitled to trial within a reasonable time or to release pending trial. Release may be conditioned by guarantees to appear for trial.
4. Everyone who is deprived of his liberty by arrest or detention shall be entitled to take proceedings by which the lawfulness of his detention shall be decided speedily by a court and his release ordered if the detention is not lawful.
5. Everyone who has been the victim of arrest or detention in contravention of the provisions of this article shall have an enforceable right to compensation.

Article 6

1. In the determination of his civil rights and obligations or of any criminal charge against him, everyone is entitled to a fair and public hearing within a reasonable time by an independent and impartial tribunal established by law. Judgment shall be pronounced publicly but the press and public may be excluded from all or part of the trial in the interest of morals, public order or national security in a democratic society, where the interests of juveniles or the protection of the private life of the parties so require, or to the extent strictly necessary in the opinion of the court in special circumstances where publicity would prejudice the interests of justice.
2. Everyone charged with a criminal offence shall be presumed innocent until proved guilty according to law.
3. Everyone charged with a criminal offence has the following minimum rights:
   (a) to be informed promptly, in a language which he understands and in detail, of the nature and cause of the accusation against him;
   (b) to have adequate time and facilities for the preparation of his defence;
   (c) to defend himself in person or through legal assistance of his own choosing or, if he has not sufficient means to pay for legal assistance, to be given it free when the interests of justice so require;
   (d) to examine or have examined witnesses against him and to obtain the attendance and examination of witnesses on his behalf under the same conditions as witnesses against him;
   (e) to have the free assistance of an interpreter if he cannot understand or speak the language used in court.

Article 7

1. No one shall be held guilty of any criminal offence on account of any act or omission which did not constitute a criminal offence under national or international law at the time when it was committed. Nor shall a heavier penalty be imposed than the one that was applicable at the time the criminal offence was committed.
2. This article shall not prejudice the trial and punishment of any person for any act or omission which, at the time when it was committed, was criminal according to the general principles of law recognized by civilized nations.

Article 8

1. Everyone has the right to respect for his private and family life, his home and his correspondence,
2. There shall be no interference by a public authority with the exercise of this right except such as is in accordance with the law and is necessary in a democratic society in the interests of national security, public safety or the economic well-being of the country, for the prevention of disorder or crime, for the protection of health or morals, or for the protection of the rights and freedoms of others.

Article 9

1. Everyone has the right to freedom of thought, conscience and religion; this right includes freedom to change his religion or belief, and freedom, either

alone or in community with others and in public or private, to manifest his religion or belief, in worship, teaching, practice and observance.

2. Freedom to manifest one's religion or beliefs shall be subject only to such limitations as are prescribed by law and are necessary in a democratic society, in the interests of public safety, for the protection of public order, health or morals, or for the protection of the rights and freedoms of others.

Article 10

1. Everyone has the right to freedom of expression. This right shall include freedom to hold opinions and to receive and impart information and ideas without interference by public authority and regardless of frontiers. This article shall not prevent States from requiring the licensing of broadcasting, television or cinema enterprises.
2. The exercise of these freedoms, since it carries with it duties and responsibilities, may be subject to such formalities, conditions, restrictions or penalties as are prescribed by law and are necessary in a democratic society, in the interests of national security, territorial integrity or public safety, for the prevention of disorder or crime, for the protection of health or morals, for the protection of the reputation or rights of others, for preventing the disclosure of information received in confidence, or for maintaining the authority and impartiality of the judiciary.

Article 11

1. Everyone has the right to freedom of peaceful assembly and to freedom of association with others, including the right to form and to join trade unions for the protection of his interests.
2. No restrictions shall be placed on the exercise of these rights other than such as are prescribed by law and are necessary in a democratic society in the interests of national security or public safety, for the prevention of disorder or crime, for the protection of health or morals or for the protection of the rights and freedoms of others. This Article shall not prevent the imposition of lawful restrictions on the exercise of these rights by members of the armed forces, of the police or of the administration of the State.

Article 12

Men and women of marriageable age have the right to marry and to found a family, according to the national laws governing the exercise of this right.

Article 13

Everyone whose rights and freedoms as set forth in this Convention are violated shall have an effective remedy before a national authority notwithstanding that the violation has been committed by persons acting in an official capacity.

Article 14

The enjoyment of the rights and freedoms set forth in this Convention shall be secured without discrimination on any ground such as sex, race, colour, language, religion, political or other opinion, national or social origin, association with a national minority, property, birth or other status.

Article 15

1. In time of war or other public emergency threatening the life of the nation any High Contracting Party may take measures derogating from its obligations under this Convention to the extent strictly required by the exigencies of the situation, provided that such measures are not inconsistent with its other obligations under international law.
2. No derogation from Article 2, except in respect of deaths resulting from lawful acts of war, or from Articles 3, 4 (paragraph 1) and 7 shall be made under this provision.
3. Any High Contracting Party availing itself of this right of derogation shall keep the Secretary-General of the Council of Europe fully informed of the measures which it has taken and the reasons therefore. It shall also inform the Secretary-General of the Council of Europe when such measures have ceased to operate and the provisions of the Convention are again being fully executed.

Article 16

Nothing in Articles 10, 11 and 14 shall be regarded as preventing the High Contracting Parties from imposing restrictions on the political activity of aliens.

Article 17

Nothing in this Convention may be interpreted as implying for any State, group or person any right to engage in any activity or perform any act aimed at the destruction of any of the rights and freedoms set forth herein or at their limitation to a greater extent than is provided for in the Convention.

Article 18

The restrictions permitted under this Convention to the said rights and freedoms shall not be applied for any purpose other than those for which they have been prescribed.

PROTOCOLS

First Protocol: Enforcement of Certain Rights and Freedoms not included in Section 1 of the Convention

The Governments signatory hereto, being Members of the Council of Europe,

Being resolved to take steps to ensure the collective enforcement of certain rights and freedoms other than those already included in Section I of the Convention for the Protection of Human Rights and Fundamental Freedoms signed at Rome on 4th November, 1950 (hereinafter referred to as 'the Convention'),

Have agreed as follows:

Article 1

Every natural or legal person is entitled to the peaceful enjoyment of his possessions. No one shall be deprived of his possessions except in the public interest and subject to the conditions provided for by law and by the general principles of international law.

The preceding provisions shall not, however, in any way impair the right of a State to enforce such laws is it deems necessary to control the use of property in accordance with the general interest or to secure the payment of taxes or other contributions or penalties.

Article 2

No person shall be denied the right to education. In the exercise of any functions which it assumes in relation to education and to teaching, the State shall respect the right of parents to ensure such education and teaching in conformity with their own religious and philosophical convictions.

Article 3

The High Contracting Parties undertake to hold free elections at reasonable intervals by secret ballot, under conditions which will ensure the free expression of the opinion of the people in the choice of the legislature.

Fourth Protocol: Securing certain Rights and Freedoms other than those included in the Convention and in Protocol No. 1

The Governments signatory hereto, being Members of the Council of Europe,

Being resolved to take steps to ensure the collective enforcement of certain rights and freedoms other than those already included in Section I of the Convention for the Protection of Human Rights and Fundamental Freedoms signed at Rome on 4 November 1950 (hereinafter referred to as 'the Convention') and in Articles 1 to 3 of the First Protocol to the Convention, signed at Paris on 20 March 1952,

Have agreed as follows:

Article 1

No one shall be deprived of his liberty merely on the ground of inability to fulfil a contractual obligation.

Article 2

1. Everyone lawfully within the territory of a State shall, within that territory, have the right to liberty of movement and freedom to choose his residence.
2. Everyone shall be free to leave any country, including his own.
3. No restrictions shall be placed on the exercise of these rights other than such as are in accordance with law and are necessary in a democratic society in the interests of national security or public safety, for the maintenance of 'ordre public', for the prevention of crime, for the protection of health and morals, or for the protection of the rights and freedoms of others.
4. The rights set forth in paragraph 1 may also be subject, in particular areas, to restrictions imposed in accordance with law and justified by the public interest in a democratic society.

Article 3

1. No one shall be expelled, by means either of an individual or of a collective measure, from the territory of the State of which he is a national.
2. No one shall be deprived of the right to enter the territory of the State of which he is a national.

Article 4

Collective expulsion of aliens is prohibited.

Seventh Protocol: Concerning Various Matters

The member States of the Council of Europe signatory hereto,

Being resolved to take further steps to ensure the collective enforcement of certain rights and freedoms by means of the Convention for the Protection of Human Rights and Fundamental Freedoms signed at Rome on 4 November 1950 (hereinafter referred to as 'the Convention'),

Have agreed as follows:

Article 1

1. An alien lawfully resident in the territory of a State shall not be expelled therefrom except in pursuance of a decision reached in accordance with law and shall be allowed:
   (a) to submit reasons against his expulsion,
   b) to have his case reviewed, and
   (c) to be represented for these purposes before the competent authority or a person or persons designated by that authority.
2. An alien may be expelled before the exercise of his rights under paragraph 1(a), (b) and (c) of this Article, when such expulsion is necessary in the interests of public order or is grounded on reasons of national security.

Article 2

1. Everyone convicted of a criminal offence by a tribunal shall have the right to have his conviction or sentence reviewed by a higher tribunal. The exercise of this right, including the grounds on which it may be exercised, shall be governed by law.
2. This right may be subject to exceptions in regard to offences of a minor character, as prescribed by law, or in cases in which the person concerned was tried in the first instance by the highest tribunal or was convicted following an appeal against acquittal.

Article 3

When a person has by a final decision been convicted of a criminal offence and when subsequently his conviction has been reversed, or he has been pardoned, on the ground that a new or newly discovered fact shows conclusively that there has been a miscarriage of justice, the person who has suffered punishment as a result of such conviction shall be compensated according to the law or the practice of the State concerned, unless it is proved that the nondisclosure of the unknown fact in time is wholly or partly attributable to him.

Article 4

1. No one shall be liable to be tried or punished again in criminal proceedings under the jurisdiction of the same State for an offence for which he has already been finally acquitted or convicted in accordance with the law and penal procedure of that State.
2. The provisions of the preceding paragraph shall not prevent the reopening of the case in accordance with the law and penal procedure of the State concerned, if there is evidence of new or newly discovered facts, or if there has been a fundamental defect in the previous proceedings, which could affect the outcome of the case.
3. No derogation from this Article shall be made under Article 15 of the Convention.

Article 5

Spouses shall enjoy equality of rights and responsibilities of a private law character between them, and in their relations with their children, as to marriage, during marriage and in the event of its dissolution. This Article shall not prevent States from taking such measures as are necessary in the interests of the children.

United Nations Convention on the Rights of the Child 1989

PREAMBLE

The states parties to the present convention,

Considering that, in accordance with the principles proclaimed in the Charter of the United Nations, recognition of the inherent dignity and of the equal and inalienable rights of all members of the human family is the foundation of freedom, justice and peace in the world,

Bearing in mind that the peoples of the United Nations have, in the Charter, reaffirmed their faith in fundamental human rights and in the dignity and worth of the human person, and have determined to promoted social progress and better standards of life in larger freedom,

Recognising that the United Nations has, in the Universal Declaration of Human Rights and in the International Covenants on Human Rights, proclaimed and agreed that everyone is entitled to all the rights and freedoms set forth therein, without distinction of any kind, such as race, colour, sex, language, religion, political or other opinion, national or social origin, property, birth or other status,

Recalling that, in the Universal Declaration of Human Rights, the United Nations has proclaimed that childhood is entitled to special care and assistance,

Convinced that the family, as the fundamental group of society and the natural environment for the growth and well-being of all its members and particularly children, should be afforded the necessary protection and assistance so that it can fully assume its responsibilities within the community,

Recognising that the child, for the full and harmonious development of his or her personality, should grow up in a family environment, in an atmosphere of happiness, love and understanding,

Considering that the child should be fully prepared to live an individual life in society, and brought up in the spirit of the ideals proclaimed in the Charter of the United Nations, and in particular in the spirit of peace, dignity, tolerance, freedom, equality and solidarity,

Bearing in mind that the need to extend particular care to the child has been stated in the Geneva Declaration of the Rights of the Child of 1924 and in the Declaration of the Rights of the Child adopted by the General Assembly on 20 November 1959 and recognised in the Universal Declaration of Human Rights, in the International Covenant on Civil and Political Rights (in particular in Articles 23 and 24), in the International Covenant on Economic, Social and Cultural Rights (in particular in Article 10) and in the statutes and relevant instruments of specialised agencies and international organisations concerned with the welfare of children,

Bearing in mind that, as indicated in the Declaration of the Rights of the Child, 'the child, by reason of his physical and mental immaturity, needs special safeguards and care, including appropriate legal protection, before as well as after birth',

Recalling the provisions of the Declaration on Social and Legal Principles relating to the Protection and Welfare of Children, with Special Reference to Foster Placement and Adoption Nationally and Internationally; the United Nations Standard Minimum Rules for the Administration of Juvenile Justice

(The Beijing Rules); and the Declaration on the Protection of Women and Children in Emergency and Armed Conflict,

Recognising that, in all countries in the world, there are children living in exceptionally difficult conditions, and that such children need special consideration,

Taking due account of the importance of the traditions and cultural values of each people for the protection and harmonious development of the child,

Recognising the importance of international co-operation for improving the living conditions of children in every country, in particular in the developing countries,

Have agreed as follows:

PART I

Article 1

For the purposes of the present Convention, a child means every human being below the age of eighteen years unless, under the law applicable to the child, majority is attained earlier.

Article 2

1. States Parties shall respect and ensure the rights set forth in the present Convention to each child within their jurisdiction without discrimination of any kind, irrespective of the child's or his or her parent's or legal guardian's race, colour, sex, language, religion, political or other opinion, national, ethnic or social origin, property, disability, birth or other status.
2. States Parties shall take all appropriate measures to ensure that the child is protected against all forms of discrimination or punishment on the basis of the status, activities, expressed opinions, or beliefs of the child's parents, legal guardians, or family members.

Article 3

1. In all actions concerning children, whether undertaken by public or private social welfare institutions, courts of law, administrative authorities or legislative bodies, the best interests of the child shall be a primary consideration.
2. States Parties undertake to ensure the child such protection and care as is necessary for his or her well-being, taking into account the rights and duties of his or her parents, legal guardians, or other individuals legally responsible for him or her, and, to this end, shall take all appropriate legislative and administrative measures.
3. States Parties shall ensure that the institutions, services and facilities responsible for the care or protection of children shall conform with the standards established by competent authorities, particularly in the areas of safety, health, in the number and suitability of their staff, as well as competent supervision.

Article 4

States Parties shall undertake all appropriate legislative, administrative, and other measures for the implementation of the rights recognised in the present

Convention. With regard to economic, social and cultural rights, States Parties shall undertake such measures to the maximum extent of their available resources and, where needed, within the framework of international co-operation.

Article 5

States Parties shall respect the responsibilities, rights and duties of parents or, where applicable, the members of the extended family or community as provided for by local custom, legal guardians or other persons legally responsible for the child, to provide, in a manner consistent with the evolving capacities of the child, appropriate direction and guidance in the exercise by the child of the rights recognised in the present Convention.

Article 6

1. States Parties recognise that every child has the inherent right to life.
2. States Parties shall ensure to the maximum extent possible the survival and development of the child.

Article 7

1. The child shall be registered immediately after birth and shall have the right from birth to a name, the right to acquire a nationality and, as far as possible, the right to know and be cared for by his or her parents.
2. States Parties shall ensure the implementation of these rights in accordance with their national law and their obligations under the relevant international instruments in this field, in particular where the child would otherwise be stateless.

Article 8

1. States Parties undertake to respect the right of the child to preserve his or her identity, including nationality, name and family relations as recognised by law without unlawful interference.
2. Where a child is illegally deprived of some or all of the elements of his or her identity, States Parties shall provide appropriate assistance and protection, with a view to speedily re-establishing his or her identity.

Article 9

1. States Parties shall ensure that a child shall not be separated from his or her parents against their will, except when competent authorities subject to judicial review determine, in accordance with applicable law and procedures, that such separation is necessary for the best interests of the child. Such determination may be necessary in a particular case such as one involving abuse or neglect of the child by the parents, or one where the parents are living separately and a decision must be made as to the child's place of residence.
2. In any proceedings pursuant to paragraph 1 of the present Article, all interested parties shall be given an opportunity to participate in the proceedings and make their views known.
3. States Parties shall respect the right of the child who is separated from one or both parents to maintain personal relations and direct contact with both parents on a regular basis, except if it is contrary to the child's best interests.

4. Where such separation results from any action initiated by a State Party, such as the detention, imprisonment, exile, deportation or death (including death arising from any cause while the person is in the custody of the State) of one or both parents or of the child, that State Party shall, upon request, provide the parents, the child or, if appropriate, another member of the family with the essential information concerning the whereabouts of the absent member(s) of the family unless the provision of the information would be detrimental to the well being of the child. States Parties shall further ensure that the submission of such a request shall of itself entail no adverse consequences for the person(s) concerned.

Article 10

1. In accordance with the obligation of States Parties under Article 9, paragraph 1, applications by a child or his or her parents to enter or leave a State Party for the purpose of family reunification shall be dealt with by States Parties in a positive, humane and expeditious manner. States Parties shall further ensure that the submission of such a request shall entail no adverse consequences for the applicants and for the members of their family.
2. A child whose parents reside in different States shall have the right to maintain on a regular basis, save in exceptional circumstances personal relations and direct contacts with both parents. Towards that end and in accordance with the obligation of States Parties under Article 9, paragraph 2, States Parties shall respect the right of the child and his or her parents to leave any country, including their own, and to enter their own country. The right to leave any country shall be subject only to such restrictions as are prescribed by law and which are necessary to protect the national security, public order (*ordre public*), public health or morals or the rights and freedoms of others and are consistent with the other rights recognised in the present Convention.

Article 11

1. States Parties shall take measures to combat the illicit transfer and non-return of children abroad.
2. To this end, States Parties shall promote the conclusion of bilateral or multilateral agreements or accession to existing agreements.

Article 12

1. States Parties shall assure to the child who is capable of forming his or her own views the right to express those views freely in all matters affecting the child, the views of the child being given due weight in accordance with the age of maturity of the child.
2. For this purpose, the child shall in particular be provided the opportunity to be heard in any judicial and administrative proceedings affecting the child, either directly, or through a representative or an appropriate body, in a manner consistent with the procedural rules of national law.

Article 13

1. The child shall have the right to freedom of expression; this right shall include freedom to seek, receive and impart information and ideas of all

kinds, regardless of frontiers, either orally, in writing or in print, in the form of art, or through any other media of the child's choice.

2. The exercise of this right may be subject to certain restrictions, but these shall only be such as are provided by law and are necessary:
   (a) For respect of the rights or reputations of others; or
   (b) For the protection of national security or of public order (*ordre public*), or of public health or morals.

Article 14

1. States Parties shall respect the right of the child to freedom of thought, conscience and religion.
2. States Parties shall respect the rights and duties of the parents and, when applicable, legal guardians, to provide direction to the child in the exercise of his or her right in a manner consistent with the evolving capacities of the child.
3. Freedom to manifest one's religion or beliefs may be subject only to such limitations as are prescribed by law and are necessary to protect public safety, order, health or morals, or the fundamental rights and freedoms of others.

Article 15

1. States Parties recognise the rights of the child to freedom of association and to freedom of peaceful assembly.
2. No restrictions may be placed on the exercise of these rights other than those imposed in conformity with the law and which are necessary in a democratic society in the interests of national security or public safety, public order (*ordre public*), the protection of public health or morals or the protection of the rights and freedoms of others.

Article 16

1. No child shall be subjected to arbitrary or unlawful interference with his or her privacy, family, home or correspondence, nor to unlawful attacks on his or her honour and reputation.
2. The child has the right to the protection of the law against such interference or attacks.

Article 17

States Parties recognise the important function performed by the mass media and shall ensure that the child has access to information and material from a diversity of national and international sources, especially those aimed at the promotion of his or her social, spiritual and moral well-being and physical and mental health. To this end, States Parties shall:

(a) Encourage the mass media to disseminate information and material of social and cultural benefit to the child and in accordance with the spirit of Article 29;
(b) Encourage international co-operation in the production, exchange and dissemination of such information and material from a diversity of cultural, national and international sources;
(c) Encourage the production and dissemination of children's books;

(d) Encourage the mass media to have particular regard to the linguistic needs of the child who belongs to a minority group or who is indigenous;
(e) Encourage the development of appropriate guidelines for the protection of the child from information and material injurious to his or her well-being, bearing in mind the provisions of Articles 13 and 18.

Article 18

1. States Parties shall use their best efforts to ensure recognition of the principle that both parents have common responsibilities for the upbringing and development of the child. Parents or, as the case may be, legal guardians, have the primary responsibility for the upbringing and development of the child. The best interests of the child will be their basis concern.
2. For the purpose of guaranteeing and promoting the rights set forth in the present Convention, States Parties shall render appropriate assistance to parents and legal guardians in the performance of their child-rearing responsibilities and shall ensure the development of institutions, facilities and services for the care of children.
3. States Parties shall take all appropriate measures to ensure that children of working parents have the right to benefit from child-care services and facilities for which they are eligible.

Article 19

1. States Parties shall take all appropriate legislative, administrative, social and educational measures to protect the child from all forms of physical or mental violence, injury or abuse, neglect or negligent treatment, maltreatment or exploitation, including sexual abuse, while in the care of parent(s), legal guardian(s), or any other person who has the care of the child.
2. Such protective measures should, as appropriate, include effective procedures for the establishment of social programmes to provide necessary support for the child and for those who have the care of the child, as well as for other forms of prevention and for identification, reporting, referral, investigation, treatment and follow-up of instances of child maltreatment described heretofore, and, as appropriate, for judicial involvement.

Article 20

1. A child temporarily or permanently deprived of his or her family environment, or in whose own best interests cannot be allowed to remain in that environment, shall be entitled to special protection and assistance provided by the State.
2. States Parties shall in accordance with their national laws ensure alternative care for such a child.
3. Such care could include, *inter alia*, foster placement, *kafalah* of Islamic law, adoption or if necessary placement in suitable institutions for the care of children. When considering solutions, due regard shall be paid to the desirability of continuity in a child's upbringing and to the child's ethnic, religious, cultural and linguistic background.

Article 21

States Parties that recognise and/or permit the system of adoption shall ensure that the best interests of the child shall be the paramount consideration and they shall:

(a) Ensure that the adoption of a child is authorised only by competent authorities who determine, in accordance with applicable law and procedures and on the basis of all pertinent and reliable information, that the adoption is permissible in view of the child's status concerning parents, relatives and legal guardians and that, if required, the persons concerned have given their informed consent to the adoption on the basis of such counselling as may be necessary;

(b) Recognise that inter-country adoption may be considered as an alternative means of child's care, if the child cannot be placed in a foster or an adoptive family or cannot in any suitable manner be cared for in the child's country of origin;

(c) Ensure that the child concerned by inter-country adoption enjoys safeguards and standards equivalent to those existing in the case of national adoption;

(d) Take all appropriate measures to ensure that, in inter-country adoption, the placement does not result in improper financial gain for those involved in it;

(e) Promote, where appropriate, the objectives of the present article by concluding bilateral or multilateral arrangements or agreements, and endeavour, within this framework, to ensure that the placement of the child in another country is carried out by competent authorities or organs.

Article 22

1. States Parties shall take appropriate measures to ensure that a child who is seeking refugee status or who is considered a refugee in accordance with applicable international or domestic law and procedures shall, whether unaccompanied or accompanied by his or her parents or by any other person, receive appropriate protection and humanitarian assistance in the enjoyment of applicable rights set forth in the present Convention and in other international human rights or humanitarian instruments to which the said States are Parties.
2. For this purpose, States Parties shall provide, as they consider appropriate, co-operation in any efforts by the United Nations and other competent inter-governmental organisations or non-governmental organisations co-operating with the United Nations to protect and assist such a child and to trace the parents or other members of the family of any refugee child in order to obtain information necessary for reunification with his or her family. In cases where no parents or other members of the family can be found the child shall be accorded the same protection as any other child permanently or temporarily deprived of his or her family environment for any reason, as set forth in the present Convention.

Article 23

1. States Parties recognise that a mentally or physically disabled child should enjoy a full and decent life, in conditions which ensure dignity, promote self-reliance and facilitate the child's active participation in the community.

2. States Parties recognise the right of the disabled child to special care and shall encourage and ensure the extension, subject to available resources, to the eligible child and those responsible for his or her care, of assistance for which application is made and which is appropriate to the child's condition and to the circumstances of the parents or others caring for the child.
3. Recognising the special needs of a disabled child, assistance extended in accordance with paragraph 2 of the present article shall be provided free of charge, whenever possible, taking into account the financial resources of the parents or others caring for the child, and shall be designed to ensure that the disabled child has effective access to and receives education, training, health care services, rehabilitation services, preparation for employment and recreation opportunities in a manner conducive to the child's achieving the fullest possible social integration and individual development, including his or her cultural and spiritual development.
4. States Parties shall promote, in the spirit of international co-operation, the exchange of appropriate information in the field of preventive health care and of medical, psychological and functional treatment of disabled children, including dissemination of and access to information concerning methods of rehabilitation, education and vocational services, with the aim of enabling States Parties to improve their capabilities and skills and to widen their experience in these areas. In this regard, particular account shall be taken of the needs of developing countries.

Article 24

1. States Parties recognise the right of the child to the enjoyment of the highest attainable standard of health and to facilities for the treatment of illness and rehabilitation of health. States Parties shall strive to ensure that no child is deprived of his or her right of access to such health care services.
2. States Parties shall pursue full implementation of this right and, in particular, shall take appropriate measures:
   (a) To diminish infant and child mortality;
   (b) To ensure the provision of necessary medical assistance and health care to all children with emphasis on the development of primary health care;
   (c) To combat disease and malnutrition, including within the framework of primary health care, through, *inter alia*, the application of readily available technology and through the provision of adequate nutritious foods and clean drinking-water, taking into consideration the dangers and risks of environmental pollution;
   (d) To ensure appropriate pre-natal and post-natal health care for mothers;
   (e) To ensure that all segments of society, in particular parents and children, are informed, have access to education and are supported in the use of basic knowledge of child health and nutrition, the advantages of breast-feeding, hygiene and environmental sanitation and the prevention of accidents;
   (f) To develop preventive health care, guidance for parents and family planning education and services.
3. States Parties shall take all effective and appropriate measures with a view to abolishing traditional practices prejudicial to the health of children.

4. States Parties undertake to promote and encourage international co-operation with a view to achieving progressively the full realisation of the right recognised in the present article. In this regard, particular account shall be taken of the needs of developing countries.

Article 25

States Parties recognise the right of a child who has been placed by the competent authorities for the purposes of care, protection or treatment of his or her physical or mental health, to a periodic review of the treatment provided to the child and all other circumstances relevant to his or her placement.

Article 26

1. States Parties shall recognise for every child the right to benefit from social security, including social insurance, and shall take the necessary measures to achieve the full realisation of this right in accordance with their national law.
2. The benefits should, where appropriate, be granted, taking into account the resources and the circumstances of the child and persons having responsibility for the maintenance of the child, as well as any other consideration relevant to an application for benefits made by or on behalf of the child.

Article 27

1. States Parties recognise the right of every child to a standard of living adequate for the child's physical, mental, spiritual, moral and social development.
2. The parent(s) or others responsible for the child have the primary responsibility to secure, within their abilities and financial capacities, the conditions of living necessary for the child's development.
3. States Parties, in accordance with national conditions and within their means, shall take appropriate measures to assist parents and others responsible for the child to implement this right and shall in case of need provide material assistance and support programmes, particularly with regard to nutrition, clothing and housing.
4. States Parties shall take all appropriate measures to secure the recovery of maintenance for the child from the parents or other persons having financial responsibility for the child, both within the State Party and from abroad. In particular, where the person having financial responsibility for the child lives in a State different from that of the child, States Parties shall promote the accession to international agreements or the conclusion of such agreements, as well as the making of other appropriate arrangements.

Article 28

1. States Parties recognise the right of the child to education, and with a view to achieving this right progressively and on the basis of equal opportunity, they shall, in particular:
   (a) Make primary education compulsory and available free to all;
   (b) Encourage the development of different forms of secondary education, including general and vocational education, make them available

and accessible to every child, and take appropriate measures such as the introduction of free education and offering financial assistance in case of need;

(c) Make higher education accessible to all on the basis of capacity by every appropriate means;

(d) Make educational and vocational information and guidance available and accessible to all children;

(e) Take measures to encourage regular attendance at schools and the reduction of drop-out rates.

2. States Parties shall take all appropriate measures to ensure that school discipline is administered in a manner consistent with the child's human dignity and in conformity with the present Convention.

3. States Parties shall promote and encourage international co operation in matters relating to education, in particular with a view to contributing to the elimination of ignorance and illiteracy throughout the world and facilitating access to scientific and technical knowledge and modern teaching methods. In this regard, particular account shall be taken of the needs of developing countries.

Article 29

1. States Parties agree that the education of the child shall be directed to:

(a) The development of the child's personality, talents and mental and physical abilities to their fullest potential;

(b) The development of respect for human rights and fundamental freedoms, and for the principles enshrined in the Charter of the United Nations;

(c) The development of respect for the child's parents, his or her own cultural identity, language and values, for the national values of the country in which the child is living, the country from which he or she may originate, and for civilisations different from his or her own;

(d) The preparation of the child for responsible life in a free society, in the spirit of understanding, peace, tolerance, equality of sexes, and friendship among all peoples, ethnic, national and religious groups and persons of indigenous origin;

(e) The development of respect for the natural environment.

2. No part of the present Article or Article 28 shall be construed so as to interfere with the liberty of individuals and bodies to establish and direct educational institutions, subject always to the observance of the principles set forth in paragraph 1 of the present Article and to the requirements that the education given in such institutions shall conform to such minimum standards as may be laid down by the State.

Article 30

In those States in which ethnic, religious or linguistic minorities or persons of indigenous origin exist, a child belonging to such a minority or who is indigenous shall not be denied the right, in community with other members of his or her group, to enjoy his or her own culture, to profess and practise his or her own religion, or to use his or her own language.

Article 31

1. States Parties recognise the right of the child to rest and leisure, to engage in play and recreational activities appropriate to the age of the child and to participate freely in cultural life and the arts.
2. States Parties shall respect and promote the right of the child to participate full in cultural and artistic life and shall encourage the provision of appropriate and equal opportunities for cultural, artistic, recreational and leisure activity.

Article 32

1. States Parties recognise the right of the child to be protected from economic exploitation and from performing any work that is likely to be hazardous or to interfere with the child's education, or to be harmful to the child's health or physical, mental, spiritual, moral or social development.
2. States Parties shall take legislative, administrative, social and educational measures to ensure the implementation of the present article. To this end, and having regard to the relevant provisions of other international instruments, States Parties shall in particular:
   (a) Provide for a minimum age or minimum ages for admission to employment;
   (b) Provide for appropriate regulation of the hours and conditions of employment;
   (c) Provide for appropriate penalties or other sanctions to ensure the effective enforcement of the present article.

Article 33

States Parties shall take all appropriate measures, including legislative, administrative, social and educational measures, to protect children from the illicit use of narcotic drugs and psychotropic substances as defined in the relevant international treaties, and to prevent the use of children in the illicit production and trafficking of such substances.

Article 34

States Parties undertake to protect the child from all forms of sexual exploitation and sexual abuse. For these purposes, States Parties shall in particular take all appropriate national, bilateral and multilateral measures to prevent:

(a) The inducement or coercion of a child to engage in any unlawful sexual activity;
(b) The exploitative use of children in prostitution or other unlawful sexual practices;
(c) The exploitative use of children in pornographic performances and materials.

Article 35

States Parties shall take all appropriate national, bilateral and multilateral measures to prevent the abduction of, the sale of or traffic in children for any purpose or in any form.

Article 36

States Parties shall protect the child against all other forms of exploitation prejudicial to any aspects of the child's welfare.

Article 37

States Parties shall ensure that:

(a) No child shall be subjected to torture or other cruel, inhuman or degrading treatment or punishment. Neither capital punishment nor life imprisonment without possibility of release shall be imposed for offences committed by persons below eighteen years of age;

(b) No child shall be deprived of his or her liberty unlawfully or arbitrarily. The arrest, detention or imprisonment of a child shall be in conformity with the law and shall be used only as a measure of last resort and for the shortest appropriate period of time;

(c) Every child deprived of liberty shall be treated with humanity and respect for the inherent dignity of the human person, and in a manner which takes into account the needs of persons of his or her age. In particular, every child deprived of liberty shall be separated from adults unless it is considered in the child's best interest not to do so and shall have the right to maintain contact with his or her family through correspondence and visits, save in exceptional circumstances;

(d) Every child deprived of his or her liberty shall have the right to prompt access to legal and other appropriate assistance, as well as the right to challenge the legality of the deprivation of his or her liberty before a court or other competent, independent and impartial authority, and to a prompt decision on any such action.

Article 38

1. States Parties undertake to respect and to ensure report for rules of international humanitarian law applicable to them in armed conflicts which are relevant to the child.
2. States Parties shall take all feasible measures to ensure that persons who have not attained the age of fifteen years do not take a direct part in hostilities.
3. States Parties shall refrain from recruiting any person who has not attained the age of fifteen years into their armed forces. In recruiting among those persons who have attained the age of fifteen years but who have not attained the age of eighteen years, States Parties shall endeavour to give priority to those who are oldest.
4. In accordance with their obligations under international humanitarian law to protect the civilian population in armed conflicts, States Parties shall take all feasible measures to ensure protection and care of children who are affected by an armed conflict.

Article 39

States Parties shall take all appropriate measures to promote physical and psychological recovery and social reintegration of a child victim of: any form of neglect, exploitation, or abuse; torture or any other form of cruel, inhuman or degrading treatment or punishment; or armed conflicts. Such recovery and reintegration shall take place in an environment which fosters the health, self-respect and dignity of the child.

Article 40

1. States Parties recognise the right of every child alleged as, accused of, or recognised as having infringed the penal law to be treated in a manner consistent with the promotion of the child's sense of dignity and worth, which reinforces the child's respect for the human rights and fundamental freedoms of others and which takes into account the child's age and the desirability of promoting the child's reintegration and the child's assuming a constructive role in society.
2. To this end, and having regard to the relevant provisions of international instruments, States Parties shall, in particular, ensure that:
   (a) No child shall be alleged as, be accused of, or recognised as having infringed the penal law by reason of acts or omissions that were not prohibited by national or international law at the time they were committed;
   (b) Every child alleged as or accused of having infringed the penal law has at least the following guarantees:
      (i) To be presumed innocent until proven guilty according to law;
      (ii) To be informed promptly and directly of the charges against him or her, and, if appropriate, through his or her parents or legal guardians, and to have legal or other appropriate assistance in the preparation and presentation of his or her defence;
      (iii) To have the matter determined without delay by a competent, independent and impartial authority or judicial body in a fair hearing according to law, in the presence of legal or other appropriate assistance and, unless it is considered not to be in the best interest of the child, in particular, taking into account his or her age or situation, his or her parents or legal guardians;
      (iv) Not to be compelled to give testimony or to confess guilt; to examine or have examined adverse witnesses and to obtain the participation and examination of witnesses on his or her behalf under conditions of equality;
      (v) If considered to have infringed the penal law, to have this decision and any measures imposed in consequence thereof reviewed by a higher competent, independent and impartial authority or judicial body according to law;
      (vi) To have the free assistance of an interpreter if the child cannot understand or speak the language used;
      (vii) To have his or her privacy fully respected at all stages of the proceedings.
3. States Parties shall seek to promote the establishment of laws, procedures, authorities and institutions specifically applicable to children alleged as, accused of, or recognised as having infringed the penal law, and, in particular:
   (a) The establishment of a minimum age below which children shall be presumed not to have the capacity to infringe the penal law;
   (b) Whenever appropriate and desirable, measures for dealing with such children without resorting to judicial proceedings, providing that human rights and legal safeguards are fully respected.

4. A variety of dispositions, such as care, guidance and supervision orders; counselling; probation; foster care; education and vocational training programmes and other alternatives to institutional care shall be available to ensure that children are dealt with in a manner appropriate to their well-being and proportionate both to their circumstances and the offence.

Article 41

Nothing in the present Convention shall affect any provisions which are more conducive to the realisation of the rights of the child and which may be contained in:

(a) The law of a State Party; or
(b) International law in force for that State.

PART II

Article 42

States Parties undertake to make the principles and provisions of the Convention widely known, by appropriate and active means, to adults and children alike.

Article 43

1. For the purpose of examining the progress made by States Parties in achieving the realisation of the obligations undertaken in the present Convention, there shall be established a Committee on the Rights of the Child, which shall carry out the functions hereinafter provided.
2. The Committee shall consist of ten experts of high moral standing and recognised competence in the field covered by this Convention. The members of the Committee shall be elected by States Parties from among their nationals and shall serve in the personal capacity, consideration being given to equitable geographical distribution, as well as to the principal legal systems.
3. The members of the Committee shall be elected by secret ballot from a list of persons nominated by States Parties. Each State Party may nominate one person from among its own nationals.
4. The initial election to the Committee shall be held no later than six months after the date of the entry into force of the present Convention and thereafter every second year. At least four months before the date of each election, the Secretary-General of the United Nations shall address a letter to State Parties inviting them to submit their nominations within two months. The Secretary-General shall subsequently prepare a list in alphabetical order of all persons thus nominated, indicating States Parties which have nominated them, and shall submit it to the States Parties to the present Convention.
5. The elections shall be held at meetings of States Parties convened by the Secretary-General at United Nations Headquarters. At those meetings, for which two thirds of States Parties shall constitute a quorum, the persons elected to the Committee shall be those who obtain the largest number of votes and an absolute majority of the votes of the representatives of States Parties present and voting.

6. The members of the Committee shall be elected for a term of four years. They shall be eligible for re-election if renominated. The term of five of the members elected at the first election shall expire at the end of two years; immediately after the first election; the names of these five members shall be chosen by lot by the Chairman of the meeting.
7. If a member of the Committee dies or resigns or declares that for any other cause he or she can no longer perform the duties of the Committee, the State Party which nominated the member shall appoint another expert from among its nationals to serve for the remainder of the term, subject to the approval of the Committee.
8. The Committee shall establish its own rules of procedure.
9. The Committee shall elect its officers for a period of two years.
10. The meetings of the Committee shall normally be held at United Nations Headquarters or at any other convenient place as determined by the Committee. The Committee shall normally meet annually. The duration of the meetings of the Committee shall be determined, and reviewed, if necessary, by a meeting of the States Parties to the present Convention, subject to the approval of the General Assembly.
11. The Secretary-General of the United Nations shall provide the necessary staff and facilities for the effective performance of the functions of the Committee under the present Convention.
12. With the approval of the General Assembly, the members of the Committee established under the present Convention shall receive emoluments from United Nations resources on such terms and conditions as the Assembly may decide.

Article 44

1. States Parties undertake to submit to the Committee, through the Secretary-General of the United Nations, reports on the measures they have adopted which give effect to the rights recognised herein and on the progress made on the enjoyment of those rights:
   (a) Within two years of the entry into force of the Convention for the State Party concerned;
   (b) Thereafter every five years.
2. Reports made under the present Article shall indicate factors and difficulties, if any, affecting the degree of fulfilment of the obligations under the present Convention. Reports shall also contain sufficient information to provide the Committee with a comprehensive understanding of the implementation of the Convention in the country concerned.
3. A State Party which has submitted a comprehensive initial report to the Committee need not, in its subsequent reports submitted in accordance with paragraph 1(b) of the present Article, repeat basic information previously provided.
4. The Committee may request from States Parties further information relevant to the implementation of the Convention.
5. The Committee shall submit to the General Assembly, through the Economic and Social Council, every two years, reports on its activities.
6. States Parties shall make their reports widely available to the public in their own countries.

Article 45

In order to foster the effective implementation of the Convention and to encourage international co-operation in the field covered by the Convention:

(a) The specialised agencies, the United Nations Children's Fund, and other United Nations organs shall be entitled to be represented at the consideration of the implementation of such provisions of the present Convention as fall within the scope of their mandate. The Committee may invite the specialised agencies, the United Nations Children's Fund and other competent bodies as it may consider appropriate to provide expert advice on the implementation of the Convention in areas falling within the scope of their respective mandates. The Committee may invite the specialised agencies, the United Nations Children's Fund, and other United Nations organs to submit reports on the implementation of the Convention in areas falling within the scope of their activities;

(b) The Committee shall transmit, as it may consider appropriate, to the specialised agencies, the United nations Children's Fund and other competent bodies, any reports from States Parties that contain a request, or indicate a need, for technical advice or assistance, along with the Committee's observations and suggestions, if any, on these requests or indications;

(c) The Committee may recommend to the General Assembly to request the Secretary-General to undertake on its behalf studies on specific issues relating to the rights of the child;

(d) The Committee may make suggestions and general recommendations based on information received pursuant to Articles 44 and 45 of the present Convention. Such suggestions and general recommendations shall be transmitted to any State Party concerned and reported to the General Assembly, together with comments, if any, from States Parties.

PART III

Article 46

The present Convention shall be open for signature by all States.

Article 47

The present Convention is subject to ratification. Instruments of ratification shall be deposited with the Secretary-General of the United Nations.

Article 48

The present Convention shall remain open for accession by any States. The instruments of accession shall be deposited with the Secretary-General of the United Nations.

Article 49

1. The present Convention shall enter into force on the thirtieth day following the date of deposit with the Secretary-General of the United Nations of the twentieth instrument of ratification or accession.

2. For each State ratifying or acceding to the Convention after the deposit of the twentieth instrument of ratification or accession, the Convention shall enter into force on the thirtieth day after the deposit by such State of its instrument of ratification or accession.

Article 50

1. Any State Party may propose an amendment and file it with the Secretary-General of the United Nations. The Secretary-General shall thereupon communicate the proposed amendment to States Parties, with a request that they indicate whether they favour a conference of States Parties for the purpose of considering and voting upon the proposals. In the event that, within four months from the date of such communication, at least one third of the States Parties favour such a conference, the Secretary-General shall convene the conference under the auspices of the United Nations. Any amendment adopted by a majority of States Parties present and voting at the conference shall be submitted to the General Assembly for approval.
2. An amendment adopted in accordance with paragraph 1 of the present article shall enter into force when it has been approved by the General Assembly of the United Nations and accepted by a two-thirds majority of States Parties.
3. When an amendment enters into force, it shall be binding on those States Parties which have accepted it, other States Parties still being bound by the provisions of the present Convention and any earlier amendments which they have accepted.

Article 51

1. The Secretary-General of the United Nations shall receive and circulate to all States the text of reservations made by States at the time of ratification or accession.
2. A reservation incompatible with the object and purpose of the present Convention shall not be permitted.
3. Reservations may be withdrawn at any time by notification to that effect addressed to the Secretary-General of the United Nations, who shall then inform all States. Such notification shall take effect on the date on which it is received by the Secretary-General.

Article 52

A State Party may denounce the present Convention by written notification to the Secretary-General of the United Nations. Denunciation becomes effective one year after the date of receipt of the notification by the Secretary-General.

Article 53

The Secretary-General of the United Nations is designated as the depositary of the present Convention.

Article 54

The original of the present Convention, of which the Arabic, Chinese, English, French, Russian and Spanish texts are equally authentic, shall be deposited with the Secretary-General of the United Nations.

In witness thereof the undersigned plenipotentiaries, being duly authorised thereto by their respective Governments, have signed the present Convention.

International Covenant on Economic, Social and Cultural Rights 1966

Entry into force: 3 January 1966

Article 10

The States Parties to the present Covenant recognize that:

1. The widest possible protection and assistance should be accorded to the family, which is the natural and fundamental group unit of society, particularly for its establishment and while it is responsible for the care and education of dependent children. Marriage must be entered into with the free consent of the intending spouses.
2. Special protection should be accorded to mothers during a reasonable period and after childbirth. During such period working mothers should be accorded paid leave or leave with adequate social security benefits.
3. Special measures of protection and assistance should be taken on behalf of all children and young persons without any discrimination for reasons of parentage or other conditions. Children and young persons should be protected from economic and social exploitation. Their employment in work harmful to their morals or health or dangerous to life or likely to hamper their normal development should be punishable by law. States should also set age limits below which the paid employment of child labour should be prohibited and punishable by law.

Article 12

1. The States Parties to the present Covenant recognize the right of everyone to the enjoyment of the highest attainable standard of physical and mental health.
2. The steps to be taken by the States Parties to the present Covenant to achieve the full realization of this right shall include those necessary for:
   (a) The provision for the reduction of the stillbirth-rate and of infant mortality and for the healthy development of the child;
   (b) The improvement of all aspects of environmental and industrial hygiene;
   (c) The prevention, treatment and control of epidemic, endemic, occupational and other diseases;
   (d) The creation of conditions which would assure to all medical service and medical attention in the event of sickness.

Article 13

1. The State Parties to the present Covenant recognize the right of everyone to education. They agree that education shall be directed to the full development of the human personality and the sense of its dignity, and shall strengthen the respect for human rights and fundamental freedoms. They further agree that education shall enable all persons to participate effectively in a free society, promote understanding, tolerance and friendship among all nations and all racial, ethnic or religious groups, and further the activities of the United Nations for the maintenance of peace.
2. The States Parties to the present Covenant recognize that, with a view to achieving the full realization of this right:

(a) Primary education shall be compulsory and available free to all;
(b) Secondary education in its different forms, including technical and vocational secondary education, shall be made generally available and accessible to all by every appropriate means, and in particular by the progressive introduction of free education;
(c) Higher education shall be made equally accessible to all, on the basis of capacity, by every appropriate means, and in particular by the progressive introduction of free education;
(d) Fundamental education shall be encouraged or intensified as far as possible for those persons who have not received or completed the whole period of their primary education;
(e) The development of a system of schools at all levels shall be actively pursued, an adequate fellowship system shall be established, and the material conditions of teaching staff shall be continuously improved.

3. The States Parties to the present Covenant undertake to have respect for the liberty of parents and, when applicable, legal guardians to choose for their children schools, other than those established by the public authorities, which conform to such minimum educational standards as may be laid down or approved by the State and to ensure the religious and moral education of their children in conformity with their own convictions.
4. No part of this article shall be construed so as to interfere with the liberty of individuals and bodies to establish and direct educational institutions, subject always to the observance of the principles set forth in paragraph 1 of this article and to the requirement that the education given in such institutions shall conform to such minimum standards as may be laid down by the State.

Article 14

Each State Party to the present Covenant which, at the time of becoming a Party, has not been able to secure in its metropolitan territory or other territories under its jurisdiction compulsory primary education, free of charge, undertakes, within two years, to work out and adopt a detailed plan of action for the progressive implementation, within a reasonable number of years, to be fixed in the plan of the principle of compulsory education free of charge for all.

Additional Protocol to the American Convention on Human Rights in the area of Economic, Social and Cultural Rights 1988 ("Protocol of San Salvador")

Article 13: Right to education

1. Everyone has the right to education.
2. The States Parties to this Protocol agree that education should be directed towards the full development of the human personality and human dignity and should strengthen respect for human rights, ideological pluralism, fundamental freedoms, justice and peace. They further agree that education ought to enable everyone to participate effectively in a democratic and pluralistic society and achieve a decent existence and should foster understanding, tolerance and friendship among all nations and all racial, ethnic or religious groups and promote activities for the maintenance of peace.
3. The States Parties to this Protocol recognize that in order to achieve the full exercise of the right to education:
   (a) primary education should be compulsory and accessible to all without cost;
   (b) secondary education in its different forms, including technical and vocational secondary education, should be made generally available and accessible to all by every appropriate means, and in particular, by the progressive introduction of free education;
   (e) programs of special education should be established for the handicapped, so as to provide special instruction and training to persons with physical disabilities or mental deficiencies.
4. In conformity with the domestic legislation of the States Parties, parents should have the right to select the type of education to be given to their children, provided that it conforms to the principles set forth above.
5. Nothing in this Protocol shall be interpreted as a restriction of the freedom of individuals and entities to establish and direct educational institutions in accordance with the domestic legislation of the States Parties.

Protocol No. 1 to the Convention for the Protection of Human Rights and Fundamental Freedoms, 1952

Entry into force: 18 May 1954.

Article 2

No person shall be denied the right to education. In the exercise of any functions which it assumes in relation to education and to teaching, the State shall respect the right of parents to ensure such education and teaching in conformity with their own religious and philosophical convictions.

Protocol No. 7 to the Convention for the Protection of Human Rights and Fundamental Freedoms, 1984

Entry into force: 1 November 1988.

Article 5

Spouses shall enjoy equality of rights and responsibilities of a private law character between them, and in their relations with their children, as to marriage, during marriage and in the event of its dissolution. This Article shall not prevent States from taking such measures as are necessary in the interests of the children.

International Convention for the Suppression of the Traffic in Women and Children 1921 as amended by 1947 Protocol

Article 1

The High Contracting Parties agree that, in the event of their not being already Parties to the Agreement of May 18, 1904, and not being already Parties to the Agreement of May, 1904, and the Convention of May 4, 1910, mentioned above they will transmit, with the least possible delay, their ratification of, or adhesions to instruments in the manner laid down therein.

Article 2

The High Contracting Parties agree to take all measures to discover and prosecute persons who are engaged in the traffic in children of both sexes and who commit offences within the meaning of Article 1 of the Convention of May 4, 1910.

Article 3

The High Contracting Parties agree to take the necessary steps to secure ???ment of attempts to commit, and within legal limits, of acts preparatory to the commission of the offences specified in Articles 1 and 2 of the Convention of May 4, 1910.

Article 4

The High Contracting Parties agree that, in cases where there are no extradition conventions in force between them, they will take all measures within their power to extradite or provide for the extradition of persons accused or convicted of the offences specified in Articles 1 and 2 of the Convention of May 4, 1910.

Article 5

In paragraph B of the Final Protocol of the Convention of 1910, the words "twenty completed years of age" shall be replaced by the words "twenty-one completed years of age".

Article 6

The High Contracting Parties agree, in case they have not already taken legislative or administrative measures regarding licensing and supervision of employment agencies and offices, to prescribe such regulations as are required to secure the protection of women and children seeking employment in another country.

Article 7

The High Contracting Parties undertake in connection with immigration and emigration to adopt such administrative and legislative measures as are required to check the traffic in women and children. In particular, they undertake to make such regulations as are required for the protection of women and children travelling on emigrant ships, not only at the points of departure and arrival, but also during the journey and to arrange for the exhibition, in railway stations and in ports, of notices warning women and children of the danger of the traffic and indicating the places where they can obtain accommodation and assistance.

Article 8

The present Convention, of which the French and the English texts are both authentic, shall bear this day's date, and shall be open for signature until March 31, 1922.

Article 9

The present Convention is subject to ratification. As from 1 January 1948 instruments of ratification shall be transmitted to the Secretary-General of the United Nations, who will notify the receipt of them to Members of the United Nations and to non-member States to which the Secretary-General has communicated a copy of the Convention. The instruments of ratification shall be deposited in the archives of the Secretariat of the United Nations.

In order to comply with the provisions of Article 18 of the Covenant of the League of Nations, the Secretary-General will register the present Convention upon the deposit of the first ratification.

Article 10

Members of the United Nations may acceede to the present Convention.

The same applies to non-member States to which the Economic and Social Council of the United Nations may decide officially to communicate the present Convention.

Accession will be noted to the Secretary-General of the United Nations, who will notify all Members of the United Nations and the non-member States to which the Secretary-General has communicated a copy of the Convention.

Article 11

The present Convention shall come into force in respect of each Party on the date of the deposit of its ratification or act of accession.

Article 12

The present Convention may be denounced by any State which is a Party thereto, on giving twelve months' notice of its intention to denounce.

Denunciation shall be effected by notification in writing addressed to the Secretary-General of the United Nations. Copies of such notification shall be transmitted forthwith by him to all Members of the United Nations and to non-member States to which the Secretary-General has communicated a copy of the Convention. The denunciation shall take effect one year after the date on which it was notified to the Secretary-General of the United Nations, and shall operate only in respect of the notifying Power.

Article 13

A special record shall be kept by the Secretary-General of the United Nations, showing which of the parties have signed, ratified, acceded to or denounced the present Convention. This record shall be open at all times to any Member of the United Nations or any non-member State to which the Secretary-General has communicated a copy of the Convention; it shall be published as often as possible, in accordance with the directions of the Economic and Social Council of the United Nations.

International Convention on the Protection of the Rights of all Migrant Workers and their Families, 1990

PART 1

SCOPE AND DEFINITIONS

Article 1

1. The present Convention is applicable, except as otherwise provided hereafter, to all migrant workers and members of their families without distinction of any kind such as sex, race, colour, language, religion or conviction, political or other opinion, national, ethnic or social origin, nationality, age, economic position, property, marital status, birth or other status.
2. The present Convention shall apply during the entire migration process of migrant workers and members of their families, which comprises preparation for migration, departure, transit and the entire period of stay and remunerated activity in the State of employment as well as return to the State of origin or the State of habitual residence.

PART II

NON-DISCRIMINATION WITH RESPECT TO RIGHTS

Article 7

States Parties undertake, in accordance with the international instruments concerning human rights, to respect and to ensure to all migrant workers and members of their families within their territory or subject to their jurisdiction the rights provided for in the present Convention without distinction of any kind such as sex, race, colour, language, religion or conviction, political or other opinion, national ethnic or social origin, nationality, age, economic position, property, marital status, birth or other status.

PART III

HUMAN RIGHTS OF ALL MIGRANT WORKERS AND MEMBERS OF THEIR FAMILIES

Article 8

1. Migrant workers and members of their families shall be free to leave any State, including their State of origin. This right shall not be subject to any restrictions except those that are provided by law, are necessary to protect national security, public order (*ordre public*), public health or morals or the rights and freedoms of others and are consistent with the other rights recognized in this Part of the Convention.
2. Migrant workers and members of their families shall have the right at any time to enter and remain in their State of origin.

Article 9

The right of life of migrant workers and members of their families shall be protected by law.

Article 10

No migrant worker or member of his or her family shall be subjected to torture or to cruel, inhuman or degrading treatment or punishment.

Article 11

1. No migrant worker or member of his or her family shall be held in slavery or servitude.
2. No migrant worker or member of his or her family shall be required to perform forced or compulsory labour.
3. Paragraph 2 of this Article shall not be held to preclude, in States where imprisonment with hard labour may be imposed as a punishment for a crime, the performance of hard labour in pursuance of a sentence to such punishment by a competent court.
4. For the purpose of this Article the term 'forced or compulsory labour' shall not include:
   (a) Any work or service not referred to in paragraph 3 of this Article normally required of a person who is under detention in consequence of a lawful order of a court or of a person during conditional release from such detention;
   (b) Any service exacted in cases of emergency or calamity threatening the life or well-being of the community;
   (c) Any work or service that forms part of normal civil obligations so far as it is imposed also on citizens of the State concerned.

Article 12

1. Migrant workers and members of their families shall have the right to freedom of thought, conscience and religion. This right shall include freedom to have or to adopt a religion or belief of their choice and freedom either individually or in community with others and in public or private to manifest their religion or belief in worship, observance, practice and teaching.
2. Migrant workers and members of their families shall not be subject to coercion that would impair their freedom to have or to adopt a religion or belief of their choice.
3. Freedom to manifest one's religion or belief may be subject only to such limitations as are prescribed by law and are necessary to protect public safety order, health or morals or the fundamental rights and freedoms of others.
4. States Parties to the present Convention undertake to have respect for the liberty of parents, at least one of whom is a migrant worker, and, when applicable, legal guardians to ensure the religious and moral education of their children in conformity with their own convictions.

Article 13

1. Migrant workers and members of their families shall have the right to hold opinions without interference.

2. Migrant workers and members of their families shall have the right to freedom of expression; this right shall include freedom to seek, receive and impart information and ideas of all kinds, regardless of frontiers, either orally, in writing or in print, in the form of art or through any other media of their choice.
3. The exercise of the rights provided for in paragraph 2 of this Article carries with it special duties and responsibilities. It may therefore be subject to certain restrictions, but these shall only be such as are provided by law and are necessary:
   (a) For respect of the rights or reputation of others;
   (b) For the protection of the national security of the States concerned or of public order (*ordre public*) or of public health or morals;
   (c) For the purpose of preventing any propaganda for war;
   (d) For the purpose of preventing any advocacy of national, racial or religious hatred that constitutes incitement to discrimination, hostility or violence.

Article 14

No migrant worker or member of his or her family shall be subjected to arbitrary or unlawful interference with his or her privacy, family, home, correspondence or other communications, or to unlawful attacks on his or her honour and reputation. Each migrant worker and member of his or her family shall have the right to the protection of the law against such interference or attacks.

Article 15

No migrant worker or member of his or her family shall be arbitrarily deprived of property, whether owned individually or in association with others. Where, under the legislation in force in the State of employment, the assets of a migrant worker or a member of his or her family are expropriated in whole or in part, the person concerned shall have the right to fair and adequate compensation.

Article 16

1. Migrant workers and members of their families shall have the right to liberty and security of person.
2. Migrant workers and members of their families shall be entitled to effective protection by the State against violence, physical injury, threats and intimidation, whether by public officials or by private individuals, groups or institutions.
3. Any verification by law enforcement officials of the identity of migrant workers or members of their families shall be carried out in accordance with procedures established by law.
4. Migrant workers and members of their families shall not be subjected individually or collectively to arbitrary arrest or detention; they shall not be deprived of their liberty except on such grounds and in accordance with such procedures as are established by law.
5. Migrant workers and members of their families who are arrested shall be informed at the time of arrest as far as possible in a language they understand of the reasons for their arrest and they shall be promptly informed in a language they understand of any charges against them.

6. Migrant workers and members of their families who are arrested or detained on a criminal charge shall be brought promptly before a judge or other officer authorized by law to exercise judicial power and shall be entitled to trial within a reasonable time or to release. It shall not be the general rule that while awaiting trial they shall be detained in custody, but release may be subject to guarantees to appear for trial, at any other stage of the judicial proceedings and, should the occasion arise, for the execution of the judgment.
7. When a migrant worker or a member of his or her family is arrested or committed to prison or custody pending trial or is detained in any other manner:
   (a) The consular or diplomatic authorities of his or her State of origin or of a State representing the interests of that State shall, if he or she so requests, be informed without delay of his or her arrest or detention and of the reasons therefor;
   (b) The person concerned shall have the right to communicate with the said authorities. Any communication by the person concerned to the said authorities shall be forwarded without delay, and he or she shall also have the right to receive communications sent by the said authorities without delay;
   (c) The person concerned shall be informed without delay of this right and of rights deriving from relevant treaties, if any, applicable between the States concerned, to correspond and to meet with representatives of the said authorities and to make arrangements with them for his or her legal representation.
8. Migrant workers and members of their families who are deprived of their liberty by arrest or detention shall be entitled to take proceedings before a court, in order that that court may decide without delay on the lawfulness of their detention and order their release if the detention is not lawful. When they attend such proceedings, they shall have the assistance, if necessary without cost to them, of an interpreter, if they cannot understand or speak the language used.
9. Migrant workers and members of their families who have been victims of unlawful arrest or detention shall have an enforceable right to compensation.

Article 17

1. Migrant workers and members of their families who are deprived of their liberty shall be treated with humanity and with respect for the inherent dignity of the human person and for their cultural identity.
2. Accused migrant workers and members of their families shall, save in exceptional circumstances, be separated from convicted persons and shall be subject to separate treatment appropriate to their status as unconvicted persons. Accused juvenile persons shall be separated from adults and brought as speedily as possible for adjudication.
3. Any migrant worker or a member of his or her family who is detained in a site of transit or in a State of employment for violation of provisions relating to migration, shall be held, in so far as practicable, separately from convicted persons or persons detained pending trial.
4. During any period of imprisonment in pursuance of a sentence imposed by a court of law, the essential aim of the treatment of a migrant worker or a

member of his or her family shall be his or her reformation and social rehabilitation. Juvenile offenders shall be separated from adults and be accorded treatment appropriate to their age and legal status.

5. During detention or imprisonment, migrant workers and members of their families shall enjoy the same rights as nationals to visits by members of their families.
6. Whenever a migrant worker is deprived of his or her liberty, the competent authorities of the State concerned shall pay attention to the problems that may be posed for members of his or her family, in particular for spouses and minor children.
7. Migrant workers and members of their families who are subjected to any form of detention or imprisonment in accordance with the law in force in the State of employment or in the State of transit shall enjoy the same rights as nationals of those States who are in the same situation.
8. If a migrant worker or a member of his or her family is detained for the purpose of verifying any infraction of provisions related to migration, he or she shall not bear any costs arising therefrom.

Article 18

1. Migrant workers and members of their families shall have the right to equality with nationals of the State concerned before the courts and tribunals. In the determination of any criminal charge against them or of their rights and obligations in a suit of law, they shall be entitled to a fair and public hearing by a competent, independent and impartial tribunal established by law.
2. Migrant workers and members of their families who are charged with a Criminal offence shall have the right to be presumed innocent until proven guilty according to law.
3. In the determination of any criminal charge against them, migrant workers or members of their families shall be entitled to the following minimum guarantee
   (a) To be informed promptly and in detail in a language they understand of the nature and cause of the charge against them;
   (b) To have adequate time and facilities for the preparation of their defence and to communicate with counsel of their own choosing;
   (c) To be tried without undue delay;
   (d) To be tried in their presence and to defend themselves in person or through legal assistance of their own choosing; to be informed, if they do not have legal assistance, of this right; and to have legal assistance assigned to them in any case where the interests of justice so require and without payment by them in any such case if they do not have sufficient means to pay for it;
   (e) To examine or have examined the witnesses against them and to obtain attendance and examination of witnesses on their behalf under the same conditions as witnesses against them;
   (f) To have the free assistance of an interpreter if they cannot understand or speak the language used in court;
   (g) Not to be compelled to testify against themselves or to confess guilt.

4. In the case of juvenile persons, the procedure shall be such as will take account of their age and the desirability of promoting their rehabilitation.
5. Migrant workers and members of their families convicted of a crime have the right to their conviction and sentence being reviewed by a higher tribunal according to law.
6. When a migrant worker or member of his or her family has, by a decision, been convicted of a criminal offence and when subsequently his conviction has been reversed or he or she has been pardoned on the ground that a new or newly discovered fact shows conclusively that there has been a miscarriage of justice, the person who has suffered punishment as a result of such conviction shall be compensated according to law, unless it is proved that the non-discovery of the unknown fact in time is wholly or partly attributable to that person.
7. No migrant worker or member of his or her family shall be liable to be punished again for an offence for which he or she has already been finally cotnvicted or acquitted in accordance with the law and penal procedure of the State concerned.

Article 19

1. No migrant worker or member of his or her family shall be held guilty of criminal offence on account of any act or omission that did not constitute a criminal offence under national or international law at the time when the criminal offence was committed, nor shall a heavier penalty be imposed than the one applicable at the time when it was committed. If, subsequent to the commission of the offence, provision is made by law for the imposition of a lighter penalty she shall benefit thereby.
2. Humanitarian considerations related to the status of a migrant worker in particular with respect to his or her right of residence or work, should be taken into account in imposing a sentence for a criminal offence committed by a migrant worker or a member of his or her family.

Article 20

1. No migrant worker or member of his or her family shall be imprisoned merely on the ground of failure to fulfil a contractual obligation.
2. No migrant worker or member of his or her family shall be deprived of his or her authorization of residence or work permit or expelled merely on the ground of failure to fulfil an obligation arising out of a work contract unless fulfilment of that obligation constitutes a condition for such authorization or permit.

Article 21

It shall be unlawful for anyone, other than a public official duly authorized by law, to confiscate, destroy or attempt to destroy identity documents, documents authorizing entry to or stay, residence or establishment in the national territory or work permits. No authorized confiscation of such documents shall take place without delivery of a detailed receipt. In no case shall it be permitted to destroy the passport or equivalent document of a migrant worker or a member of his or her family.

Article 22

1. Migrant workers and members of their families shall not be subject to measures of collective expulsion. Each case of expulsion shall be examined and decided individually.
2. Migrant workers and members of their families may be expelled from the territory of a State Party only in pursuance of a decision taken by the competent authority in accordance with law.
3. The decision shall be communicated to them in a language they understand. Upon their request where not otherwise mandatory, the decision shall be communicated to them in writing and, save in exceptional circumstances on account of national security, the reasons for the decision likewise stated. The persons concerned shall be informed of these rights before or at the latest at the time the decision is rendered.
4. Except where a final decision is pronounced by a judicial authority, the person concerned shall have the right to submit the reason against his or her expulsion and to have his or her case reviewed by the competent authority, unless compelling reasons of national security require otherwise. Pending such review, the person concerned shall have the right to seek a stay of the decision of expulsion.
5. If a decision of expulsion that has already been executed is subsequently annulled, the person concerned shall have the right to seek compensation according to law and the earlier decision shall not be used to prevent him or her from re-entering the State concerned.
6. In case of expulsion, the person concerned shall have a reasonable opportunity before or after departure to settle any claims for wages and other entitlements due to him or her and any pending liabilities.
7. Without prejudice to the execution of a decision of expulsion, a migrant worker or a member of his or her family who is subject to such a decision may seek entry into a State other than his or her State of origin.
8. In case of expulsion of a migrant worker or a member of his or her family the costs of expulsion shall not be borne by him or her. The person concerned may be required to pay his or her own travel costs.
9. Expulsion from the State of employment shall not in itself prejudice any rights of a migrant worker or a member of his or her family acquired in accordance with the law of that State, including the right to receive wages and other entitlements due to him or her.

Article 23

Migrant workers and members of their families shall have the right to have recourse to the protection and assistance of the consular or diplomatic authorities of their State of origin or of a State representing the interests of that State whenever the rights recognized in the present Convention are impaired. In particular, in case of expulsion, the person concerned shall be informed of this right without delay and the authorities of the expelling State shall facilitate the exercise of such right.

Article 24

Every migrant worker and every member of his or her family shall have the right to recognition everywhere as a person before the law.

Article 25

1. Migrant workers shall enjoy treatment not less favourable than that which applies to nationals of the State of employment in respect of remuneration and:
   (a) Other conditions of work, that is to say overtime, hours of work, weekly rest, holidays with pay, safety, health, termination of the employment relationship and any other conditions of work which, according to national law and practice, are covered by this term;
   (b) Other terms of employment, that is to say minimum age of employment, restriction on home work and any other matters which, according to national law and practice, are considered a term of employment.
2. It shall not be lawful to derogate in private contracts of employment from the principle of equality of treatment referred to in paragraph 1 of this article.
3. States Parties shall take all appropriate measures to ensure that migrant workers are not deprived of any rights derived from this principle by reason of any irregularity in their stay or employment. In particular, employers shall not be relieved of any legal or contractual obligations, nor shall their obligations be limited in any manner by reason of any such irregularity.

Article 26

1. States Parties recognize the right of migrant workers and members of their families:
   (a) To take part in meetings and activities of trade unions and of any other associations established in accordance with law, with a view to protecting their economic, social, cultural and other interests, subject only to the rules of the organization concerned;
   (b) To join freely any trade union and any such association as aforesaid, subject only to the rules of the organization concerned;
   (c) To seek the aid and assistance of any trade union and of any such association as aforesaid.
2. No restrictions may be placed on the exercise of these rights other than those that are prescribed by law and which are necessary in a democratic society in the interests of national security, public order (*ordre public*) or the protection of the rights and freedoms of others.

Article 27

1. With respect to social security, migrant workers and members of their families shall enjoy in the State of employment the same treatment granted to nationals in so far as they fulfil the requirements provided for by the applicable legislation of that State and the applicable bilateral and multilateral treaties. The competent authorities of the State of origin and the State of employment can at any time establish the necessary arrangements to determine the modalities of application of this norm.
2. Where the applicable legislation does not allow migrant workers and members of their families a benefit, the States concerned shall examine the possibility of reimbursing interested persons the amount of contributions made by them with respect to that benefit on the basis of the treatment granted to nationals who are in similar circumstances.

Article 28

Migrant workers and members of their families shall have the right to receive any medical care that is urgently required for the preservation of their life or the avoidance of irreparable harm to their health on the basis of equality of treatment with nationals of the State concerned. Such emergency medical care shall not be refused to them by reason of any irregularity with regard to stay or employment.

Article 29

Each child of a migrant worker shall have the right to a name, to registration of birth and to a nationality.

Article 30

Each child of a migrant worker shall have the basic right of access to education on the basis of equality of treatment with nationals of the State concerned. Access to public pre-school educational institutions or schools shall not be refused or limited by reason of the irregular situation with respect to stay or employment of either parent or by reason of the irregularity of the child's stay in the State of employment.

Article 31

1. States Parties shall ensure respect for the cultural identity of migrant workers and members of their families and shall not prevent them from maintaining their cultural links with their State of origin.
2. States Parties may take appropriate measures to assist and encourage efforts in this respect.

Article 45

1. Members of the family of migrant workers shall, in the State of employment, enjoy equality of treatment with nationals of that State in relation to:
    (a) Access to educational institutions and services, subject to the admission requirements and other regulations of the institutions and services concerned;
    (b) Access to vocational guidance and training institutions and services, provided that requirements for participation are met;
    (c) Access to social and health services, provided that requirements for participation in the respective schemes are met;
    (d) Access to and participation in cultural life.
2. States of employment shall pursue a policy, where appropriate in collaboration with the States of origin, aimed at facilitating the integration of children of migrant workers in the local school system, particularly in respect of teaching them the local language.
3. States of employment shall to facilitate for the children of migrant workers the teaching of their mother tongue and culture and, in this regard, States of origin shall collaborate whenever appropriate.
4. States of employment may provide special schemes of education in the mother tongue of children of migrant workers, if necessary in collaboration with the States of origin.

American Convention on Human Rights 1969 ("Pact of San José, Costa Rica")

Entry into force: 18 July 1978.

Article 4: Right to life

1. Every person has the right to have his life respected. This right shall be protected by law, and, in general, from the moment of conception. No one shall be arbitrarily deprived of his life.
5. Capital punishment shall not be imposed upon persons who, at the time the crime was committed, were under 18 years of age or over 70 years of age; nor shall it applied to pregnant women.

Article 5: Right to humane treatment

1. Every person has the right to have his physical, mental, and moral integrity respected.
5. Minors while subject to criminal proceedings shall be separated from adults and brought before specialized tribunals, as speedily as possible, so that they may be treated in accordance with their status as minors.

Article 12: Freedom of conscience and religion

4. Parents or guardians, as the case may be, have the right to provide for religious and moral education of their children, or wards, that is in accord with their own convictions.

Article 13: Freedom of thought and expression

1. Everyone has the right to freedom of thought and expression. This right includes freedom to seek, receive, and impart information and ideas of all kinds, regardless of frontiers, either orally, in writing, in print, in the form of art, or through any other medium of one's choice.
2. The exercise of the right provided for in the foregoing paragraph shall not be subject to prior censorship but shall be subject to subsequent imposition of liability, which shall be expressly established by law to the extent necessary in order to ensure:
   (a) respect for the rights or reputations of others; or
   (b) the protection of national security, public order, or public health or morals.
4. Notwithstanding the provisions of paragraph 2 above, public entertainments may be subject by law to prior censorship, for the sole purpose of regulating access to them for the moral protection of childhood and adolescence.

Article 15: Right to the formation and the protection of families

1. The family is the natural and fundamental element of society and ought to be protected by the State, which should see to the improvement of its spiritual and material conditions.
2. Everyone has the right to form a family, which shall be exercised in accordance with the provisions of the pertinent domestic legislation.

3. The States Parties hereby undertake to accord adequate protection to the family unit and in particular:
   (a) to provide special care and assistance to mothers during a reasonable period before and after childbirth;
   (b) to guarantee adequate nutrition for children at the nursing stage and during school attendance years;
   (c) to adopt special measures for the protection of adolescents in order to ensure the full development of their physical, intellectual and moral capacities;
   (d) to undertake special programs of family training so as to help create a stable and positive environment in which children will receive and develop the values of understanding, solidarity, respect and responsibility.

Article 16: Rights of children

Every child, whatever his parentage, has the right to the protection that his status as a minor requires from his family, society and the State. Every child has the right to grow under the protection and responsibility of his parents: save in exceptional, judicially-recognized circumstances, a child of young age ought not to be separated from his mother. Every child has the right to free and compulsory education, at least in the elementary phase, and to continue his training at higher levels of the educational system.

Article 17: Rights of the family

1. The family is the natural and fundamental group unit of society and is entitled to protection by society and the State.

RELEVANT CHILD PROVISIONS

3. No marriage shall be entered into without the free and full consent of the intending spouses.
4. The States Parties shall take appropriate steps to ensure the equality of rights and the adequate balancing of responsibilities of the spouses as to marriage, during marriage, and in the event of its dissolution. In case of dissolution, provision shall be made for the necessary protection of any children solely on the basis of their own best interests.
5. The law shall recognize equal rights for children born out of wedlock and those born in wedlock.

Article 18: Right to a name

Every person has the right to a given name and to the surnames of his parents or that of one of them. The law shall regulate the manner in which this right shall be ensured for all, by the use of assumed names if necessary.

Article 19: Rights of the child

Every minor child has the right to the measures of protection required by his condition as a minor, on the part of his family, society and the State.

Children and War

CHILDREN AND WAR

Children are increasingly finding themselves targeted in armed conflict. UNICEF has concluded that in the last decade alone some two million children have been killed, with a further five million disabled, twelve million made homeless and one million orphaned. In parts of Africa there is such increasing concern that children are being forcibly recruited into armed forces and often given life-threatening tasks such as planting land mines, that the Ottawa Treaty of 1998 that Diana, Princess of Wales supported before her death is hoped to eradicate.

Child civilians should be distinguished from child soldiers. The latter can serve as fighters from the age of fifteen pursuant to Article 77(2) of the Geneva Protocol I 1977 additional to the Geneva Conventions of August 1994 and Relating to the Victims of International Armed Conflicts (1977 GP I) and the UN Convention on the Rights of the Child 1989 Article 38(2). The UN Convention states that 'a child means every human being under the age of eighteen years, unless under the law applicable to the child, majority is attained earlier'. The Hague and European Conventions define a 'child' as being below the age of sixteen. Otherwise, human rights instruments and international treaties do not define when childhood comes to an end.

Children are granted special status in the arena of armed conflict in international and humanitarian law and in Conventions because, pursuant to the Declaration on the Rights of the Child 1924, 'mankind owes to the child the best it has to give', the child is vulnerable and represents the continuity of life through the next generation.

Western legal systems protect children through domestic statutes of a civil or criminal nature. In less sophisticated countries norms and customs of behaviour offer limited protection. International human rights instruments make no direct reference to children specifically in armed conflict. A child might have to fall back upon the contents of other Conventions relating to 'man' generally, though such Conventions could be interpreted as also incorporating children.

Whilst states can technically derogate from their international obligations by informing states parties to such Conventions of such a wish, such derogation supposedly cannot relate to children. The American Convention on Human Rights 1969 forbids derogation regarding the rights of the child even in wartime. The following Conventions exist and can be relied upon to ensure the protection of children:

1. The Convention on the Prevention and Punishments of the Crime of Genocide 1948 mentions children in terms of anyone prohibiting their being transferred from one religious group to another.

2. The Convention on the Elimination of All Forms of Discrimination Against Women 1979 also relates to children.
3. The International Convention on the Protection of the Rights of All Migrant Workers and their Families 1990 relates to children.
4. The Universal Declaration of Human Rights seeks a common standard for all people of all nations.
5. The International Convention on Civil and Political Rights 1966 establishes economic, social and cultural rights. Article 10(3) states that special measures of protection and assistance should be taken on behalf of all children and young persons without discrimination.
6. The Covenant on Civil and Political Rights 1966 also establishes rights that can be said to relate to children. Article 24(1) states that 'every child shall have without discrimination as to race, colour, sex, language, religion, national or social origin, property or birth, the right to such measures of protection as are required by its status as a minor, on the part of his family, society or the state.'

The Human Rights Committee confirmed that under Article 24, states should adopt measures ensuring that everyone enjoys the rights provided for in the Covenant. General regional human rights instruments include:

1. The American Declaration on the Rights and Duties of Man 1948.
2. The American Convention on Human Rights 1969.
3. The African Charter on Human and People's Rights 1981.
4. The Charter on the Rights and Welfare of the Child 1990.
5. The draft Pacific Charter on Human Rights, and
6. The Arab Charter on Human Rights.

The report adopted at the Rio Conference on Environment and Development 1992 urged countries to combat human rights abuses against young people. The Vienna Declaration and Programme of Action, set out in the Vienna Conference 1993, plans action to combat emergencies resulting from armed conflict, for the implementation of human rights norms, and other measures to 'facilitate assistance to children in war zones'. The Programme of Action of the Cairo Conference 1994 emphasised the need to empower and educate female children. The Declaration and Platform for Action of the Beijing Conference in 1995 also referred to the specific situation of the child.

Article 5(1)(d) of the Convention for the Protection of Human Rights and Fundamenal Freedoms permits the deprivation of a child's liberty in certain circumstances. The Geneva Protocol 1925, the Geneva Convention 1949, the Geneva Protocol I 1977, the Geneva Protocol II 1977 and the Inhumane Weapons Convention 1980 set out standards and issues regarding civilians and armed conflict that can extend to children. Upon the establishment of an International Criminal Court, voted for on 17 July 1998, prosecutions could be brought before it regarding the maltreatment of children forced into armed conflict as soldiers, for example.

The Chemical Weapons Convention 1993 provides for the prospect that civilians, including children, be protected from direct and indiscriminate attack. The Geneva Convention 1949 contains seventeen substantive Articles for the protection of children in armed conflict with nine in the 1977 Articles. Article 77(1) of the Convention was the first time there was specific reference to children in territories of the parties of conflict, with children being the object of special respect and protected against indecent assault.

The Geneva Conventions refer to zones for the protection of children and the concept of 'zones of peace' to permit humanitarian aid. UNICEF has successfully negotiated in the past what has been referred to as 'days of tranquillity' in El Salvador, the Lebanon and the Sudan. The Conventions permit the removal of children from areas besieged, with the 1977 Convention emphasising the evacuation of separated or orphaned children. Article 23 of the 1949 Convention refers to free passage for essential foodstuffs, clothing and tonics intended for children under fifteen. The 1977 Convention provides for children receiving essential supplies, with the death penalty for those under eighteen forbidden for those in armed conflict. In addition, children in occupied territories are entitled to special treatment with regard to orphaned or separated childen. Children should only be detained if parents are themselves detained and should certainly not be separated from their parents under Articles 82 and 89. Under Article 24 children should not be left to fend for themselves but be received into a neutral country and those under the age of twelve should be specifically identified by name tag.

The Inhumane Weapons Convention 1980 Article (6)(b) prohibits booby traps associated with children's toys, with states parties not entitled to recruit anyone under the age of fifteen into armed conflict. The Coalition to Stop the Use of Child Soldiers has campaigned since the adoption of the Optional Protocol to the UN Convention on the Rights of the Child to raise the minimum age for military recruitment from fifteen to eighteen. In 1994 the draft Declaration on the Rights of Children in Armed Conflict, the Declaration of Amsterdam, sought to set out final legal and policy issues regarding the treatment of children in armed conflict for the UN to adopt, an adoption that cannot come too soon.

Geneva Convention Relative to the Protection of Civilian Persons in Time of War 1949

Entry into force: 21 October 1950

Article 14

In time of peace, the High Contracting Parties and, after the outbreak of hostilities, the Parties thereto, may establish in their own territory and, if the need arises, in occupied areas, hospital and safety zones and localities so organized as to protect from the effects of war, wounded, sick and aged persons, children under fifteen, expectant mothers and mothers of children under seven.

Upon the outbreak and during the course of hostilities, the Parties concerned may conclude agreements on mutual recognition of the zones and localities they have created. They may for this purpose implement the provisions of the Draft Agreement annexed to the present Convention, with such amendments as they may consider necessary.

The Protecting Powers and the International Committee of the Red Cross are invited to lend their good offices in order to facilitate the institution and recognition of these hospital and safety zones and localities.

Article 17

The Parties to the conflict shall endeavour to conclude local agreements for the removal from besieged or encircled areas, of wounded, sick, infirm, and aged persons, children and maternity cases, and for the passage of ministers of all religions, medical personnel and medical equipment on their way to such areas.

Article 24

The Parties to the conflict shall take the necessary measures to ensure that children under fifteen, who are orphaned or are separated from their families as a result of the war, are not left to their own resources, and that their maintenance, the exercise of their religion and their education are facilited in all circumstances. Their education shall, as far as possible, be entrusted to persons of a similar cultural tradition.

The Parties to the conflict shall facilitate the reception of such children in a neutral country for the duration of the conflict with the consent of the Protecting Power, if any, and under due safe-guards for the observance of the principles stated in the first paragraph.

They shall, furthermore, endeavour to arrange for all children under twelve to be identified by the wearing of identity discs, or by some other means.

Article 38

With the exception of special measures authorized by the present Convention, in particularly by Article 27 and 41 thereof, the situation of protected persons shall continue to be regulated, in principle, by the provisions concerning aliens in time of peace. In any case, the following rights shall be granted to them:

(1) they shall be enabled to receive the individual or collective relief they may be sent to them.

(2) they shall, if their state of health so requires, receive medical attention and hospital treatment to the same extent as the nationals of the State concerned.

(3) they shall be allowed to practise their religion and to receive spiritual assistance from ministers of their faith.
(4) if they reside in an area particularly exposed to the dangers of war, they shall be authorized to move from that area to the same extent as the nationals of the State concerned.
(5) children under fifteen years, pregnant women and mothers of children under seven years shall benefit by any preferential treatment to the same extent as the nationals of the State concerned.

Article 50

The Occupying Power shall, with the cooperation of the national and local authorities, facilitate the proper working of all institutions devoted to the care and education of children.

The Occupying Power shall take all necessary steps to facilitate the identification of children and the registration of their parentage. It may not, in any case, change their personal status, nor enlist them in formations or organizations subordinate to it.

Should the local institutions be inadequate for the purpose, the Occupying Power shall make arrangements for the maintenance and education, if possible by persons of their own nationality, language and religion, of children who are orphaned or separated from their parents as a result of the war and who cannot be adequately cared for by a near relative or friend.

A special section of the Bureau set up in accordance with Article 136 shall be responsible for taking all necessary steps to identify children whose identity is in doubt. Particulars of their parents or other near relatives should always be recorded if available.

The Occupying Power shall not hinder the application of any preferential measures in regard to food, medical care and protection against the effects of war which may have been adopted prior to the occupation in favour of children under fifteen years, expectant mothers, and mothers of children under seven years.

Article 68

Protected persons who commit an offence which is solely intended to harm the Occupying Power, but which does not constitute an attempt on the life or limb of members of the occupying forces or administration, nor a grave collective danger, nor seriously damage the property of the occupying forces or administration or the installations used by them, shall be liable to internment or simple imprisonment, provided the duration of such internment or imprisonment is proportionate to the offence committed. Furthermore, internment or imprisonment shall, for such offences, be the only measure adopted for depriving protected persons of liberty. The courts provided for under Article 66 of the present Convention may at their discretion convert a sentence of imprisonment to one of internment for the same period.

The penal provisions promulgated by the Occupying Power in accordance with Articles 64 and 65 may impose the death penalty on a protected person only in cases where the person is guilty of espionage, of serious acts of sabotage against the military installations of the Occupying Power or of intentional offences which have caused the death of one or more persons, provided that such offences were punishable by death under the law of the occupied territory in force before the occupation began.

The death penalty may not be pronounced on a protected person unless the attention of the court has been particularly called to the fact that since the accused is not a national of the Occupying Power, he is not bound to it by any duty of allegiance.

In any case, the death penalty may not be pronounced on a protected person who was under eighteen years of age at the time of the offence.

Article 76

Protected persons accused of offences shall be detained in the occupied country, and if convicted they shall serve their sentences therein. They shall, if possible, be separated from other detainees and shall enjoy conditions of food and hygiene which will be sufficient to keep them in good health, and which will be at least equal to those obtaining in prisons in the occupied country.

They shall receive the medical attention required by their state of health.

They shall also have the right to receive any spiritual assistance which they may require.

Women shall be confined in separate quarters and shall be under the direct Supervision of women.

Proper regard shall be paid to the special treatment due to minors.

Protected persons who are detained shall have the right to be visited by delegates of the Protecting Power and of the International Committee of the Red Cross, in accordance with the provisions of Article 143.

Such persons shall have the right to receive at least one relief parcel monthly.

Article 82

The Detaining Power shall, as far as possible, accommodate the internees according to their nationality, language and customs. Internees who are nationals of the same country shall not be separated merely because they have different languages.

Throughout the duration of their internment, members of the same family, and in particular parents and children, shall be lodged together in the same place of internment, except when separation of a temporary nature is necessitated for reasons of employment or health or for the purposes of enforcement of the provisions of Chapter IX of the present Section. Internees may request that their children who are left at liberty without parental care shall be interned with them.

Wherever possible, interned members of the same family shall be housed in the same premises and given separate accommodation from other internees, together with facilities for leading a proper family life.

FOOD AND CLOTHING

Article 89

Daily food rations for internees shall be sufficient in quantity, quality and variety to keep internees in a good state of health and prevent the development of nutritional deficiencies. Account shall also be taken of the customary diet of the internees.

Internees shall also be given the means by which they can prepare for themselves any additional food in their possession.

Sufficient drinking water shall be supplied to internees. The use of tobacco shall be permitted.

Internees who work shall receive additional rations in proportion to the kind of labour which they perform.

Expectant and nursing mothers and children under fifteen years of age, shall be given additional food, in proportion to their physiological needs.

Article 94

The Detaining Power shall encourage intellectual, educational and recreational pursuits, sports and games amongst internees, whilst leaving them free to take part in them or not. It shall take all practicable measures to ensure the exercise thereof in particular by providing suitable premises.

All possible facilities shall be granted to internees to continue their studies or to take up new subjects. The education of children and young people shall be ensured: they shall be allowed to attend schools either within the place of internment or outside.

Internees shall be given opportunities for physical exercise, sports and outdoor games. For this purpose, sufficient open spaces shall be set aside in all places of internment. Special playgrounds shall be reserved for children and young people.

RELEASE, REPATRIATION AND ACCOMMODATION IN NEUTRAL COUNTRIES

Article 132

Each interned person shall be released by the Detaining Power as soon as the reasons which necessitated his internment no longer exist.

The Parties to the conflict shall, moreover, endeavour during the course of hostilities, to conclude agreements for the release, the repatriation, the return to places of residence or the accommodation in a neutral country of certain classes of internees, in particular children, pregnant women and mothers with infants and young children, wounded and sick, and internees who have been detained for a long time.